ENVIRONMENTAL AND ARCHITECTURAL ACOUSTICS

ENVIRONMENTAL AND ARCHITECTURAL ACOUSTICS

Z. Maekawa
Environmental Acoustics Laboratory
Kobe University
Osaka
Japan

and

P. Lord
Department of Applied Acoustics
University of Salford
UK

E & FN SPON
An Imprint of Chapman & Hall
London · Glasgow · New York · Tokyo · Melbourne · Madras

Published by E & FN Spon, an imprint of Chapman & Hall, 2–6 Boundary Row, London SE1 8HN, UK

Chapman & Hall, 2–6 Boundary Row, London SE1 8HN, UK

Blackie Academic & Professional, Wester Cleddens Road, Bishopbriggs, Glasgow G64 2NZ, UK

Chapman & Hall Inc., One Penn Plaza, 41st Floor, New York, NY 10119, USA

Chapman & Hall Japan, Thomson Publishing Japan, Hirakawacho Nemoto Building, 6F, 1-7-11 Hirakawa-cho, Chiyoda-ku, Tokyo 102, Japan

Chapman & Hall Australia, Thomas Nelson Australia, 102 Dodds Street, South Melbourne, Victoria 3205, Australia

Chapman & Hall India, R. Seshadri, 32 Second Main Road, CIT East, Madras 600 035, India

First published in 1968 in Japan as *Architectural Acoustics*

© 1994 Z. Maekawa and P. Lord

Typeset in 10/12pt Times by Compuscript Ltd, Shannon Industrial Estate, Co. Clare, Ireland.

Printed in Great Britain by St. Edmundsbury Press, Bury St. Edmunds, Suffolk.

ISBN 0 419 15980 0

A catalogue record for this book is available from the British Library

Library of Congress Cataloging-in-Publication Data

Maekawa, Z.
    Environmental and architectural acoustics / Z. Maekawa, P. Lord.
        p.   cm.
    Includes bibliographical references and index.
    ISBN 0–419–15980–0
    1. Soundproofing. 2. Vibration. 3. Architectural acoustics.
I. Lord, P. (Peter). II. Title.
TH1725.M34 1993
693'. 834–dc20   92–47247
                                                                        CIP

♾ Printed on permanent acid-free text paper, manufactured in accordance with ANSI/NISO Z39.48-1992 and ANSI/NISO Z39.48-1984 (Permanence of Paper).

FOREWORD

My involvement with this book is a very modest one. It has been my task to help Professor Maekawa to present his work in a way which would be easily understood by the English-speaking reader. This has proved to be an interesting exercise because it has revealed the basic mathematical understanding expected of a Japanese student of architecture, that, beneath the discipline of the artist, lurks an engineer.

The book not only follows some fairly well-trodden paths but points to new directions in acoustics which are just being investigated and are not well established. They are referred to in order to make it clear to the reader that here is a subject, albeit with a basis in classical physics, which is still expanding and developing, and that one must always beware of adopting an inflexible approach to the solution of acoustic problems, whether it be in architectural acoustics or noise control.

In preparing this version of Professor Maekawa's book, I have had considerable help from my secretary, Barbara Mather, for which I thank her.

P. LORD

PREFACE

This book is intended to present the practical technology needed to achieve a more acceptable acoustic environment for human life.

In the early 20th century, W.C. Sabine started to investigate the acoustics of a lecture room with a view to obtaining good speech intelligibility. This developed into a major study which we now see as the precursor of 'Architectural Acoustics'. This work also called into play an understanding of 'Noise Control' and 'Sound Insulation', both coming under the heading of Environmental Acoustics, which has even more significance in the noise polluted world of today.

There are two aspects to the acoustic environment, one public or social, the other personal. Broadly speaking, the former deals with the outdoor environment, the latter with the indoor environment. The extraordinary development of industry and increasing speed of transportation produces very high levels of noise in the outdoor environment; consequently it is now of vital necessity to establish a technology of 'Environmental Acoustics' based on 'Architectural Acoustics' with its multi-disciplinary foundation.

After achieving a quiet space, then what are the criteria for 'good acoustics'? This question is examined under the heading of Room Acoustics—a major part of 'Architectural Acoustics'. Hence the title of this book.

This text should serve as a useful foundation, not only for students of architecture or environmental engineering, but also students and engineers meeting acoustics for the first time. Furthermore, in order to provide the fundamental knowledge necessary for understanding a more specialised text on acoustics, Chapter 10 has been added.

The book is based on my lectures at Kobe University and two or three other colleges, and on many research papers on acoustical problems solved by myself over a period of nearly 40 years. (Included in the text are some problems which the reader should try to solve.)

I wrote a book on 'Architectural Acoustics' in Japanese, published in 1968 and revised in 1978, and have used material from it in the more basic parts of this book, but the manuscript for this book is a totally new production. Of course, science makes rapid progress and a book should be revised more or less every ten years, so I would welcome any suggestions from readers for corrections or improvements.

It is my great pleasure to have, as co-author, Peter Lord, who was suggested by the publishers. He is a long-standing professional friend of mine from 1968, the date of the first issue of the Journal 'Applied Acoustics'. We also worked together as members of the 'International Commission on Acoustics' (1984–1990).

Much material and data resulting from research has been quoted in this book and so I would like to express my sincere appreciation to the authors of that research, and also Professor H. Tachibana of the University of Tokyo for his helpful suggestions. My special thanks go to Professor Em. T. David Terasaki of the University of Hawaii for his professional advice on translation in the early stages. I am also indebted to Dr. Yoichi Ando, Dr. M. Morimoto and Mr. K. Sakagami of the Kobe University, and wish to thank my many graduate students for their kind help in preparing this book.

Z. Maekawa

CONTENTS

Chapter 1

FUNDAMENTALS OF SOUND WAVES AND HEARING

Sound can be visualised physically as a wave motion which is transmitted through a whole range of elastic media. It is called a 'sound wave'. On the other hand, it is also a sensation subjectively perceived by the ear which is stimulated by the sound wave. This is referred to as auditory sensation, a phenomenon which is the subject of advanced research and comes under the general heading of psycho-physiology.

1.1 SOUND WAVES

A sound wave is transmitted through a medium which has both inertia and elasticity. The space in which sound waves travel is called the 'sound field'. In a sound field the medium particles exhibit a repetitive movement backwards and forwards about their original position. Since a particle in the medium causes a neighbouring particle to be displaced by ξ, the repetitive movement produces a wave motion, i.e. vibration which is transmitted from particle to particle successively in the medium. The direction of the particle's movement is the same as that of the transmission path of the sound wave. Therefore, it is called a 'longitudinal wave'. As shown in Fig. 1.1 the medium particles are crowded together at a certain point, producing a high pressure while at a neighbouring point they are dispersed resulting in a reduced pressure. Two such points of condensation and rarefaction exist alternately in the wave motion. Thus, at a fixed point, the dense and rare parts of the wave arrive alternately and the pressure consequently repeatedly rises and falls. This pressure fluctuation is called 'sound pressure' p and the velocity of motion of the particles of the medium is called the 'particle velocity' v.

The number of fluctuations in 1 s is called the 'frequency' generally expressed by f, the unit of which is the Hertz (Hz). The distance which

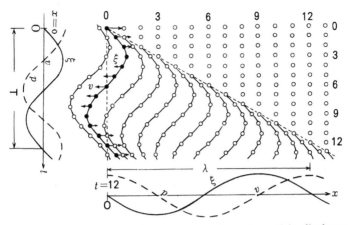

Fig. 1.1. Particle movement and wave propagation: ξ, particle displacement; v, particle velocity; p, sound pressure; λ, wavelength; and T, period.

a sound travels in 1 s is called the 'sound speed' and generally denoted by c (m/s). If we let λ represent the 'wavelength' then

$$\lambda = c/f \, (m) \tag{1.1}$$

In order to express the wave motion in the form of a mathematical equation, the displacement ξ of a medium particle in the x direction is expressed as follows,

$$\xi = AF(t - x/c) \tag{1.2}$$

where F is a function which has two independent variables, time t and distance x; c is a constant and A is the amplitude which is constant in this case. When a sound source produces simple harmonic motion the equation becomes

$$\xi = A \cos \omega(t - x/c) = A \cos(\omega t - kx) \tag{1.3}$$

where ω is the angular frequency; $\omega = 2\pi f$ and $k = \omega/c$. The sound pressure and the particle velocity can also be expressed in the same form. In eqn (1.3) when t becomes $(t + 1)$ and x becomes $(x + c)$,

$$\xi = A \cos \omega[(t + 1) - (x + c)/c] = A \cos \omega(t - x/c)$$

Therefore, the expression does not change. This means the phenomenon shifts through a distance c in 1 s, therefore, c is the sound speed. If we consider a certain position, for instance, where $x = 0$ in eqn (1.3) then $\xi = A \cos \omega t$ which means that it is a sine wave motion. Also at a certain time, for example when $t = 0$, $\xi = A\cos(-kx)$ which shows that the positions of moving particles also follow a sinusoidal pattern. In this case $kx = 2\pi(x/\lambda)$, therefore, when (x/λ) is an integer the values of ξ are the same, and it is found that particles separated by λ are in the same phase. Also, $k = \omega/c = 2\pi/\lambda$ and is called 'wavelength constant' or 'wave number'.

In the mathematical description of wave motion use is made of complex number representation. For instance, the sound pressure p can be expressed as:

$$p = Pe^{j\omega(t-x/c)} = Pe^{j(\omega t - kx)} \tag{1.4}$$

where P is the pressure amplitude and $j = \sqrt{-1}$. Using Euler's formula

$$p = P[\cos(\omega t - kx) + j\sin(\omega t - kx)]$$

Therefore, if the real part is taken, the relationship has the same form as eqn (1.3) which represents a physical phenomenon while the imaginary part can be considered as something additional for calculation convenience.

The sound wave propagates in a spherical shape from a sound source whose dimension is relatively small compared to the wavelength. It is called a 'spherical wave' and the sound source is referred to as a 'point source'. Although an actual sound source has a finite size, it can be considered as a point source when the source is located from an observer at a sufficiently large distance compared to its size. When the sound source is located very far away then the 'wave front' approximates to a plane and the sound may be treated as a 'plane wave'. Strictly speaking, a plane wave propagates only in one direction, and in a plane perpendicular to this direction its sound pressure and particle velocity are uniform and have the same phase.

1.2 SPEED OF SOUND

The sound speed c in a fluid whose density is ρ and has a volume elasticity κ is given by

$$c = \sqrt{\frac{\kappa}{\rho}} \quad \text{(m/s)} \tag{1.5}$$

In the case of a gas, the pressure variations associated with the sound wave are adiabatic, therefore, when the ratio of specific heats under conditions of constant pressure and constant volume is γ (see Section 10.1).

$$\kappa = \gamma P_0 \quad \text{where } P_0 \text{ is the atmospheric pressure} \qquad (1.6)$$

In the air at 0°C and 1 atm of pressure $\gamma = 1 \cdot 41$, $P = 101,300 \, (\text{N}/\text{m}^2) = 1,013$ (mbar, or h Pa), $\rho = 1 \cdot 29 \, (\text{kg}/\text{m}^3)$ and $c = 331 \cdot 5 \, (\text{m}/\text{s})$.

Since ρ varies with temperature while the atmospheric pressure remains substantially constant, at t°C the sound speed becomes

$$c = 331 \cdot 5 \left(1 + \frac{t}{273}\right)^{1/2} \doteqdot 331 \cdot 5 + 0 \cdot 61 t \quad (\text{m}/\text{s}) \qquad (1.7)$$

Therefore, 340 (m/s) is generally used for calculation at normal temperatures. Also the effect due to humidity is negligible.

The sound speed of a longitudinal wave in a solid whose density is ρ and Young's modulus E is expressed in the same form as follows:

$$c = \sqrt{\frac{E}{\rho}} \qquad (1.8)$$

As shown in Table 1.1 the sound speed in a solid is much larger than in air except in the case of rubber which is used as a special building material.

Table 1.1
Sound Speed and Characteristic Impedance of Various Materials

Material	Sound speed c (m/s)	Density (kg/m^3)	Characteristic impedance c $(kg/m^2 . s)$
Air (one atmospheric pressure, 20°C)	343·5	1·205	415
Water	1,460	1,000	146×10^4
Rubber	35–230	1,010–1,250	$3 \cdot 5$–28×10^4
Cork	480	240	12×10^4
Timber (pine, cypress)	3,300	400–700	$1 \cdot 3$–$2 \cdot 3 \times 10^6$
Iron	5,000	7,800	$39 \cdot 0 \times 10^6$
Concrete	3,500–5,000	2,000–2,600	7–13×10^6
Glass	4,000–5,000	2,500–5,000	10–25×10^6
Marble	3,800	2,600	$9 \cdot 9 \times 10^6$
Sand	1,400–2,600	1,600	$2 \cdot 3$–$4 \cdot 2 \times 10^6$

Equation (1.8) can be used to find the Young's modulus E of a material, from the measured value of c under suitable conditions. In a solid not only longitudinal waves but transverse waves are also produced, therefore, every part of a building structure is subjected to complex vibrations (see Chapter 6).

1.3 IMPEDANCE

Generally, when some effect is produced by an alternating action at a point, (Action)/(Effect) = Z called the 'Impedance' at the point. For instance, in an electric circuit where an alternating action due to an electric voltage E produces an alternating electric current I,

$$E/I = Z_e \qquad (1.9a)$$

which is the 'electrical impedance' at the point in the circuit. If E is a steady voltage and I is the direct current, then this expression is recognised simply as Ohm's Law.

Also in a mechanical vibrating system when an external force F is applied and a velocity v is produced,

$$F/v = Z_m \qquad (1.9b)$$

called the 'mechanical impedance'.

In the case of sound, when the sound pressure p is the action and produces a particle velocity v,

$$p/v = Z \qquad (1.9c)$$

called the impedance for the sound wave at the point.

Strictly speaking, since in this case both the sound pressure and particle velocity are considered over unit area, Z in eqn (1.9c) is the 'specific acoustic impedance' or 'acoustic impedance density'. In a pipe whose cross-sectional area is S, a volume velocity Sv is produced by a sound pressure p,

$$p/Sv = Z_A \qquad (1.10)$$

called the 'Acoustic Impedance' (see Section 10.2). These impedances relating to vibration are expressed by complex quantities because (Action) and (Effect) are generally not in the same phase, thus

$$Z = R + jX = |Z|e^{j\varphi} = |Z| < \varphi \qquad (1.11)$$

where, the absolute value of $|Z| = \sqrt{R^2 + X^2}$, and the phase angle $\varphi = \tan^{-1}(X/R)$.

When a plane wave propagates in free space through a medium without any loss, the acoustic impedance is always a real number which is a product of the medium density ρ and sound speed c (see Section 10.1),

$$Z = p/v = \rho c \qquad (1.12)$$

This Z has a specific value for the medium and is called the 'characteristic impedance', or 'specific acoustic resistance' as it is a real number. For air in its standard condition the value is 415 (kg/m^2 s = MKS rayl). Characteristic impedance values for various materials are shown in Table 1.1. The reciprocal of a impedance is called 'admittance'.

1.4   SOUND INTENSITY AND LEVEL

A.   Sound Intensity

The energy passing through unit cross-sectional area normal to the direction of sound propagation in unit time (1 s) is termed the 'sound intensity'. This is regarded as a power/unit area. As mentioned above, when (sound pressure) is substituted for (electric voltage) and (particle velocity) to (electric current) sound intensity corresponds to electric power, since the sound transmission path is analogous to the electric circuit. As is well known, (electric power) = (electric voltage) × (electric current), therefore sound intensity I can be expressed as follows:

$$I = pv \quad (W/m^2) \qquad (1.13)$$

From eqn (1.12)

$$I = p^2/\rho c = \rho c v^2 \qquad (1.14)$$

Thus, clearly sound intensity is proportional to the square of the sound pressure and the particle velocity, respectively.

Here, in eqn (1.13) and (1.14) both sound pressure and particle velocity should be effective values, as in the case of the electric alternating current. The 'effective value' is the root mean square (r.m.s.) of the instantaneous values as indicated in Fig. 1.2 where there is no minus sign because of squaring. In the case of a sinusoidal vibration with amplitude A and period T, the r.m.s. value is as follows:

$$\text{r.m.s.} = \sqrt{\frac{1}{T}\int_0^T (A\cos\omega t)^2 \, dt} = \frac{A}{\sqrt{2}} = 0\cdot707A \qquad (1.15)$$

Unless otherwise stated the magnitude of the sound pressure and the particle velocity are shown as effective values.

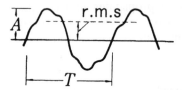

Fig. 1.2. Effective values.

B. Sound Energy Density

The sound intensity of a plane wave I is equal to the energy travelling a distance c (m) through unit area for 1 s, therefore, the sound energy density E in this space will be,

$$E = I/c = p^2/\rho c^2 \quad (\text{W} \cdot \text{s/m}^3 = \text{J/m}^3) \tag{1.16}$$

where c is the sound speed. Using energy density since there is no need then to consider direction, determination of a sound field becomes much simpler in a room in which reflected sounds are travelling in all directions.

C. Decibel Scale

In practice, when the sound intensity or sound pressure is measured, a logarithmic scale is used in which the unit is the 'decibel' (dB). It derives from the auditory sensation of man which can perceive a very wide range of sound intensities, i.e. the maximum to minimum energy ratio is more than $10^{13} : 1$. Also the sensation is logarithmically proportional to the intensity of the stimulus (Weber–Fechner's law: see Section 1.8C).

Originally, the scale expressed the logarithm of the ratio of two powers W_1 to W_0 called the 'Bell' but as it is too coarse a unit one-tenth of it is used and called the 'decibel' (dB).

$$\text{Number of decibels} = 10 \log_{10}\left(\frac{W_1}{W_0}\right) = 10 \log_{10}(n) \text{ dB} \tag{1.17a}$$

It is used not only to make relative comparisons but also to express absolute values by reference to a standard value. With a standard value of $W_0 = 10^{-12}$ (watt), the sound of W (watt) is expressed as

$$\text{Sound power level,} \quad L_w = 10 \log_{10}\left(\frac{W}{10^{-12}}\right) \text{ dB} \tag{1.17b}$$

A magnitude on such a logarithmic scale is generally called a 'level'.

Thus, the 'sound intensity level' I (W/m^2) is expressed as follows,

$$\text{Sound intensity level} = 10_{10} \log\left(\frac{I}{I_0}\right) \text{dB} \qquad (1.18)$$

where, $I_0 = 10^{-12}$ (W/m^2).

Then from eqn (1.14) the 'sound pressure level' L_p is obtained as follows:

$$L_p = 10\log_{10}\left(\frac{p^2}{p_0^2}\right) = 20\log_{10}\left(\frac{p}{p_0}\right) \text{dB} \qquad (1.19)$$

where, $p_0 = 2 \times 10^{-5}$ (N/m^2) $= 20 \ \mu$Pa is the reference value for air. It is much easier to measure sound pressure than intensity, therefore, generally a sound field is expressed by the sound pressure level which is, of course, equal to the sound intensity level for a plane wave in free space. In other instances it is common practice to evaluate the strength of sound in terms of sound pressure level. For the calculation of the sound field in a room the sound energy density is often used and compared directly as follows.

$$\text{The energy density level} = 10\log_{10}\left(\frac{E}{E_0}\right) \text{dB} \qquad (1.20)$$

Where an arbitrary value can be used for E_0 for purposes of convenience in calculation. As described above although the value is expressed in dB, the reference value used should be clearly defined.

[Ex. 1.1] $L_1 = 10\log_{10} n$(dB) and $L_2 = 20\log_{10} n$(dB) are plotted graphically in Fig. 1.3.

D. Energy Summation and Average Using Decibels

(a) Suppose we wish to find the level of sound L_3 (dB) resulting from two sounds L_1 (dB) and L_2 (dB) which exist simultaneously and comprise noise of random frequency. Let their energy densities be E_1 and E_2, respectively. Then since $E_3 = E_1 + E_2$

$$L_3 = 10\log_{10}\left(\frac{E_3}{E_0}\right) = 10\log_{10}\left(\frac{E_1 + E_2}{E_0}\right)$$

$$= 10\log_{10}(10^{L_1/10} + 10^{L_2/10}) \text{ dB} \qquad (1.21)$$

This calculation is made easier by using Fig. 1.4. However, when L_1 and L_2 (dB) have the same or nearly the same frequency content as pure

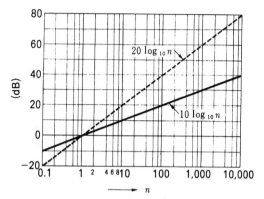

Fig. 1.3. Decibel scale.

tones the above equation can not be used because of interference (see Section 1.6); the reader must beware of the nature of the sound sources.

[Ex. 1.2]   When the energy summation L_3 is obtained from the expression $L_3 = L_1 + D$ (dB), with above notation the value of D vs $(L_1 - L_2)$ can be obtained from eqn (1.21) with the proviso $(L_1 > L_2)$ as follows:

$$D = 10 \log(1 + 10^{(L_1 - L_2)/10})$$

and Fig. (1.4) is derived.

(b) When there are n sources of sound of L_n (dB) with energy density E_n, the average level $\overline{L}$ is given by

$$\overline{L} = 10 \log_{10} \left(\frac{E_1 + E_2 + \cdots + E_n}{n E_0} \right) \text{ dB} \qquad (1.22a)$$

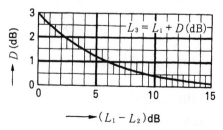

Fig. 1.4.   Summation of L_1 (dB) and L_2 (dB), $(L_1 > L_2)$.

or in terms of sound pressure P_n,

$$\bar{L} = 10 \log_{10} \left(\frac{p_1^2 + p_2^2 + \cdots + p_n^2}{np_0^2} \right) \text{dB} \qquad (1.22b)$$

In practice

$$\bar{L} = 10 \log_{10} \frac{1}{n} (10^{(L_1/10)} + 10^{(L_2/10)} + \cdots + 10^{(L_n/10)}) \text{ dB} \quad (1.22c)$$

is used.

When the difference between maximum and minimum values among the L_n is not greater than 3 (or 5) dB, the arithmetic mean can be used within an error of $0 \cdot 3$ (or $0 \cdot 7$) dB in place of $\bar{L}$.

1.5 REFLECTION, ABSORPTION AND TRANSMISSION

A. Absorption Coefficient and Transmission Loss

When a sound hits a wall, its energy is divided into three parts. If the sound incident on a wall has energy E_i, a part of the sound energy E_r is reflected back while a part E_a is absorbed in a wall. The rest E_t is transmitted as shown in Fig. 1.5. So we may write

$$E_i = E_r + E_a + E_t$$

Then, the 'absorption coefficient' α is defined as follows:

$$\alpha = \frac{E_i - E_r}{E_i} = \frac{E_a + E_t}{E_i} \qquad (1.23)$$

which means that all portions of the sound except that which is reflected is considered to be absorbed. The 'transmission coefficient' τ is defined as follows:

$$\tau = \frac{E_t}{E_i} \qquad (1.24)$$

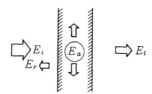

Fig. 1.5. Reflection, absorption and transmission.

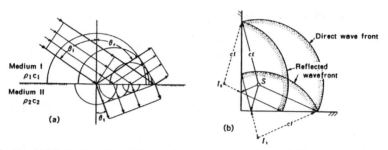

Fig. 1.6. (a) Reflection and refraction drawn by Huygens Principle and (b) wave fronts of direct and reflected sounds.

This can be expressed in dB and is called 'Transmission Loss' or 'Sound Reduction Index' denoted by TL or R respectively and defined as follows:

$$\text{TL (or R)} = 10 \log_{10} \frac{1}{\tau} = 10 \log \frac{E_i}{E_t} \text{ dB} \qquad (1.25)$$

In practice this is the term commonly used to describe sound insulation.

[Ex. 1.3] For an open window Fig. 1.5 $E_r = 0$, $E_a = 0$. Therefore $E_i = E_\tau$ and the absorption coefficient $\alpha = 1$. The transmission coefficient $\tau = 1$ which means complete transmission, therefore, TL = 0 (dB). So in this case it is seen that a material which has a large absorption coefficient is no good for sound insulation.

B. Reflection, Refraction and Diffraction

(a) A plane sound wave incident on a boundary between two different media shows the same phenomena of reflection and refraction as an optical wave. In Fig. 1.6(a),

the angle of incidence θ_i = angle of reflection θ_r (1.26)

With angle of refraction θ_t,

$$\frac{\sin \theta_i}{\sin \theta_t} = \frac{c_1}{c_2} \qquad (1.27)$$

where c_1 and c_2 are the sound speeds in the respective media. These relations are explained by 'Huygens principle'.

On the basis of these rules the sound paths and wave fronts are drawn graphically in Fig. 1.6(b) where I_1 and I_2 are the mirror images

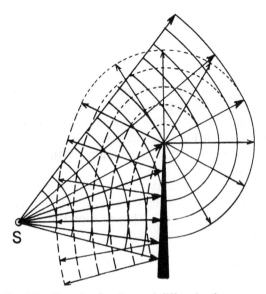

Fig. 1.7. Sound reflection and diffraction by screen.

of the sound. The line showing the sound path is called a 'sound ray' and the surface connecting vibrating particles in the same phase is called a 'wave front'. The wave front created by the sound waves emerging from the sound source after t seconds forms a sphere of radius ct with its centre at the source of mirror image. However, for valid application of this reflection rule the reflection plane should be sufficiently large compared to the wavelength.

(b) Even if an obstacle exists in the space in which the sound wave propagates the sound wave goes behind the body as shown in Fig. 1.7. This phenomenon is called 'diffraction'. The sound attenuation due to the diffraction depends on the size of the obstacle; the smaller the sound wavelength than the body the larger the attenuation and vice versa. The attenuation shall be obtained by the wave theory described later (see Section 10.14). In the case of an uneven reflecting surface, although when the wavelength is very small the sound reflects from each portion of concave or convex surface just as in optics, there is almost no effect when the size of concave or convex portion is small compared to the sound wavelength. In optics since the wavelength of light is very small, a distinct shadow is produced and reflected paths follow graphical drawing, whereas in acoustics, because the wavelength of sound is relatively large (in the audible range from 2 cm to 17 m) and is close to the sizes of objects in our environment, the sound field is very complicated.

C. Coefficients of Reflection, Transmission and Absorption

(a) Suppose the boundary plane between two media is infinitely large and a plane sound wave travelling in medium I is normally incident on the plane, as shown in Fig. 1.8, where ($\theta_i = \theta_r = 0$ in Fig. 1.6(a)), then the relationships between the magnitude of the reflected and the transmitted sound is derived as follows:

At the boundary two conditions of continuity must be fulfilled on both sides, i.e. (1) there must be continuity of sound pressure and (2) the particle velocities are equal. Though sound pressure has no direction, velocity is a vector quantity hence

$$\begin{cases} p_i + p_r = p_t & (1.28a) \\ v_i - v_r = v_t & (1.28b) \end{cases}$$

Both equations must be satisfied simultaneously. Substituting eqn (1.12) into eqn (1.28b)

$$\frac{p_i}{Z_1} - \frac{p_r}{Z_1} = \frac{p_t}{Z_2} \tag{1.29}$$

where $Z_1 = \rho_1 c_1$ and $Z_2 = \rho_2 c_2$.

Eliminating p_t from eqn (1.28a) and (1.29), the 'sound pressure reflection coefficient' r_p is given by

$$r_p = \frac{p_r}{p_i} = \frac{Z_2 - Z_1}{Z_2 + Z_1} \tag{1.30}$$

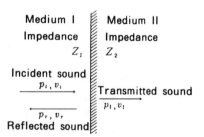

Medium I
Impedance
Z_1

Medium II
Impedance
Z_2

Incident sound
p_i, v_i

Transmitted sound
p_t, v_t

p_r, v_r
Reflected sound

Fig. 1.8. Reflection and transmission at the boundaryplane between two media.

Similarly, eliminating p_r from the equations, the 'sound pressure trans-mission coefficient' t is given by

$$t_p = \frac{p_t}{p_i} = \frac{2Z_2}{Z_1 + Z_2} \tag{1.31}$$

Therefore the two coefficients are determined from the characteristic impedances.

[Ex. 1.4] From the above conditions the reflection coefficient r_v and transmission coefficient t_v can be obtained in a similar manner for particle velocity as follows:

$$r_v = \frac{v_r}{v_i} = \frac{Z_2 - Z_1}{Z_2 + Z_1} \tag{1.32a}$$

$$t_v = \frac{v_t}{v_i} = \frac{2Z_1}{Z_1 + Z_2} \tag{1.32b}$$

(b) When considering the relationship between the aforementioned absorption coefficient and sound pressure reflection coefficient, since reflected incident sound energies in eqn (1.23) are proportional to $|p_r|^2$ and $|p_i|^2$, respectively

$$\frac{E_r}{E_i} = \frac{|p_r|^2}{|p_i|^2} = |r_p|^2$$

Therefore,

$$\alpha = 1 - |r_p|^2 = 1 - \left| \frac{Z_2 - Z_1}{Z_2 + Z_1} \right|^2 \tag{1.33}$$

When the medium I is air, $Z_1 = \rho c$, and medium II is an absorptive material, $Z_2 = Z$, the absorption coefficient of the material becomes,

$$\alpha = 1 - \left| \frac{(Z/\rho c) - 1}{(Z/\rho c) + 1} \right|^2 = 1 - \left| \frac{z - 1}{z + 1} \right|^2 \tag{1.34}$$

Thus the absorption coefficient is determined by z, the ratio of the impedance Z to the characteristic impedance of the air.

$Z/\rho c = z$ is called the 'acoustic impedance ratio' or 'normalised impedance' of the material surface.

1.6 INTERFERENCE, BEATS AND STANDING WAVES

A. Interference and Beats

When two waves of the same frequency propagate simultaneously, the vibration amplitude at each point of the medium is determined by the summation of the amplitude of each individual wave. This is the principle of superposition in a linear system. Therefore, the amplitude increases where the waves meet in phase and decreases where they are out of phase. Such phenomena, where more than two sound waves overlap and cause this amplitude change, are called 'interference'. When a pure tone is generated in a room, multiple reflected sounds are propagated from various directions, then very complicated 'interference patterns' are produced in the space.

A phenomenon known as 'beats' which is produced by two sounds whose frequencies are slightly different is due to an amplitude pulsation, i.e. a change in time recognised at an observation point. The number of beats per second is equal to the difference in frequency of the two sounds. This phenomenon is used to measure precisely or tune the frequency of a sound when the other sound's frequency is recognised as a standard.

B. Standing Waves

When two sound waves of the same frequency are travelling in opposite directions, the further from a reference point the more the phase shifts back and forth between the two waves. Therefore, at a certain point where the waves are in phase, the amplitude becomes a maximum, producing an 'antinode' while at another distance the amplitude becomes a minimum, producing a 'node' with the waves out of phase. Thus, antinode and node are observed alternately so the identical motion repeats at every point and the wave form does not proceed. This phenomenon is called a 'standing wave' which is the simplest example of interference. A complicated interference pattern produced in a three-dimensional room is also called a standing wave since the wave form does not move.

Expressing the sound pressure of a plane wave incident normally on a hard wall as

$$P_i = A \sin(\omega t + kx)$$

and for the reflected wave as

$$P_r = B \sin(\omega t - kx)$$

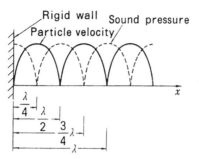

Fig. 1.9. Standing wave.

then when they are superposed

$$P = P_i + P_r = A \sin(\omega t + kx) + B \sin(\omega t - kx)$$
$$= (A + B)\sin \omega t \cos kx + (A - B)\cos \omega t \sin kx$$

For simplification, assuming that the sound is completely reflected, i.e.
$A = B$,

$$P = 2A \sin \omega t \cos kx \qquad (1.35)$$

Since $\cos kx$ is the function expressing the form of the wave in space,
when $kx = x(2\pi/\lambda) = n\pi$, i.e. $x = n(\lambda/2)(n = 0, 1, 2, 3, \ldots)$ the sound
pressure becomes a maximum and when $kx = x(2\pi/\lambda) = (2n + 1)\pi/2$,
i.e. $x = (2n + 1)\lambda/4$ the sound pressure becomes zero (Fig. 1.9). This is
the sound pressure pattern of a standing wave.

[Ex. 1.5]   In order to obtain the particle velocity pattern of a standing
wave, when a plane wave is incident on a hard wall, a similar expression
to sound pressure can be used. The velocity pattern is as shown in Fig.
1.9 by the solid curve, with zero velocity at the position of maximum
sound pressure and maximum velocity at zero pressure.

1.7   REVERBERATION

When a sound source starts to supply sound energy in a room, it needs
some time to build up an equilibrium sound level. Afterwards, if the
sound source stops, the sound will still be heard for sometime until it
decays away completely as shown in Fig. 1.10. Such a phenomenon in
which the sound remains even after the termination of the source is
called 'reverberation'.

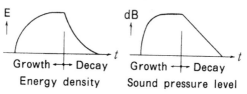

Fig. 1.10.   Sound growth and decay in a room.

To evaluate reverberation numerically, the 'reverberation time' is defined as the time required for the average sound energy density to decay by 60 dB from an equilibrium level. Since the time of W.C. Sabine in 1900 (Lit. B2), who studied the phenomenon, reverberation time has been used as the most important indicator of the acoustic characteristics or the auditory environment of a room. Sabine found, from many experimental results, that the larger the volume V (m³) of the room, the longer the reverberation time T and the more absorptive the materials and objects in the room, the shorter the reverberation time. Therefore,

$$T = K \frac{V}{A} \; (S) \tag{1.36}$$

where the constant $K = 0 \cdot 16$ and A is the total absorption. A can be obtained as follows:

$$A = S\bar{\alpha} \; (m^2) \tag{1.37}$$

where S (m²) is the total surface area inside the room and the average absorption coefficient is $\bar{\alpha}$. The total absorption is expressed by

$$A = \Sigma S_i \bar{\alpha}_i (m^2) \tag{1.38a}$$

where α_i is the absorption coefficient of the corresponding area S_i and $\Sigma S_i \alpha_i$ is the sum of the absorptions of all the different surfaces in the room.

When there is furniture and people present for which the surface area cannot be determined, each individual unit of absorption described as Aj (m²) is used. Therefore the total absorption can be obtained as follows:

$$A = \Sigma S_i \alpha_i + A_j \; (m^2) \tag{1.38b}$$

α_i is variable depending on the frequencies of sounds, as shown in Table A.2 in Appendixes, however, generally the value at 500 Hz is taken as representative. There will be more detailed discussion in Chapters 3 and 4.

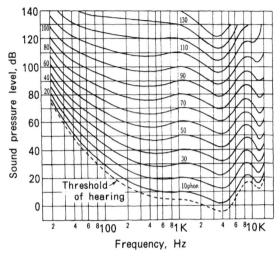

Fig. 1.11. Equal loudness contours (ISO).

1.8 LOUDNESS AND LOUDNESS LEVEL OF SOUND

'Loud' or 'silent' describes a sound which produces a large or small auditory sensation which is related to the physical intensity of the sound. However, the subjective sensation is not in simple proportion to the objective intensity, so another scale needs to be used.

A. Loudness Level

The 'loudness level' of a sound is defined as the sound pressure level in (dB) of a standard frequency, 1000 Hz, pure tone which is heard with loudness equal to that of the sound, and measured in 'Phon'. The curves shown in Fig. 1.11 which connects the equal loudness levels of each sound pressure level for each frequency of pure tone are called 'equal loudness contours'.

The figures are based on the average values of tests carried out with numerous young persons aged from 18 to 20 years. We can observe the following in Fig. 1.11.

(1) Generally speaking, below 500 Hz the auditory sensitivity is reduced with decreasing frequency. At 100 Hz, for example on the curve for 10 phon the sound pressure level is 20 dB higher than at 1000 Hz which means the sensitivity is only 1/100 of the

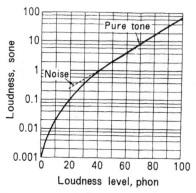

Fig. 1.12. Loudness (sone) vs loudness level (phon).

standard; at 40 Hz, $1/10\,000$; and at 25 Hz, less than $1/1\,000\,000$ of the 1000 Hz standard.

(2) This fall in sensitivity becomes less pronounced at higher levels of the range.

(3) Maximum sensitivity exists between 3000 and 5000 Hz, where it reaches 10 times the standard.

B. Loudness

The loudness level can define sounds which are heard as equally loud, but cannot be used to compare directly sounds at different levels. For example, a sound of 100 phon is not heard as twice as loud as one of 50 phon. As a result of experiments carried out by Fletcher, a relationship was established between loudness level in phons and subjective loudness in 'sones'. The unit of loudness is a sone which is defined as the loudness of a 1000 Hz tone of loudness level 40 phon. If the sound is heard twice as loud as 1 sone, its loudness equals 2 sones, and if 10 times as loud the loudness is 10 sones. The relationship between loudness and the loudness level is obtained by experiments and standardised in Fig. 1.12.

C. Weber–Fechner's Law

As shown in Fig. 1.11, the maximum to minimum energy ratio in the audible sound pressure level range is as much as $10^{13}:1$. Due to Weber–Fechner's law, however, the just noticeable difference in the physical stimulus for the smallest change of human sensation called 'differential limen' is proportional to the original amount of physical stimulus, i.e. not only in hearing but all sensations (magnitude) are logarithmically proportional to the intensity of the stimulus. Therefore the decibel scale can be applied to the measurement of sound and is also very convenient for the handling of large numbers.

1.9   AUDITORY SENSATION AREA

Ears can hear a wide range of sound pressures and frequencies as shown by the equal loudness contours in Fig. 1.11. The minimum sound pressure which is perceived as a sound is called the 'minimum audible field (MAF)' indicated by a dotted line in the Figure. The maximum audible value is not so clearly defined, a sound pressure level higher than 110 dB causes an uncomfortable sensation in the ear and at still higher levels, a feeling of pain. There is a threshold of feeling beyond which the sound is perceived not as sound but as pain, and its intensity level is about 130–140 dB for almost all frequencies and is accompanied by the risk of irreparable nerve damage.

The differential limen in sound intensity is about 1 dB, although it varies in a complicated way depending on frequency and sound intensity, and also on the hearing ability of the individual person.

The range of frequencies which can be heard as a sound is shown in Fig. 1.11 and extends from about 20 to 20 000 Hz. The differential limen in frequency is about 0·7% above 500 Hz, and 3–4 Hz below 500 Hz, but may vary depending on the sound intensity and also on the individual person.

This auditory sensation area is based on tests with many young people who have good hearing. However, over 20 years old, the auditory sensation shows a noticeable falling off especially at high frequencies with increasing age. That is, the threshold of hearing, MAF, is shifting upward in Fig. 1.11. The amount of this shift is called 'hearing loss' and is measured in dB.

1.10   PITCH AND TONE

A.   Sound Scale (Pitch)

We have the ability to sense whether the pitch of a sound is high or low. This perception of the pitch of a sound depends mainly on the sound's frequency. It is, however, rather complicated since the intensity and the wave shape may affect our sensation. A sound which has a constant pitch is called a 'tone'. When the duration is too short, we may not perceive the pitch.

Weber–Fechner's law may also be applied to frequency perception. $\text{Log}_2(f_2/f_1)$ is defined as the octave number, i.e. one octave in the case where f_2 is twice f_1. This is the basis of the musical scale where we have a similar sensation when the frequency is doubled. In engineering we always identify the octave by its position on the frequency scale, though in psychoacoustics the pitch scale is in 'mel', a number which permits summation in a similar way to 'sone' in loudness.

[Ex. 1.6]   The frequencies of sounds at octave intervals, above and below 1000 Hz are, for example, 500, 250 and 125 Hz for the lower ones and 2000, 4000 and 8000 Hz for the higher. These frequencies are equally spaced on a logarithmic scale.

The sound generated from a musical instrument has many component tones of various frequencies and is called a 'complex tone'. The tone of the lowest frequency is called the 'fundamental' and all other tones are known as 'overtones'. If the frequencies of the overtones are an integral multiple of the fundamental, they are called 'harmonics'. The pitch of a complex sound is perceived as that of the frequency which is the highest common factor of the frequencies of all the component sounds. Therefore a complex sound whose overtones consist of harmonics only has a pitch which is that of the fundamental even if that fundamental is actually absent.

[Ex. 1.7]   The pitch of a complex sound consisting of components 100, 150, 200 and 300 Hz is in fact the pitch of 50 Hz which is the highest common factor for the components. Thus, even a loudspeaker which cannot produce a frequency less than 100 Hz, has a pitch equivalent to 50 Hz. This 50 Hz is called the 'missing fundamental'.

B.   Timbre and Spectrum

We can distinguish the difference between tones produced by different musical instruments, even if they have the same pitch and intensity, because they possess their own 'timbre'. A 'pure tone' which is represented by a pure sine wave, produces the simplest timbre while a complex tone changes the timbre depending on its component tones. The timbre can be physically compared by means of the 'spectrum' of the sound obtained by frequency analysis.

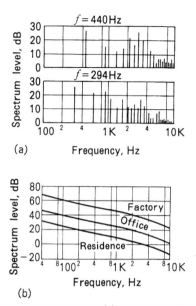

(a)

(b)

Fig. 1.13. Examples of sound spectra: (a) Spectrum of violin sound; and (b) Spectrum of long-time average of environmental noise.

The sound spectrum is measured by the 'spectrum level'. The spectrum level of the frequency f is the sound intensity level in a 1-Hz bandwidth. The spectrum of a musical tone is discontinuous as shown in Fig. 1.13(a) because it consists of harmonics, while the spectrum of noise is generally continuous as shown in Fig. 1.13(b).

The sound whose spectrum level is equal and uniformly continuous for the whole range of frequencies is called 'white noise', analogous to the optical phenomenon of white light which has a continuous spectrum.

When a noise is to be analysed for noise control purposes, generally a frequency bandwidth of 1 or 1/3 octave is used. Thus the measured sound intensity level in the frequency band is called 1 or 1/3 octave band level, and the result is described as a 'band spectrum'.

Although we have no pitch sensation with the white noise itself we sense the pitch of the various bands filtered with 1 or 1/3 octave band filters. These 'band noises' are often used as source signals for acoustic measurements.

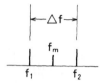

Fig. 1.14. Frequency band: Δf, band width; f_m, centre frequency; f_1 and f_2, cut off frequencies.

[Ex. 1.8] In Fig. 1.14 the centre frequency f_m for the octave and 1/3 octave band and the bandwidth Δf have the following relationship for 1 octave band

$$f_2 = 2f_1, \qquad \frac{f_m}{f_1} = \frac{f_2}{f_m} = \frac{2f_1}{f_m}$$

$$f_m = \sqrt{f_1 f_2} = \sqrt{2}\, f_1, \qquad \Delta f = f_1 = \frac{1}{\sqrt{2}} f_m = 0 \cdot 707 f_m$$

for 1/3 octave band

$$\frac{f_m}{f_1} = \frac{f_2}{f_m} = 2^{1/6}$$

$$\Delta f = f_2 - f_1 = f_m(2^{1/6} - 2^{-1/6}) = 0 \cdot 23 f_m$$

[Ex. 1.9] The relationships between spectrum level, octave band level and 1/3 octave band level for a white noise with intensity $I_s/1$ Hz at frequency f are derived as follows for the spectrum level:

$$L_s = 10 \log_{10} \frac{I_s}{I_0} \text{ (dB)}$$

for octave band level:

$$L_1 = 10 \log \frac{\Delta f I_s}{I_0} = 10 \log \frac{I_s}{I_0} + 10 \log \Delta f = L_s + 10 \log 0 \cdot 707 f_m$$

for 1/3 octave band level:

$$L_{1/3} = L_s + 10 \log 0 \cdot 23 f_m$$

Thus, the band level is raised by 3 dB/octave when the frequency is increased in any bandwidth.

C. Timbre of Musical Instruments

Although the highest fundamental tone for the musical scale is about 4000 Hz, the timbre of each individual instrument is different depending upon the harmonic structure which may include very high frequencies as shown in Fig. 1.13(a). Furthermore, there are noise-like sounds from musical instruments due to frictional noises at the start of the passage of the bow across a violin string, spectrum shift during the starting transient in the build up and the decay of sound in the piano string and so on, all of which contribute to what we call timbre. The frequency range necessary to transmit exactly the timbre is generally from 30 Hz to 16 000 Hz, i.e. almost the whole audible frequency range depending on the instrument.

1.11   AUDITORY MASKING

When we want to hear a sound in a noisy environment, we often experience difficulty hearing the sound clearly. So we can say that the noise masks the sound, a phenomenon referred to as the 'masking effect'. The explanation is that the noise dulls the auditory sensation, as a result the threshold of hearing is raised. The amount of masking is measured by this threshold shift in dB.

A.   Masking Due to Pure Tones

Figure 1.15(a) is an example of an actual measurement and shows that a pure tone of 1200 Hz with a 100 dB ('masker') raises the threshold of hearing for pure tones ('maskee') up to 70 or 80 dB in the frequency range above 1000 Hz. Similarly for pure tones masked by other frequencies, so that:

(1) The closer the masker frequency, the stronger the masking of the maskee frequency. In closest proximity, however, we can easily recognise the maskee due to audible beats.

(2) The louder the masker, the stronger the masking effect. And in a frequency range higher than the masker we perceive stronger masking than in a frequency range lower than the masker.

B.   Masking Due to White Noise

The threshold of hearing is shifted due to the presence of white noise as shown in Fig. 1.15(b) and the masking effect is almost uniform for all frequencies.

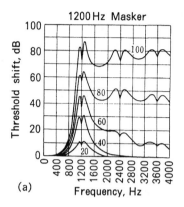

(a)

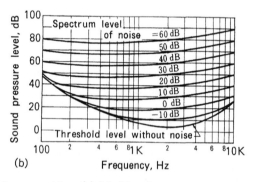

(b)

Fig. 1.15. Auditory masking: (a) Masking due to pure tones; and (b) Masking
due to white noise.

1.12   BINAURAL EFFECTS AND AUDITORY
LOCALISATION

Since the ears are located on either side of the head, the incident sound
wave to either ear may not be identical unless it comes from the median
plane. Because of the separate locations of ears and depending on the
sound wave direction, the amplitude as well as the phase (arrival time)
must be different at both ears.

Thus, hearing with two ears one can localise the sound source, i.e.
recognise the direction of the sound source and distance, thus giving

rise to a spatial impression. This is called the 'binaural' as opposed to 'monaural' effect which scarcely creates such a sensation.

As regards localisation of direction, the most effective auditory cues are the differences in sound pressure and the arrival time at the two ears. The former is more effective for frequencies higher than about 1500 Hz, and the latter more effective for frequencies lower than 1500 Hz.

Binaural localisation in the horizontal plane is accurate to about 1–3° near 0° just in front of the listener under the condition of a quiet, echo free environment while at 60° to the side of the listener the localisation ability rapidly deteriorates and is more than 40° around 90° to the listener. In the vertical plane localisation is poorer than in the horizontal plane.

Localisation of a pure tone is difficult, and, in a room, almost impossible due to the standing wave pattern but easy for complex sounds such as clicks and for bands of noise since they have many overtones.

In a room with many reflections arriving from various directions, we can still locate a sound source, due to the 'law of the first wave front' or 'precedence effect' which ignores the later arrivals.

In a noisy environment we can still extract those sounds we wish to hear, a phenomenon called the 'cocktail party effect'. Then, we have the experience of selecting a sound made much easier with binaural hearing.

With regard to assessing the distance of a sound source we have unfortunately insufficient data as yet to explain the phenomenon in the same terms as directional location. So far the problem remains an interesting challenge for those working in the field of psycho-physics.

1.13 NATURE OF SPEECH

A. Spectrum and Level Distribution of Speech

The spectrum of speech measured and averaged over a long-time interval at 1 m from the speaker's mouth is shown in Fig. 1.16 and is the average for ordinary people. Since the figure shows the intensity per Hz, by integrating the whole range of frequency, the overall intensity level is obtained at about 65 dB. However, speech is a complicated sound whose intensity and spectrum are fluctuating with time, therefore it is necessary to describe it statistically. Each syllable of speech lasts about

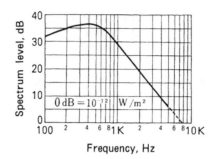

Fig. 1.16. Long-time average spectrum of the human voice.

1/8 s so that the sampling interval of 1/8 s is said to be sufficient. In Fig. 1.17, the abscissa shows the relative values of speech intensity level referred to the long-time interval average value, while the ordinate shows the time rate, i.e. the samples which exceed that level expressed as a percentage of the total. This characteristic is shown to be common to both male and females and also for any language. It shows that the long-time average level is only exceeded for 20% of the time while levels over $+12$ dB are about 1% of the whole time and the level difference between maximum and minimum level (dynamic range) is found to be 45–55 dB. There is a variation from 40 dB for shouting to -40 dB the minimum level referred to the average value.

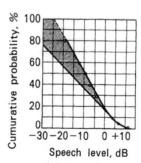

Fig. 1.17. Ogive of speech level distribution at 1/8-s interval.

B. Directivity of Human Voice

The sound intensity of the human voice has 'directivity' caused by diffraction by the head as shown in Fig. 1.18. Although over the whole

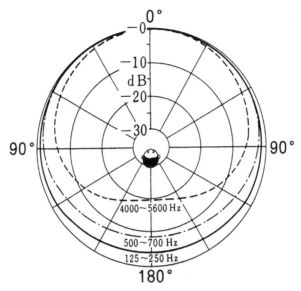

Fig. 1.18.   Directivity of human voice.

frequency range the difference is only -5 dB for the back of the head compared to the front. In the more important range for speech above 2000 Hz the difference is more than -15 dB.

C. Vowel and Consonant

Human speech generally consists of vowels and consonants. The vowel sounds are produced by vocal cords with expiration, while the consonants are produced by the noise of air movement through the vocal tract, i.e. throat, nostril, mouth over the tongue and lips. The frequency spectra of both types of sounds are formed by the resonant cavities in the vocal tract. The spectra of vowels have their own almost constant frequency ranges which are called 'formant' frequencies. The pitch of the voice is based on the frequency of the vocal chords, i.e. about 100 Hz for male and 200–300 Hz for female voice as fundamental frequencies. It is an important characteristic that formants are almost stable, when the fundamental tone is varied.

The consonants are produced during the transient state of speech, so that the lapse time is very short and frequency components tend to be in the higher frequency range. The energy content in consonants is unfortunately so small that they are easily masked by noise, although they are critical for speech intelligibility.

1.14   INTELLIGIBILITY OF SPEECH

The determination of speech intelligibility is important for evaluating an acoustic environment directly and synthetically, a technique which has its origins in the evaluation of telecommunication systems.

A.   Percentage Articulation

The percentage of meaningless spoken syllables correctly written down by listeners is called 'Percentage Articulation (P.A.)'. Knudsen (see Lit. B4) reported that on the basis of experiment P.A. can be expressed as

$$P.A. = 96 k_i k_r k_n k_s \quad (\%) \tag{1.39}$$

where k_i, k_r, k_n and k_s (see Fig. 1.19) are the coefficients determined by the average intensity level, reverberation time, noise level, and room shape, respectively. k_i becomes a maximum for 60–80 dB and falls

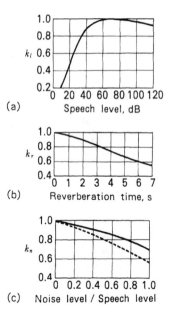

Fig. 1.19. Reduction factors on percentage articulation: (a) speech level; (b) reverberation time; and (c) noise level.

rapidly below 40 dB. k_r decreases when the reverberation increases. This is explained by the fact that the preceding sound overlaps and masks the succeeding one. Also the larger the noise level, the more the masking, then, k_n decreases. In the figure the solid line shows the case where the speaker is situated in a noisy environment and deliberately controls his voice intensity, whereas the dotted line shows the situation where the speaker is in a different room, or the speech is recorded, so that there is no control of speech level. Although k_s is said to be defined by room shape, it may include other uncertain factors such as echo etc. The fact that even when every coefficient is 1 indicating the best condition P.A. becomes 96% instead of 100% is interpreted as the syllable itself possessing some obscurity.

B. Speech Intelligibility

Even if the syllables are not fully recognised, the words or phrases are rather easily understood due to sequence or context. The percentage of correctly received phrases is called 'speech intelligibility'. The relationship between syllable articulation and speech intelligibility is shown in Fig. 1.20.

PROBLEMS 1

1. In a plane wave when the displacement of a medium is expressed as

$$\xi = A e^{j\omega(t-x/c)},$$

   show that the particle velocity $v = j\omega\xi$, and the acceleration $dv/dt = -\omega^2\xi$

2. When a plane wave is incident on the boundary between two media at an angle of incidence θ_i, show that the sound pressure reflection coefficient r_p can be expressed as follows,

$$r_p = \frac{Z_2 \cos \theta_i - Z_1 \cos \theta_t}{Z_2 \cos \theta_i + Z_1 \cos \theta_t}$$

   (Refers to Figs 1.6(a) and 1.8).

3. There are a number of fans of the same type and size in a room. When a fan runs the average sound pressure level in the room is 55 dB. When 2, 3, 4, ... and 10 fans run successively, calculate the average sound pressure levels at every stage in the room.

4. When a noise survey is carried out in a noisy factory, sound pressure levels of 58, 63, 59, 62, 64 and 61 dB are obtained at six points. Calculate the average sound pressure level in the room, and compare it to the arithmetic mean.

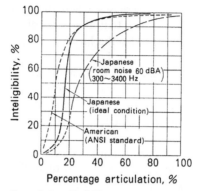

Fig. 1.20. Speech intelligibility vs percentage articulation.

5. White noise has a spectrum level of 30 dB. Calculate octave band levels at the centre frequencies 100 Hz, 200 Hz, 500 Hz and 1000 Hz. And also calculate 1/3 octave band levels for the same frequencies.

6. Describe fully the sound measuring units (dB), (phon) and (sone).

Chapter 2

NOISE AND VIBRATION—MEASUREMENT AND RATING

Any sound which a listener finds undesirable is defined as 'noise'. Even beautiful music when it disturbs someone's study or sleep is perceived as noise. Vibration should also be considered as an environmental factor which brings disturbance to human comfort and activities.

2.1   MEASUREMENT OF SOUND / NOISE

A.   Sound Level Meter

The instrumentation must comply with specifications given in IEC Publication 651, Type 1 for precision sound level meters, and Type 2 for ordinary sound level meters. Although many countries have their own national standards, in general they follow the relevant International Standards. IEC: International Electrotechnical Commission.

a.   Construction of Sound Level Meter

An example of a sound level meter is shown in Fig. 2.1. An omni-directional microphone converts the sound pressure into electrical volt-age, which is amplified, passes through a frequency-weighting network which approximates to the ear's characteristics, and causes an indicator to respond. The measured value is obtained by summing the coarse

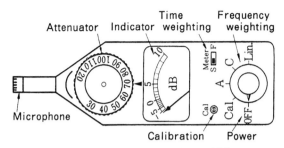

Fig. 2.1. Example of a Sound Level Meter.

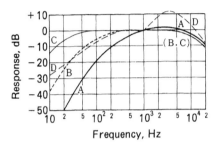

Fig. 2.2. Frequency weighting characteristics.

value set by the attenuator and the value of the meter deflection shown in Fig. 2.1.

b. Frequency Weighting
Frequency-weighting networks approximate the frequency response of the ear. 'A' and 'C' weighting responses are shown in Fig. 2.2 and Table 2.1; a flat response is added in precision sound level meters. Frequency-weightings 'A' and 'C' are internationally standardised to approximate the 40 and 100 phon curves, respectively, as shown in the equal loudness contours (Fig. 1.11). The intermediate weighting 'B' of Fig. 2.2 is no longer used; 'D' weighting, however, has been proposed as an international standard (IEC Pub. 537-1976) for rating aircraft noise which will be discussed later.

The measured value dBA* using frequency-weighting 'A' is regarded as a close approximation to the noise level perceived by human ears.

Table 2.1

International Standard of Frequency-Weighting for Sound Level Meters

Frequency	Weighting (dB)		Tolerances (dB)	
(Hz)	A	C	Type 1	Type 2
16	−56·7	−8·5	+3 −∞	+5 −∞
31·5	−39·4	−3·0	±1·5	±3
63	−26·2	−0·8	±1·5	±2
125	−16·1	−0·2	±1	±1·5
250	−8·6	0	±1	±1·5
500	−3·2	0	±1	±1·5
1 000	0	0	±1	±1·5
2 000	+1·2	−0·2	±1	±2
4 000	+1·0	−0·8	±1	±3
8 000	−1·1	−3·0	+1·5 −3	±5
16 000	−6·6	−8·5	+3 −∞	+5 −∞

The value dBC* using frequency-weighting 'C' is taken as an approximate value of the sound pressure level based on the flat weighting characteristic. In noise surveys both dBA and dBC values should be recorded; then, from the difference between them, one can find which frequency range is dominant, either above or below 1 kHz.

c. Time Weighting

The detector-indicator gives the r.m.s. value of the signal, with 'F' (fast) and 'S' (slow) time-weighting characteristics. The averaging circuit has two time-constants: 125 ms for 'F' and 1000 ms for 'S' (see Section 10.2E). The detector-indicator should also respond to tone bursts as specified in Fig. 2.3.

The other time-weighting 'I' is also specified for measurements of peak r.m.s. values of impulsive signals. With 'I' time-weighting, the averaging circuit has a 35 ms time-constant so that the rise time is about four times faster than with 'F' time-weighting, but the decay rate is very slow, i.e. 2·9 dB/s in order to catch the maximum displayed level of the indicator.

---

*dB(A) or dB(C) are also used, but omission of the parentheses is preferred throughout this book.

	Duration of test tone burst T, s	Max. response refer to continuous level a, dB	Tolerances for type 1, Type 2		Maximum overshoot b, dB
F	0.2	− 1.0	± 1	$^{+1}_{-2}$	1.1
S	0.5	− 4.1	± 1	± 2	1.6

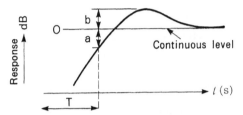

Fig. 2.3. Time-weighting characteristics of the indicator (IEC Pub. 651).

d. Correction for Background Noise

The reading on a sound level meter shows a total sound pressure level from many noise sources surrounding the microphone and is referred to as 'ambient noise'. When only a 'specific noise' emitted from a specific source is to be measured, the effect of residual noise must be excluded. The ambient noise remaining at the microphone position when the specific noise is suppressed is called 'background noise' or 'residual noise'. Unless the background noise level is sufficiently low compared with the one to be measured, proper measurement cannot be carried out. So specifying the sound to be measured as S (signal), where $S = L_1$ dB, the background noise N, where $N = L_2$ dB, then $(L_1 - L_2)$ dB is called the 'SN ratio'. When S coexists with N, the measurable level L_3 dB may be obtained from eqn (1.21). Referring to Fig. 1.4, when the SN ratio is greater than 10 dB, the background noise can be ignored.

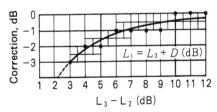

Fig. 2.4. Correction to background noise for a specific noise measurement.

When L_2 and L_3 are measured, L_1 may be obtained from Fig. 2.4 by the same process as in Fig. 1.4. However, if $(L_3 - L_2)$ is smaller than 3 dB, the L_1 value may not be reliable.

[Ex. 2.1]   In a factory the noise level including the noise generated by a machine is 92 dB and with the machine stopped is 87·5 dB, so to obtain the machine noise level

$$L_3 - L_2 = 92 - 87 \cdot 5 = 4 \cdot 5 \text{ dB}$$

From Fig. 2.4 the correction is $-2 \cdot 0$ dB. Hence,

$$L_1 = 92 - 2 = 90 \text{ dB}$$

e.   Other Undesirable Effects and their Remedies

1. *Effect due to reflection and diffraction:* The measurement position should be at least 1 m from any wall, the ground and other objects. When an obstacle approaches the sight-line from source to microphone, a deviation may occur in the measured values. Moreover, the microphone shall be as far as possible from the observer, and if possible on a tripod or fixed stand.

2. *Wind effect:* Outdoors and at positions receiving wind: for example, when located near a blower system, it is difficult to get a correct value of noise level due to wind-induced noise. A windscreen or windshield is essential in order to carry out correct measurements.

3. *Vibration effect:* Where subject to vibration, as in a vehicle or on board ship, it is advisable and effective to hold the microphone and the meter in the hand or support them on a flexible piece of plastic foam to reduce the vibration.

4. *Effect due to electromagnetic fields:* Measurements should not be carried out near an electric motor or transformer unless a condenser microphone is used. Caution is required in order to avoid induced currents in the microphone cable and other parts of the instrumentation.

5. *Effects due to temperature and humidity:* The standard conditions are a temperature of 20°C and 65% relative humidity. When the sensitivity changes by more than $0 \cdot 5$ dB with any other changes in condition, corrections must be provided by the manufacturer.

B.   Frequency Analysis

Frequency analysis of noise is indispensable for the purpose of not only realising the various effects of noise but also preventing them. Fre-

Table 2.2
Frequency of One Octave Band Filter (Hz)

Centre frequency	31·5	63	125	250	500	1,000	2,000	4,000	8,000	16,000
Cut off frequency	22·5	45	90	180	355	710	1,410	2,820	5,630	11,300	22,500

quency analysis is performed by measuring the output of a sound level meter through a band filter which passes only a particular frequency range between f_1 and f_2 (Hz). In the analysing process $f_2 - f_1 = \Delta f$ (Hz) is called the 'band width' or 'pass band' where f_1 and f_2 are the 'cut-off frequencies' and $f_m = \sqrt{f_1 \times f_2}$ is called the 'centre or mid frequency'. There are two types of analysers, i.e. where the ratio f/f_m is constant and where the bandwidth Δf is constant. Although the frequency component details become clearer as the filter band width narrows, more time and effort are required for analysis; therefore, it is necessary to select the analyser which is most appropriate for the analysis of the particular noise.

a.   Octave-band Analyser
When the band width is one octave, i.e. $f_2 = 2f_1$, the band filter is called an 'octave-band filter', while an 'octave-band analyser', which consists of several series of octave-band filters, is used for band-level measurements by switching to each serial band (see Table 2.2). Figure 2.5 shows an example of the standard octave-band filter performance specified by

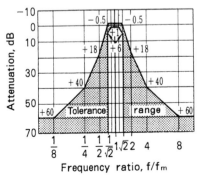

Fig. 2.5.   Frequency characteristics of octave band pass filter
(IEC Pub. 225).

Table 2.3
Serial Number Used in 1/3 Octave Band Centre Frequency

1	1.25	1.6	2	2.5	3.15	4	5	6.3	8	10

the IEC. The portable version of this analyser attached to a sound level meter is very simple and convenient to use for analysing noise in the field and on building sites.

b. 1/3 Octave-band Analyser

Where more detailed analysis is required, 1/3 octave-band filters, which are produced by dividing the octave band width into three equal parts (see Table 2.3), are used. The data obtained by a 1/3 octave-band analyser are often used in various evaluations required in architectural acoustics mainly in laboratory measurements.

c. Other Types of Narrow-band Analyser

In some special cases, for example, in investigations of the noise source, other narrow band widths are required to obtain greater resolution. For this purpose a 'tunable band pass filter', of constant ratio down to 1%, or a 'heterodyne analyser', of equal band width down to about 3 Hz, is used for continuous frequency analysis by sweeping the filters.

d. Arrangement and Conversion of Analysed Data

1. The analysed values should be plotted at the centre frequency of each particular band as shown in Fig. 2.6. The band width should be given for these plottings.
2. The relationship between band level L_b and spectrum level L_s is expressed as follows:

$$L_s = L_b - 10 \log_{10} \Delta f \text{ (dB)} \qquad (2.1)$$

derived from [Ex. 1.9] based on the assumption that levels within Δf are uniformly continuous.

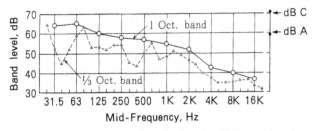

Fig. 2.6. Frequency analysis by 1 and 1/3 Octave band.

3. The total 'over all' level L_{OA} is obtained from the various band levels $L_1, L_2, \ldots, L_n$ as follows:

$$L_{OA} = 10 \log_{10} \frac{\Sigma P_n^2}{P_0^2} = 10 \log_{10}\left(\Sigma 10^{L_n/10}\right) \qquad (2.2)$$

where P_n indicates the sound pressure in each band level. Hence, using eqn (1.21) and Fig. 1.4, a successive calculation is carried out as follows: first the energy sum L_{12} for L_1 and L_2, then the sum for L_{12} and L_3 and so on.

4. In order to obtain dBA values, A-weighting values shown in Table 2.1 are added to all measured band levels, L_n, to obtain the 'over all' total level.

C. Automatic Measurement

In order to achieve accurate measurement, analysis and recording and also to save labor, automatic processing has been developed.

a. Level Recorder

This apparatus records sound levels automatically on a paper chart running at constant speed by means of a pen, the movement of which coincides with fluctuations in sound level. Several types of level recorders are shown in Table 2.4.

There are some automatic analysis systems for steady sound combining one of these level recorders with one of the frequency analysers mentioned above.

b. Magnetic Tape Recorders

For analysis of transient or irregularly fluctuating noise, a magnetic tape recorder recording the output signal from a sound level meter is ideal,

Table 2.4
Level recorders, Types and Characteristics

Mechanism type	Size	Pen (writing) speed*		Characteristics
Galvanometer	small and light	high,	Exponentially variable speed	Approximates to sound level meter indicator
Servomotor	small and light	low,	Constant speed	Automatic balancing type, good accuracy for general physical measurement
Moving coil	large and heavy	high,		

*High speed is suitable for measurement of reverberation time (Fig. 3.16) but poor for impact sound measurement.

and can be made to replay the recording many times in order to carry out the analysis by the various techniques mentioned above. It is very useful, especially for minimizing both time spent on site and apparatus employed. Various types of tape recorders shown in Table 2.5 can be used for different frequency ranges.

c. Real Time Analyser

When the signals change rapidly in both amplitude and frequency, they can be processed simultaneously through all the filters covering the

Table 2.5
Magnetic Tape Recorders, Types and Characteristics

Type	Frequency range	SN ratio	Channel	
1. DR	20 Hz–20(−100) kHz	> 50 dB	2–24	Convertible on frequency*
2. FM	DC-1(−50) kHz	> 40 dB	4–21	
3. PCM	DC-20 kHz	> 70 dB	2–16	For low and audio frequency
4. DAT	1 Hz–22 kHz	> 90 dB	2	

1. DR = Direct Recording of analog signal for sound analysis.
2. FM = Frequency Modulation recording for vibration and sound analysis.
3. PCM = Pulse Code Modulation with video or DAT cassettes.
4. DAT = Digital Audio Tape recording for high quality reproduction.
*For frequency conversion, tape speeds are proportionally changed.

frequency range concerned by means of a real time analyser and the output fed to a continuous display on a screen. The latter can display a series of instantaneous octave or 1/3 octave band spectra which are renewed many times per second. The output can then be recorded using a level recorder or other type of printer.

d. Digitisation and Signal Processing

1. Other instruments are available where the indicator needle of the sound level meter is replaced with a digital display which gives consecutive instantaneous maximum values for prescribed periods such as every 1–5 s. This information can then be printed out.
2. Statistical quantities such as *Percentile level* L_N *or* $L_{AN,T}$ the equivalent continuous A-weighted sound level $L_{Aeq,T}$ and other quantities specified in international standards for rating other types of fluctuating noise (see Section 2.2C) to be described later can be calculated and indicated by a digital processor. These instruments are convenient for continuous observation and for monitoring at fixed positions as well as for the simultaneous recording at many different site positions.
3. Another form of narrow band spectrum analyser is available. It is a fully digitised instrument based on FFT (Fast Fourier Transform) techniques (see Section 10.3). The time history of noise is captured with an A–D (analog–digital) converter and displayed directly on the screen. Quick transformations between the time and frequency domains are effected with a push-button and any of 400 or more discrete lines of the spectrum can be selected with a cursor, both values of frequency and level being displayed in digital form on the screen. This function can also be performed by a general purpose desktop computer with appropriate software.

D. Sound Intensity Measurement

With the rapid development of digital techniques, sound intensity measurements are now easily made with the aid of specially-designed instrumentation systems. Sound intensity is a product of sound pressure and particle velocity as shown in eqn (1.13), which is a vector quantity as the particle velocity has both magnitude and direction. There are two principles upon which the design of the sound intensity probe is based;

i.e. one has a pressure-sensitive microphone and a velocity sensor, the other has two pressure microphones which are located at the proper distance for measuring pressure gradient rather than particle velocity. Both systems are fully digitised and the intensity measurement is carried out automatically. It is, however, difficult to take measurements at more points than would be necessary in making sound pressure measurements; also the directional characteristics have to be taken into consideration. Nevertheless, intensity measurements are now being used for all kinds of acoustic assessments because the sound energy flow in any sound field can be visualised and so many acoustical quantities are defined or specified using sound energy as their basis: for example, sound power of noise sources, absorption coefficient and transmission loss etc. (see Lit. B38).

2.2 NOISE RATING (Lit. B24)

A. Noise Pollution
Any sound undesired by the recipient is classed as noise, as it detracts from the quality of human life. An outline of the impact of noise on comfort is discussed in the following:

a. Annoyance to Daily Life
Because of masking due to noise, the comprehension of speech and music is affected due to decrease in intelligibility (Fig. 1.19). Background noise occurring in telephone, radio and television communication causes poor information transfer, affecting daily social life and productivity. Too much noise is psychologically unacceptable and causes annoyance and interferes with concentration, resulting in a decrease in efficiency leading to misconduct and errors. It also disturbs rest and sleep.

b. Physiological Effects
Noise may cause temporary or permanent disorder in all the physiological functions of the digestive, respiratory organs, circulation and nervous systems. Ando & Hattori (1970) reported some effects on foetal life due to aircraft noise near an airport. It is becoming clear that such environmental noise affects the growth of children.

The most distinct physiological effect is hearing loss. When a momentary hearing loss occurs due to exposure to short duration high level noise, a rise in the threshold of audibility called 'TTS' (temporary threshold shift) is observed which may be recovered with time. However, people working for long hours in extremely noisy factories may risk permanent damage to their hearing referred to as 'PTS' (permanent threshold shift).

c. Social Effects

Alongside or near noisy trunk roads or busy airports the demand for land use is reduced, resulting in lowering land values. Transport noise is also affecting not only human health but cattle and poultry growth, resulting in some lawsuit cases for compensation for decrease of milk and egg production. Thus, noise nuisance is becoming omnipresent in our society.

B. Steady Noise Rating

The effect of noise varies largely depending not only on its intensity but on frequency and the time-varying pattern. As far as the frequency is concerned, noise whose major components are at high frequencies and/or containing pure tones appears noisier. As regards the time domain, generally an interrupted and/or impulsive noise is more annoying than a steady one. Even though the physical stimulus is identical, the effect will vary greatly depending on the listener's physiological and psychological state.

An ideal noise-rating system would be one in which all influencing factors are combined into a unique rating scale suitable for all kinds of noise. However, it is extremely difficult to unify the physical, physiological reactions to noise. Therefore, at present, depending on the ultimate aim, the following assessment methods are employed.

a. Loudness Level (phon) and A-weighted Sound Pressure Level (dBA)

When measuring the physical magnitude of the frequency spectrum of a steady sound, a couple of subjective judging methods are used such as loudness 'sones' and loudness level 'phons'. Although they require much processing for evaluation it has been shown that 'phon' values correspond to L_A (dBA) measured by a simple sound level meter over a wide range of levels. So A-weighted sound level is now commonly used.

Table 2.6 shows acceptable value of dBA for various occupied environments.

Table 2.6
Recommended Range of NCB Curves for Various Occupied Activity
Areas (Beranek, 1988)

Type of space	NCB curve	dBA
Broadcast and recording studios (distant microphone used)	10	18
Concert halls, opera houses, and recital halls	10–15	18–23
Large theatres, churches and auditoriums	< 20	< 28
Television and recording studio (close microphone used)	< 25	< 33
Small theatres, auditoriums, churches, music, rehearsal rooms, large meeting and conference rooms	< 30	< 38
Bedrooms, hospitals, hotels, residences, apartments, etc.	25–40	33–48
Classrooms, libraries, small offices, and conference rooms. Living rooms, and drawing rooms in dwellings	30–40	38–48
Large offices, receptions, retail shops and stores, cafeterias, restaurants, etc.	35–45	43–53
Lobbies, laboratory, drafting rooms, and general offices	40–50	48–58
Kitchens, laundries, computer and maintenance shops	45–55	53–63
Shops, garages, etc. (for just acceptable telephone)	50–60	58–68
For work spaces where speech is not required	55–70	63–78

b. Noisiness and PNL (PNdB)

Kryter (1959) proposed a new subjective rating scale (mainly for the assessment of aircraft noise) which classifies 'noisiness' in units of 'noy' following Stevens' method relating 'loudness' to units of 'sone' (see Section 10.5). The noise level derived from this new scale is called PNL (perceived noise level) whose unit is PNdB (see Section 10.6). Since this method involves much processing, a simplified method using dBD values measured with a sound level meter with the frequency-weighting 'D' (Fig. 2.2) can be used. For example, in the case of noise from jet aircraft

$$PNL = dBD + 7 \qquad (2.3)$$

or, using dBA value measured with the usual A-weighting

$$PNL = dBA + 13 \qquad (2.4)$$

which is recognised as a good approximation to the perceived noise level. For other noise sources further research is still needed.

c. Assessment of Frequency Characteristics

(1) Speech Interference Level (SIL). In order to assess the disturbance caused in speech communication by noise, the arithmetic mean value of

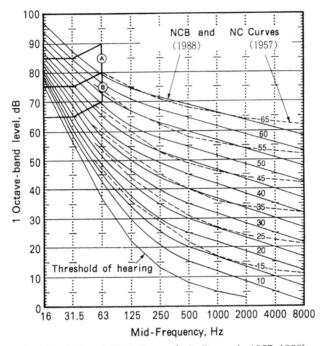

Fig. 2.7.   NC and NCB Curves (L.L. Beranek, 1957, 1988).

4 octave band levels, at mid-frequencies of 500, 1000, 2000 and 4000 Hz is often used in U.S.A.

(2) NC and NCB curves. Beranek (1957) developed Noise Criteria (NC) to deal with commercial buildings. The criteria consisted of a family of curves which related the noise spectrum to the disturbance caused in speech communication. These curves were later revised in 1988 as Balanced Noise Criteria (NCB) with improvements both at low and high frequencies, as shown in Fig. 2.7.

The NCB number of a noise can be determined by plotting the noise in octave band levels on the NCB curves. The lowest curve, which is not exceeded in any of the octave bands, is the NCB rating of the particular noise. The recommended values of NCB are given in Table 2.6 for the environmental assessment. This method is useful because any information relating to frequency necessary for noise reduction purposes can be easily extracted.

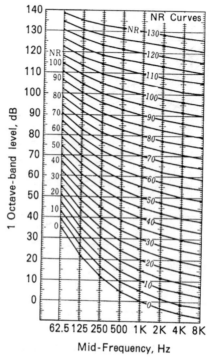

Fig. 2.8. NR Curves.

These values are applicable for background noise under the condition of all the facilities in operation in the room. Therefore the permissible value of each noise source is obtained using the correction described in Section 2.1A,d.

(3) NR Curves. The noise rating method was developed from the NC curves for wider application by a committee of ISO (International organization for standardization) as shown in Fig. 2.8. Though it was not accepted as an international standard it is widely used in Europe for steady noise rating.

(4) Hearing Damage Risk Criteria. The Japanese Industrial Hygiene Association (1966) recommended the damage-risk contours as shown in Fig. 2.9 for simple continuous noise exposure instead of the criteria issued by the Committee on Hearing and Bioacoustics (CHABA) of the U.S Academy of Sciences. These contours indicate permissible exposure

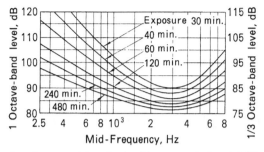

Fig. 2.9. Hearing damage risk criteria (Japanese Industrial Hygiene Assoc. 1969).

minutes against band spectrum levels which correspond to about 90 dBA in an 8-h working day, so that the TTS will not exceed 10 dB at 1 kHz and below, 15 dB at 2 kHz and 20 dB at 3 kHz and above, for the average normal listener.

However, the assessment method for risk of noise-induced hearing impairment is being discussed continuously in the Committee of ISO, since the more important recent concept is one of maximum permissible noise dose which takes into account both the time-varying noise level and its duration.

C. Time-Varying Noise Measurements and Rating

Noise is generally fluctuating with time, and its effect is highly dependent on its time-varying pattern. An intermittent or impact sound is judged as more annoying than a continuous sound. When the meter reading, however, fluctuates within a range of less than 5 dB when using the time-weighting 'S', then the noise can be treated as a steady noise and the average meter deflection taken.

a. Sampling or Statistical Measurements

(1) Discrete Noise Event having a Relatively Constant Peak. Noise like that produced by a train requires an average value from several measurements, each one taken over a specified period and time interval.

(2) Separate Noise Event having a Wide Range of Peak Values. Noise similar to that produced by aircraft needs to be expressed in terms of the number of peak values which occur during the measuring period;

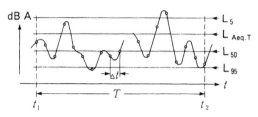

Fig. 2.10. Irregularly fluctuating noise with wide dynamic range.

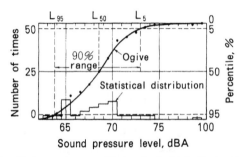

Fig. 2.11. Ogive and percentile level of widely fluctuating noise.

for example, 13 times above 80 dBA, 10 times above 90 dBA, 3 times above 100 dBA, and the maximum value 105 dBA in an interval of 1 h.

(3) Irregularly Fluctuating Noise with Wide Range in Amplitude. Noise such as occurs in the street can be obtained in terms of a 'percentile level' $L_{AN,T}$, which is obtained by using the time-weighting 'F' exceeded for N% of the time interval, T, as shown in Fig. 2.10. For example, after reading 50 samples of instantaneous level in the interval $\Delta t = 5$ s, sorting them into each level as shown in Fig. 2.11, where the median value L_{A50} lies at the centre of ogive, then the 90% variation range inclusive of 90% of the samples, which is adopted as an evaluation standard in Japan, is indicated by L_{A95} and L_{A5} on the upper abscissa.

b. Measurements Based on Sound Dosage
Generally the effect of noise on human life can be taken as approximately proportional to the total energy of the existing noise stimulus. On the other hand, environmental noise is often a combination of sounds from many sources, and the distribution of such different kinds of sound is likely to change from moment to moment. Although there is

a 'Dosimeter' measuring 'Total noise exposure level' on the market, the International Standard (ISO 1996/1) has defined the basic quantities, $L_{Aeq,T}$ and L_{AE} etc., in order to describe the noise in a community environment. The definitions are reviewed in the following:

(1) Equivalent Continuous A-weighted Sound Pressure Level. This is the level in dBA of a continuous steady sound which has the same A-weighted sound energy as the actual noise history within a specified time interval T. It is defined as:

$$L_{Aeq,T} = 10\log_{10}\left[\frac{1}{t_2 - t_1}\int_{t_1}^{t_2}\frac{P_A^2(t)}{P_0^2}\,dt\right]\text{dB} \qquad (2.5)$$

where $T = t_2 - t_1$; $P_A(t)$, instantaneous A-weighted sound pressure; P_0, reference sound pressure (20 μPa).

The simplest method of measuring $L_{Aeq,T}$ is to use an 'integrating sound level meter' (IEC Pub.804) which calculates and indicates the value of $L_{Aeq,T}$ together with the value of T automatically. Use can be made of an ordinary sound level meter by employing a sampling process. For this purpose $L_{Aeq,T}$ can be written as

$$L_{Aeq,T} = 10\log_{10}\left[\frac{1}{n}(10^{L_{A1}/10} + 10^{L_{A2}/10} + \cdots + 10^{L_{An}/10})\right]\text{dB} \quad (2.6)$$

where n = total number of samples and $L_{A1}, L_{A2}, \ldots, L_{An}$ = measured sound levels in (dBA).

When the sampling period Δt is shorter than the time constant of the measuring system, almost the same result is obtained as that obtained with the integrating sound level meter. However, in practice the recommendation is as follows:

with time-weighting 'F' $\Delta t \leq 0\cdot25$ s

with time-weighting 'S' $\Delta t \leq 2\cdot0$ s

When the noise fluctuation is small, Δt can be longer by $5\cdot0$ s, then the conventional instrument is still useable.

If the noise level fluctuations form a normal distribution then the relation with the percentile level is as follows:

$$\begin{aligned}L_{Aeq} &= L_{A10} - 1\cdot3\sigma + 0\cdot12\sigma^2\\ &= L_{A50} + 0\cdot12\sigma^2\end{aligned} \qquad (2.7)$$

where, σ is the standard deviation.

It is also said that L_{Aeq} for highway traffic noise is equivalent to $L_{A25} \sim L_{A30}$.

(2) Single Event of a Discrete Noise. The 'sound exposure level' of a discrete noise event is defined as

$$L_{AE} = 10 \log_{10} \left[\frac{1}{t_0} \int_{t_1}^{t_2} \frac{P_A^2(t)}{P_0^2} \, dt \right] \text{ dB} \tag{2.8}$$

where t_0 = reference duration of 1 s; $t_2 - t_1$ = stated time interval long enough to encompass all significant sound of a stated event.

An integrating sound level meter is a convenient instrument to use for this measurement. For an impulsive noise using an ordinary sound level meter an approximate value of L_{AE} can be obtained from the peak value by using 'S' time-weighting.

When a noise event has a rather long duration of more than several seconds, with a sampling period Δt short enough to trace the noise-varying pattern, L_{AE} can be obtained using the conventional instrument with 'S' time-weighting as follows:

$$L_{AE} = 10 \log_{10} \left[\frac{\Delta t}{t_0} (10^{L_{A1}/10} + 10^{L_{A2}/10} + \cdots + 10^{L_{An}/10}) \right] \text{ dB} \tag{2.9}$$

where the symbols are the same as in eqn (2.6).

(3) Day-night Equivalent Level. This is defined and proposed by the E.P.A. (Environmental Protection Agency) in the U.S.A. It is an average taken over 24 h with a penalty of 10 dB for night-time noise level to take into account the greater annoyance during night as follows:

$$L_{dn} = 10 \log_{10} \frac{1}{24} [15 \times 10^{L_d/10} + 9 \times 10^{(L_n + 10)/10}] \tag{2.10}$$

$$L_d = L_{eq}(7 \cdot 00 \sim 22 \cdot 00), \qquad L_n = (22 \cdot 00 \sim 7 \cdot 00)$$

The recommended criteria are shown in Table 2.7.

(4) Noise Pollution Level. Depending on the noise variation pattern, annoyance is different even for identical L_{Aeq} values; therefore, Robinson (1971) has proposed a definition of noise pollution level, L_{NP}, combining the standard deviation, σ, as follows:

$$L_{NP} + L_{Aeq} + 2 \cdot 56\sigma$$

$$\approx L_{Aeq} + (L_{10} - L_{90}) \tag{2.11}$$

where the constant $2 \cdot 56$ was obtained from social surveys and is said to be applicable for all kinds of noise, although further study is required.

Table 2.7
Permissible Values for L_{dn} and $L_{Aeq,24h}$

Purpose	Standard	Application
Audibility protection	$L_{Aeq,24h} \leq 70$	Whole areas
Outdoor activity	$L_{dn} \leq 55$	Residential areas and quiet places
	$L_{Aeq,24h} \leq 55$	School courtyard, public parks and allied spaces
Indoor activity	$L_{dn} \leq 45$	Inside residences,
	$L_{Aeq,24h} \leq 45$	Schools except residences areas

(5) WECPNL (aircraft noise rating). While various rating methods for aircraft noise have been suggested in many countries, in Japan WECPNL (Weighted Equivalent Continuous PNL) specified by the ICAO (International Civil Aviation Organisation) is used. Its principle is based on a total noise exposure using PNL. The Environment Agency of Japan has prescribed a value as shown below where, for convenience of measurement, the noise level is observed in one day,

$$\text{WECPNL} = \overline{\text{dBA}} + 10\log_{10} N - 27 \qquad (2.12)$$

where $\overline{\text{dBA}}$ is the average value of all peak levels and N is the number of flights in 1 day divided into 3 parts, i.e. daytime N_1, 7–19 h, evening N_2, 19–22 h and night-time N_3, 22–7 h with weighting factors as shown in eqn (2.13).

$$N = N_1 + 3N_2 + 10N_3 \qquad (2.13)$$

The criteria for this method of environmental assessment are shown in Table 2.8.

For annoyance assessment of aircraft noise too, if possible, it is preferable to use a simpler scale such as $L_{Aeq,T}$ or L_{NP} in common with other noises. Further research is still required to investigate this concept.

Table 2.8
Japan Environmental Standard for Aircraft Noise (1973)

Area type	WECPNL	Applicable area
I	< 70	Exclusive residential area
II	< 75	Other areas required to preserve normal life

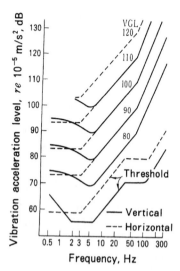

Fig. 2.12. Equal sensation curves for whole body sinusoidal vibration in both vertical and horizontal direction (Miwa 1971).

2.3   MEASUREMENT OF VIBRATION

A.   Human Sensitivity to Vibration

a.   Measurement of Equal Sensation

Unlike sound, vibration has an extra dimension, that of direction. Furthermore, owing to the complexity of the human sensitivity to vibration, research into it has taken second place to noise. Miwa & Yonekawa (1974) reviewed their experimental work and produced a chart of equal sensation curves for human response to vibration (Fig. 2.12) as a function of acceleration levels. This figure is similar to the equal loudness curves shown in Fig. 1.11. For vibration, however, there are two kinds of curve, one for vertical and the other for the horizontal vibration of the floor on which a person is assumed to be standing or sitting.

b.   Evaluation of Environmental Vibration

ISO (2631 series) is going to specify the base curves shown in Fig. 2.13 which represent magnitudes of approximately equal human response

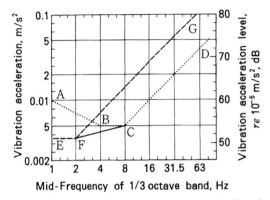

Fig. 2.13. Base curves for acceleration in environmental vibration: A–B–C–D for vertical (foot to head) direction; E–F–G, for horizontal (side to side and back to chest) direction; E–F–C–D for combined direction, used when the directions of vibration and human occupants vary or are unknown.

Table 2.9
Multiplying Factors Applied to the Base Curves Shown in Fig. 2.13 to Specify Satisfactory Magnitudes of Building Vibration

Place	Time	Continuous or intermittent vibration	Transient vibration excitation with several occurrences per day[1]
Critical working (e.g. medical operation etc.)	Day	1	1
	Night		
Residential	Day	2–4	60–90
	Night	1·4	1·4–20
Office	Day	4	128
	Night		
Workshop[2]	Day	8	128
	Night		

[1] The 'trade-off' between number of events per day and magnitudes is not well established.
[2] Working places subject to vibration, e.g. drop forges or crushers, may not be included.

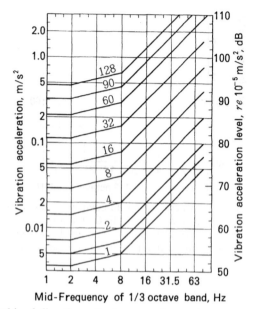

Fig. 2.14. Combined-direction criteria curves for environmental vibration, corresponding to the various multiplying factors given in Table 2.9.

with respect to human annoyance and complaints about interference with comfort. Satisfactory vibration magnitudes in the human environment should be specified in multiples of the values of the base curves. Table 2.9 shows the multiplying factors currently used to evaluate the criteria, and Fig. 2.14 shows the criteria curves specified by Table 2.9 for the base curve of combined-direction shown in Fig. 2.13.

B. Measuring Instrumentation

a. Construction of the Vibration Meter

A vibration-measuring instrument works on a similar principle to that of a sound level meter except a vibration pickup replaces the microphone. There are many types of vibration pickup for measuring various kinds of vibration such as that produced by noisy machinery; also building elements, for example, wall or floor, transmitting structure-borne sound as shown in Table 2.10. For measurement of environmental vibration the piezoelectric accelerometer shown in Fig. 2.15, is widely used, since it has very wide frequency and dynamic response with good linearity and, since its output is proportional to acceleration, integration of the output enables velocity or displacement to be measured. ISO (8041) will publish the standard for the vibration-measuring instrumentation for assessing human response to vibration.

b. Frequency Weighting

Human-response vibration-measuring instrumentation should have one or more frequency weighting characteristics corresponding to three base curves shown in Fig. 2.13 and also an optional characteristic flat to measure unweighted values, not only of vibration but also, for example, infrasound, using an auxiliary component. The instrument should satisfy the requirements of the specified weighting characteristics and tolerances in a specified frequency range.

c. Time Weighting

The detector-indicator should indicate the r.m.s. value using an averaging circuit of 1 s time-constant, i.e. the same characteristics as the 'S' time-weighting of the sound level meter as shown in Fig. 2.3, because the sensitivity of vibration is reduced when duration of vibration becomes shorter than 1 s.

d. Vibration Measurement and Analysis

The vibration pickup should be installed very firmly so as not to wobble or resonate with its own mass coupled to a soft surface. Vibration in 3 axes should be recorded and frequency analysis performed in 1/3 octaves or with narrow band filters as previously described. In all cases, the effect of ambient vibration should be excluded by using Fig. 2.4 and by taking measurements at a number of points. All instruments described in Section 2.1 are also useful as related equipment for measuring vibration.

2.4   VIBRATION POLLUTION AND ITS DISTRIBUTION

A. Generation of Vibration Pollution

Annoyance due to vibration is generated by transportation systems, factory machinery and construction work, and is transmitted chiefly through the ground but sometimes through air, causing vibration of

Table 2.10
Vibration Pick-up: Types and Characteristics

Mechanism types	Piezo-electric types	Electro-dynamic types	Resistant wire strain gauge
Weight	1–600 g	25–4000 g	1–400 g
f_0 resonant frequency	10–180 kHz	0·2–30 Hz	10–2000 Hz
Effective frequency range	1–50 000 Hz 0·1–1000 Hz	30–4000 Hz 0·2–30 Hz	0–700 Hz 0–8 Hz
Internal impedance	High capacitance	Inductance lower than 1000 Ω	100–400 Ω
Output	Proportional to acceleration at frequencies lower than f_0	Proportional to velocity at frequencies higher than f_0	Proportional to displacement
Purpose	Acceleration, velocity, displacement	Velocity, displacement	Displacement
Merits	Light weight, small size, wide range	High output voltage, cable extension is easy as its impedance is low	Light weight measurement is possible from 0 Hz
Demerits	Preamplifier is required as impedance is high	Easily affected by electromagnetic field	Low output, difficult to amplify

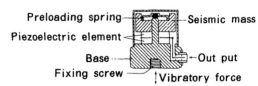

Fig. 2.15.   Construction of a piezo-electric accelerometer.

buildings and disturbance to the human environment. Not only direct human suffering but also resonance of building elements, fixtures and furniture producing noise as a secondary effect results from vibration. In severe cases physical damage such as cracking of walls and slipping roof tiles may occur.

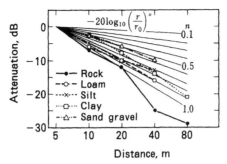

Fig. 2.16. Attenuation with distance of ground vertical vibration in different soils (Shioda).

B. Attenuation with Distance and Prevention of Transmission

Unlike noise, ground vibration is propagated by means of longitudinal, transverse and surface waves, all of which have different attenuation characteristics with frequency, direction and amplitude. Moreover, the medium consists of different kinds of soil layers whose transmission characteristics differ locally and include discontinuities due to ground water, etc., thus the transmission mechanism becomes very complicated. In addition, attenuation caused by the medium's internal losses is so variable that exact prediction of the effect of distance may be difficult. However, as shown in Fig. 2.16, the attenuation due to distance seems to be around -3 to -6 dB per doubling of distance, which applies primarily to surface waves which are largely responsible for the transmission of ground vibration (Shioda 1986). In order to block the transmission path some obstructions such as ditches and underground walls have been used for some time. In the case of ditches, where the depth is about the same as the wavelength, the amplitude ratio is often reported to be reduced by about 1/10, but there is no reliable formula as yet which can be used with confidence because of the numerous influencing factors.

C. Criteria for Rating of Vibration Pollution

The characteristics of vibration pollution may be described as follows:

1. Excluding special cases, vibration does not extend beyond 100 m from the source (in most cases, about 10–20 m).

2. In general, the vertical vibration magnitude is larger than the horizontal one.
3. The vibration frequency commonly lies in the range of 1–90 Hz.

As regards a reliable rating method or criteria for vibration pollution, we can quote only Table 2.9 and Fig. 2.14 at present. However, the more detailed evaluation methods for effects of annoyance, especially due to impulsive, intermittent and time-varying vibrations, are currently being researched. There are many difficulties to overcome, because annoyance due to vibration can be changed by its duration and the time period over which events occur; furthermore any startle factor caused by a transient vibration can be reduced by warning signals, announcement and regularity of occurrence and a suitable public relations programme.

2.5 INFRASOUND AND LOW FREQUENCY AIR VIBRATION

Infrasound is defined as sound whose frequency is lower than the minimum audible frequency, i.e. about 20 Hz. Recently, however, serious complaints on noise pollution in the frequency range about 1–100 Hz have occurred. Therefore, it is often called 'low frequency noise' or 'low frequency air vibration'.

It can be measured with instruments normally used for measuring vibration incorporating an appropriate microphone.

In the low frequency region there is such a wide scatter of individual hearing thresholds that a noise audible to one person may not be audible to another. Physiological and psychological factors differ widely between individuals which is by far the major problem in assessing response to infrasound. The effect can be very distressing for some people who are affected and who are passed back and forth between environmental and medical authorities, both failing to solve their problem (Leventhall 1987).

Infrasound is generated by large fans, diesel engines, gas turbines, combustion processes in industry and by heavy traffic; also by domestic appliances such as washing machines, waste disposal units, pumps, refrigerators and air-conditioning systems, etc.

These low-frequency air vibrations cause not only building vibration and the same effects as vibration pollution, but also unsolved effects on human bodies described above. Therefore, there is an urgent requirement to establish a rating method and countermeasures.

PROBLEMS 2

1. Noise data (band spectrum) analysed by octave band filters in an office room as shown in Table P.2.1, X. Obtain the values of dBC, dBA and NCB.

Table P.2.1
Octave band level (dB)

Freq. (Hz)	31.5	63	125	250	500	1 k	2 k	4 k	8 k
X	64	68	61	64	57	43	37	29	23
Y	64	68	61	64	61	56	45	34	26

2. In the office room mentioned above, find the reduction value in each octave band necessary to obtain NCB-45. Hence what is the dBA value? Furthermore, when NCB-40 is realised, what is the dBA value?
3. After installation of office machinery in the above room the noise data changed as shown in Table P.2.1, Y. Estimate the sound level generated by the machine in each octave band.
4. The results of a noise survey at a roadside are obtained in every 5 s as shown in Table P.2.2. Find the statistical values of L_{50}, L_5, L_{10}, L_{90} and L_{95}.

Table P.2.2
Street noise level (dBA) in 5-s intervals

68	71	70	64	65	74	65	68	69	70
73	69	72	69	65	66	69	79	66	67
68	70	69	70	71	73	68	67	70	74
65	66	65	63	63	67	70	68	70	72
69	68	68	71	70	66	65	66	65	67

5. Enumerate the factors related to 'annoyance' of noise and explain the difference between 'loudness' and 'noisiness'.

Chapter 3

ROOM ACOUSTICS

Acoustical phenomena in a closed room are the main focal problems in architectural acoustics. In this chapter fundamental theories are described and their practical applications are discussed.

3.1   SOUND FIELD IN A ROOM

A.   Characteristics of the Indoor Sound Field

While the characteristics of the outdoor sound field are rather simple because the sound wave from the source spreads out freely, assuming there is no obstacle, then attenuates with distance, the sound emitted indoors creates a very complicated sound field due to multiple reflections from walls, ceiling and floor. The characteristics of the indoor sound field are as follows. (1) The sound intensity at a receiving point remote from the source is not attenuated as much as in free space even if the distance is large. (2) Reverberation occurs due to the reflected sound arriving after the source has stopped. These two features are quite distinct from the outdoor situation and are very important. Moreover, depending upon the room shape and surface finish, peculiar phenomena like echos, flutter echos, etc, which result in a complicated acoustic field are observed. This is mainly due to the effect of surrounding walls which determine the room shape. Therefore, the purpose of the study of room acoustics is to control the above described phenomena by means of room boundary conditions such as room shape and finishing materials and to create a satisfactory acoustical environment in the space.

B. Geometrical Acoustics and Physical Acoustics

The science which handles sound energy transmission and diffusion geometrically without considering the physical wave nature of sound is called 'geometrical acoustics' whereas the science which handles the physical wave nature of sound wave is called 'wave acoustics' or 'physical acoustics'.

When the wave nature of the sound field in a room is discussed, the wave equation, as described later, has to be solved under the appropriate boundary conditions. It is possible, however, to solve only simple cases. But, very complicated problems occur in real rooms surrounded by walls whose shape and characteristics are quite varied. However, in the case of rooms with dimensions large compared with the wavelength and with a complexity of walls the sound field may be analysed rather simply with geometrical acoustics and the wave nature of sound ignored. Thus, most practical problems of room acoustics are handled with the aid of geometrical acoustics although it is necessary to have a proper understanding of wave acoustics for more accurate and effective application of the former.

3.2 NORMAL MODE OF VIBRATION IN ROOMS

When wave motion is taken into account in room acoustics, the most important and fundamental characteristic which needs to be understood is the normal mode of vibration of the room. Thus, to begin with, the simplest case of one dimensional space, i.e. the sound field in a closed pipe is discussed.

A. Normal Mode of Vibration in a Closed Pipe

a. Wave equation and its solution

In the case of a closed pipe whose internal diameter is small compared with the wavelength, the sound wave can only propagate longitudinally and not across the pipe, therefore, only one dimensional plane wave motion need be considered. The wave equation of this free vibration can be derived from the characteristics of the medium as follows (see Section 10.1)

$$\frac{\partial^2 \varphi}{\partial t^2} = c^2 \frac{\partial^2 \varphi}{\partial x^2} \tag{3.1}$$

where φ can be thought of as either the sound pressure p or the particle velocity v because both can be expressed in the same form. Hence, instead of the double process of handling p and v it is convenient to introduce a new function φ which is defined as follows,

$$\left.\begin{array}{c} v = -\dfrac{\partial \varphi}{\partial x} \\[2ex] p = \rho \dfrac{\partial \varphi}{\partial t} \end{array}\right\} \tag{3.2}$$

where p is density of medium. The minus gradient in any direction (in this case the x direction) indicates the particle velocity in that direction, hence the reason for calling φ the velocity potential. So differentiating φ with respect to t or x enables p or v to be derived by using eqn (3.2)

When the sound wave can be described by simple harmonic motion, $\varphi \propto e^{j\omega t}$ with angular frequency ω, then eqn (3.1) becomes

$$\left(\frac{d^2}{dx^2} + k^2\right)\varphi = 0 \tag{3.3}$$

where

$$k = \frac{\omega}{c}$$

The general solution of the above equation is

$$\varphi = C_1 e^{j(\omega t - kx)} + C_2 e^{j(\omega t + kx)} \tag{3.4}$$

where C_1 and C_2 are constants.

The first term describes the wave propagating in the $+x$ direction. The second term describes the wave propagating in the $-x$ direction. Alternatively the above solution can be expressed as follows:

$$\varphi = (A \cos kx + B \sin kx) e^{j\omega t} \tag{3.5}$$

where

$$A = (C_1 + C_2) \quad \text{and} \quad B = -j(C_1 - C_2)$$

b. Natural vibration in a closed pipe

Here, we discuss the case where the pipe is closed at $x = 0$ and l_x by rigid walls. The boundary condition of this space is such that the particle velocity is 0 at $x = 0$ and $x = l_x$. From eqns (3.2) and (3.5) the following is obtained.

$$v = -\frac{\partial \varphi}{\partial x} = k(A \sin kx - B \cos kx) e^{j\omega t} \tag{3.6}$$

In order to satisfy the boundary condition $B = 0$ when $x = 0$ and $\sin kl_x = 0$ when $x = l_x$.

Hence,

$$k_m l_x = m\pi, \quad (m = 0, 1, 2, 3, \dots)$$

Therefore

$$k_m \equiv \frac{\omega_m}{c} = \frac{m\pi}{l_x} \tag{3.7}$$

here, $m = 0$ is not our concern as it infers zero vibration. Then, the angular frequency with specific values is expressed as follows,

$$\omega_m = \frac{cm\pi}{l_x}$$

and frequencies satisfying the above relation are

$$f_m = \frac{\omega_m}{2\pi} = \frac{cm}{2l_x} \text{ (Hz)} \tag{3.8}$$

These are called 'normal frequencies' or 'natural frequencies' characterising 'natural vibrations' which are also known as 'normal modes of vibration'. Furthermore, at these frequencies the pipe resonates, therefore, they are called 'resonance frequencies'. The wavelengths λ_m for the above case are,

$$\lambda_m = \frac{c}{f_m} = \frac{2l_x}{m} \qquad \therefore \quad l_x = m\frac{\lambda_m}{2} \qquad (3.9)$$

This means that the frequencies where the pipe length is an integral multiple of a half wavelength are natural frequencies. There are an infinite number of normal modes of vibration from $m = 1$ to infinity.

[Ex. 3.1]   To obtain the normal mode of vibration $m = 1\text{--}3$ for a pipe of length 6.8 m. From eqn (3.8) with sound velocity $c = 340$ m,

$$f_1 = \frac{340}{2 \times 6\cdot8} = 25 \text{ Hz}, \quad f_2 = 25 \times 2 = 50 \text{ Hz}, \quad f_3 = 25 \times 3 = 75 \text{ Hz}$$

[Ex. 3.2]   For the above condition the particle velocity distribution in the pipe whose length is l_x from eqns (3.6) and (3.7) becomes

$$v = kA \sin\left(\frac{m\pi x}{l_x}\right)e^{j\omega t}$$

then the particle velocity distribution is expressed by

$$\sin\left(\frac{m\pi x}{l_x}\right) \qquad (3.10)$$

This is shown by solid lines in Fig. 3.1 for $m = 1$ to $m = 3$.

[Ex. 3.3]   For the above condition the sound pressure distribution is derived from eqns (3.2) and (3.5).

$$p = \rho\frac{\partial\varphi}{\partial t} = j\omega\rho A \cos kx e^{j\omega t} = j\omega\rho A \cos\left(\frac{m\pi x}{l_x}\right)e^{j\omega t}$$

Therefore, the pressure distribution is expressed by

$$\cos\left(\frac{m\pi x}{l_x}\right) \qquad (3.11)$$

This is shown by dotted lines in Fig. 3.1.

As discussed in the above example the sound pressure and particle velocity in the pipe in its normal mode of vibration can be determined by position. The wave is found to be a standing wave because its shape does not shift.

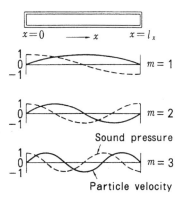

Fig. 3.1. Normal mode of vibration in a closed pipe.

B. Natural Frequency of a Rectangular Room

In ordinary rooms the sound wave has to be treated as a three-dimensional field. The velocity potential φ is given as a solution of the three-dimensional wave equation similar to the one for the one-dimensional field as follows:

$$\frac{\partial^2 \varphi}{\partial t^2} = c^2 \left(\frac{\partial^2 \varphi}{\partial x^2} + \frac{\partial^2 \varphi}{\partial y^2} + \frac{\partial^2 \varphi}{\partial z^2} \right) \tag{3.12}$$

where c is the sound speed.

Now, we choose a rectangular room with dimensions l_x, l_y and l_z for simplicity, taking the origin of coordinates as the corner of the room, as shown in Fig. 3.2. The boundary condition for a rigid wall is that the particle velocity normal to the wall is zero at the wall. The equation can be solved in a similar way to the one-dimensional case because the

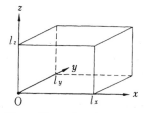

Fig. 3.2. Three-dimensional room coordinates.

three variables can be separated. With these conditions the natural frequency is obtained as follows.

$$f_n = \frac{c}{2}\sqrt{\left(\frac{n_x}{l_x}\right)^2 + \left(\frac{n_y}{l_y}\right)^2 + \left(\frac{n_z}{l_z}\right)^2} \qquad (3.13)$$

where, n_x, n_y and n_z are taken as $0, 1, 2, 3, \ldots$ etc. The particle velocity distribution in the room is expressed as a standing wave as follows:

$$\sin\left(\frac{n_x \pi x}{l_x}\right)\sin\left(\frac{n_y \pi y}{l_y}\right)\sin\left(\frac{n_z \pi z}{l_z}\right) \qquad (3.14)$$

and the pressure amplitude distribution as

$$\cos\left(\frac{n_x \pi x}{l_x}\right)\cos\left(\frac{n_y \pi x}{l_y}\right)\cos\left(\frac{n_z \pi z}{l_z}\right) \qquad (3.15)$$

These expressions correspond to eqns (3.8), (3.10) and (3.11) in the one dimensional case.

Although there are an infinite number of normal modes depending upon arbitrary combination of n_x, n_y and n_z, they are separated into three categories:

(1) *Axial mode:* for which two n's are zero, then the waves travel along one axis, parallel to two pairs of walls and are therefore called 'axial waves'.

(2) *Tangential mode:* for which one n is zero, the waves are parallel to one pair of parallel walls and are obliquely incident on two other pairs of walls. The waves are called 'tangential waves'.

(3) *Oblique mode:* for which no n is zero, then the waves are obliquely incident on all walls and called 'oblique waves'.

[Ex. 3.4] When normal modes $(2,0,0)$, $(1,1,0)$, $(2,1,0)$ exist, the sound pressure distribution can be described in a two-dimensional plane since $n_z = 0$ in eqn (3.15). And the mode $(2,0,0)$ is in one-dimension corresponding to the case of $m = 2$ in Fig. 3.1. These results are shown by contours of equal sound pressure in Fig. 3.3. On the two sides of the zero contour line of sound pressure, i.e. the node of the standing wave, the sign is reversed as shown in Fig. 3.1. For the sound pressure distribution, however, only the absolute values are given since the phase is of no interest.

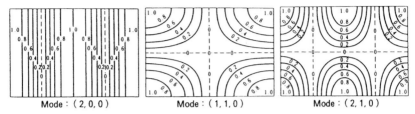

Fig. 3.3. Examples of sound pressure distribution for normal mode of vibrations.

Some interesting characteristics are illustrated by this example as follows: (1) the sound pressure is a maximum at the room corner for any mode; and (2) when any one of n_x, n_y and n_z is an odd integer the sound pressure becomes 0 at the centre of the room and so on.

C. Number of Normal Modes and their Distribution
Although the number of normal modes are infinite, when eqn (3.13) is rearranged as follows,

$$f_n = \sqrt{\left(\frac{cn_x}{2l_x}\right)^2 + \left(\frac{cn_y}{2l_y}\right)^2 + \left(\frac{cn_z}{2l_z}\right)^2} \qquad (3.16)$$

f_n is found to correspond to the distance between the origin of the rectangular coordinates and the point given by coordinates

$$\left(\frac{cn_x}{2l_x}, \frac{cn_y}{2l_y}, \frac{cn_z}{2l_z}\right)$$

Thus, if a three-dimensional lattice spaced at $c/2l_x$, $c/2l_y$ and $c/2l_z$ along the axes f_x, f_y and f_z respectively as shown in Fig. 3.4 is formed (called 'frequency space') then every node of the lattice, in the frequency space corresponds to each normal mode, and the number of normal modes is equal to the number of lattice points. Hence, the total number of normal modes less than f is equal to the total number of points within the first octant of the sphere of radius f, having its centre at the origin of coordinates. Therefore, when f increases, the number of points (normal modes) rapidly increases. In this context, f_x, f_y and f_z express the axial modes along the respective axes increasing in proportion to f while the lattice points located in the plane including 2 axes

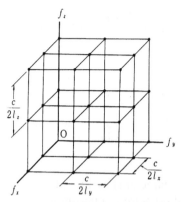

Fig. 3.4. Frequency space lattice expressing normal mode of vibration of a rectangular room.

express two-dimensional tangential modes increasing in proportion to f^2 and all other lattice points express three-dimensional oblique modes increasing in proportion to f^3. Furthermore, if we consider the density of normal modes at frequency f, axial modes are constant regardless of f while tangential modes are almost proportional to the arc length of the circle whose radius is f, therefore the modes are proportional to f. Oblique modes are proportional to the surface area of the sphere and thus proportional to f^2. In other words, as far as the distribution of natural frequencies is concerned, the higher the frequency, the larger their density and since the number of oblique modes is largest, the density is considered to be proportional to the square of the frequency.

D. Room Shape and Natural Frequency Distribution

Using eqn (3.13) depending on the particular choice of (n_x, n_y, n_z) it is possible to obtain the same value for the frequency f_n with more than one combination of (n_x, n_y, n_z). These normal modes are then referred to as 'degenerate'. Several lattice points exist on the same sphere whose centre is at the origin of coordinates in the frequency space shown in Fig. 3.4.

The degeneration of normal modes means that their non-uniform distribution makes the acoustic condition of the room undesirable and is related to the dimensional ratio $l_x : l_y : l_z$. The natural frequency distribution in two rooms whose side length ratios are 1:1:1 and

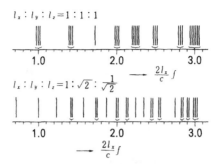

Fig. 3.5. Distribution of normal mode of vibration in two rectangular rooms.

$1/\sqrt{2}:1:\sqrt{2}$ is shown in Fig. 3.5. The normal mode degeneration of a regular cube is very distinct.

In general when the ratio of the room's length, width to height, is integrally related, e.g. 1:2:4, degeneration is emphasised and therefore, must be avoided.

The room shape can be used to eliminate degeneration and to create a uniform distribution of normal modes by having oblique boundary planes instead of parallel walls. In such an irregularly shaped room all natural frequencies may be of the oblique mode type, favourable for a uniform sound decay process. This technique is often applied in reverberation rooms where the requirement is for a diffuse sound field.

E. Transmission Characteristics

The natural frequency distribution can be obtained by measuring the transmission characteristics of the room. While generating a pure tone of constant intensity with a loudspeaker at one corner of a room and sweeping the frequency, the record of sound pressure level measured at another corner shows the transmission characteristics between the two points. Figure 3.6 illustrates this.

In general a sharp peak can be found at the normal mode frequencies of the room. Although in the low frequency range there are fewer normal modes yielding fewer resonance peaks they are nevertheless quite distinct. At higher frequencies there are many which are closer together, even overlapping and tending to produce a uniform transmission. From the above it can be seen that it is desirable to avoid degenerate normal modes and to have a uniform distribution of modes with spacing as nearly equal as possible at all frequencies.

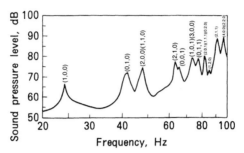

Fig. 3.6. Transmission characteristics of a rectangular room of $4 \cdot 8 \times 7 \cdot 7 \times 2 \cdot 8$ m (Kunden & Harris).

The curve shows various profiles depending upon the positions of sound source and receiver. All normal modes of vibration of the room can be observed when the sound source is located at a corner and the receiver in the other corner along a diagonal of the room (cf. [Ex. 3.4]).

F. Effect of Absorption of Walls

In order to simplify the above discussion we assumed the surrounding walls to be rigid and their surfaces completely reflective. However, they also possess some sound absorption. Therefore, the normal modes of a room generally tend to shift towards lower frequencies, and the rugged profile of the transmission characteristics are flattened. If flat transmission characteristics are desired it is necessary to select appropriate absorbing materials and construction effective for particular normal modes (see Section 4.5).

3.3   REVERBERATION TIME

A. Assumption of Diffuse Sound Field

In geometrical acoustics the sound field in a room is assumed to be completely diffuse. This means: (1) the acoustical energy is uniformly distributed throughout the entire room; and (2) at any point the sound propagation is uniform in all directions.

When the room dimensions become large, the normal modes in the low frequency range are sparsely distributed but their frequencies are below the range of audibility, while many normal modes build up in the audible frequency range. It is almost impossible to treat so many

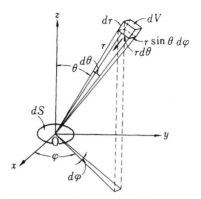

Fig. 3.7. Sound incidence from diffuse sound field.

natural frequencies as individual wave motions, therefore a statistical approach becomes necessary. In other words, wave motion need no longer be considered and geometrical acoustics seems more reasonable. Also the shape of large rooms is often irregular, sound diffusion dominates and the above assumption is satisfactory.

According to this assumption of a 'completely diffuse field' the room acoustics can be treated very simply whereas it is difficult to solve by the wave theory. Therefore, an effort to diffuse the sound field in a room must be made in order to utilise the geometrical theory.

B. Sound Incidence on Wall in Diffuse Sound Field

The energy density E in an infinitesimal volume dV at a distance r from an area dS of wall propagates in all directions in a diffuse sound field. Since the effective area dS as seen from the direction of dV is $dS \cos \theta$ (Fig. 3.7), the energy element incident on dS is as follows

$$\Delta I \, dS = \frac{dS \cos \theta}{4 \pi r^2} E \, . \, dV$$

To calculate the total energy E_i incident on dS in 1 s, the sound energy which travels a distance c is integrated for all dV within the half sphere of radius c with its centre on dS. Using polar coordinates r, θ, ψ centred at dS,

$$dV = r \, d\theta \, . \, dr \, . \, r \sin \theta \, d\theta \, d\varphi$$

Therefore

$$\Delta I \, dS = \frac{E \, dS}{4\pi} \cos\theta \sin\theta \, d\theta \, d\varphi \, dr$$

$$\therefore I \, dS = \frac{E \, dS}{4\pi} \int_0^{\pi/2} \cos\theta \sin\theta \, d\theta \int_0^{2\pi} d\varphi \int_0^c dr = \frac{c}{4} E \, dS \quad (3.17)$$

Hence, the acoustic energy I incident on unit area (1 m^2) in 1 s of the surrounding wall, i.e. the intensity, in the diffuse sound field of energy density E is expressed as follows,

$$I = \frac{c}{4} E \quad (3.18)$$

where c is the sound speed. This is an important feature of a diffuse sound field.

We should remember the above and compare it with the intensity of a plane wave at normal incidence on a wall which is, from eqn (1.16)

$$I = cE$$

C. Reverberation Theory

The reverberation time indicated by eqn (1.36) in Chapter 1 is the most fundamental concept in geometrical acoustics for evaluating the sound field in a room. The theory is based on the assumption of a diffuse sound field in a room, thus, regardless of location and effectiveness of absorbing materials and of the sound source and measuring points, the reverberation time has the same value.

a. Derivation of Sabine's Reverberation Formula

The total surface area of the surrounding walls of a room is S and the energy density of the diffuse sound field is E. The energy incident on all walls is $cES/4$ from eqn (3.18) and the absorbed energy $cES\bar{\alpha}/4$ where $\bar{\alpha}$ is the average absorption coefficient of all walls. If the sound source emits a sound power W (watt), the fundamental equation of the total energy in the room is

$$V\frac{dE}{dt} = W - \frac{cEA}{4} \quad (3.19)$$

where $A = S\bar{\alpha}$ is the room absorption as given in eqn (1.37). With $E = 0$ at $t = 0$ the solution becomes the growth formula for sound in a room

$$E = (4W/cA) \left[1 - e^{(cA/4v)t}\right]$$

The steady-state value E_0 will reached at $t = \infty$ and is given by

$$E_0 = 4W/cA \qquad (3.20)$$

Now, when the sound source stopped and starts to decay, the total energy reduction in the room is obtained by substituting $E = E_0$, $W = 0$ at $t = 0$ in the fundamental eqn (3.19)

$$E = E_0\, e^{-(cA/4V)t} \qquad (3.21)$$

This is the decay formula. Hence the decay rate becomes,

$$D = 10 \log_{10} e^{(cA/4V)} \; (\text{dB/s}) \qquad (3.22)$$

The Reverberation time T is the time required for the sound to decay by 60 dB, therefore

$$T = \frac{60}{D} = \frac{6 \times 4V}{cA \log_{10} e}$$

$$\therefore T = K \frac{V}{A} \qquad (3.23)$$

Thus, Sabine's reverberation formula (1.36) is derived.
In the above equation

$$K = \frac{24}{c \log_{10} e} = \frac{55.26}{c} \qquad (3.24)$$

Where c is the sound speed as given by eqn (1.7). K does, however, vary with temperature as shown in Fig. 3.8.

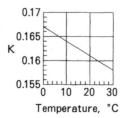

Fig. 3.8. Value of K vs air temperature in the reverberation formula.

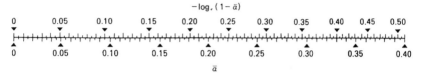

Fig. 3.9. Relationship between $\bar{\alpha}$ and $-\log_e(1 - \bar{\alpha})$.

b. Eyring's Reverberation Formula

While Sabine's formula is applicable to live rooms with low absorption and hence long reverberation times agreeing well with experimental results, the formula tends to give values which are too large for dead rooms with much absorption.

For instance, when $\bar{\alpha} \to 1$ i.e. perfect absorption, it follows that $T \to 0$, while eqn (3.23) yields a certain finite value since $A = S$. Thus, C.F. Eyring (1931) derived the following new formula correcting this defect,

$$T = \frac{KV}{-S \log_e(1 - \bar{\alpha})} \qquad (3.25)$$

where

$$-\log_e(1 - \bar{\alpha}) = \bar{\alpha} + \frac{\bar{\alpha}^2}{2} + \frac{\bar{\alpha}^3}{3} + \cdots \qquad (3.26)$$

Thus, when $\bar{\alpha} \ll 1$, we can neglect terms after the second, so the denominator becomes

$$-S \log_e(-\bar{\alpha}) = S\bar{\alpha} = A$$

Therefore the resulting equation coincides with eqn (3.23). The values of eqn (3.26) are obtained with the aid of Fig. 3.9

Eyring considered that reflected sounds were supposed to be emitted from the image sources. Therefore the endless succeeding reflections means that there are an infinite number of images at infinitely remote positions. When the sound source stops, all images stop simultaneously. At the receiving point, however, initially the direct sound from the source disappears, the reflected sound from the nearest image disappears and so on consecutively producing a step by step decay until all sounds have completely disappeared. Contrary to this concept Sabine considered that the sound decays continuously until it disappears.

A sound wave generated from a sound source reflects from a wall then reflects again from another wall, thus every sound wave travels a different distance. The average distance between reflections is called the 'mean free path'. The time from one reflection to another is p/c second where p is the mean free path and the energy for that period generated from the sound source whose power is W is Wp/c. If the average absorption coefficient of the walls is $\bar{\alpha}$, the power from the image source of the nth reflected sound becomes $W(1 - \bar{\alpha})^n$ and so the energy generated before the next reflection must be $W(1 - \bar{\alpha})^n p/c$. Thus the acoustic energy density including the nth reflected sound is as follows,

$$E_n = \frac{1}{V}\left\{\frac{p}{c}W + \sum_{n=1}^{n} \frac{p}{c}W(1 - \bar{\alpha})^n\right\} = \frac{pW}{cV\bar{\alpha}}\{1 - (1 - \bar{\alpha})^n\} \quad (3.27)$$

The energy density for steady state E_0 with $n \to \infty$ and $(1 - \bar{\alpha})^n \to 0$ is obtained as follows,

$$E_0 = \frac{pW}{cV\bar{\alpha}} \quad (3.28)$$

Comparing with eqn (3.20),

$$\frac{pW}{cV\bar{\alpha}} = \frac{4W}{cS\bar{\alpha}}$$

and so the mean free path becomes

$$p = \frac{4V}{S} \quad (3.29)$$

This shows that in a room satisfying the assumption of a diffuse sound field the mean free path is determined by V/S and is not related to the room shape. Strictly speaking, depending on the room shape and the sound source position, there must be some difference. However, eqn (3.29) gives a sufficiently good approximation except for very particular shapes. Hence, the number of reflections at walls during t second will be

$$\frac{ct}{p} = \frac{cS}{4V}t$$

Therefore, at t seconds after the sound source is stopped in the steady state the sound energy density,

$$E = E_0(1 - \bar{\alpha})^{(cS/4V)t} = E_0 e^{(cSt/4V)\log_e(1 - \bar{\alpha})} \quad (3.30)$$

This is Eyring's attenuation formula. The formula shown in eqn (3.25) can be derived from eqn (3.30) using the same process from eqn (3.21) to eqn (3.23).

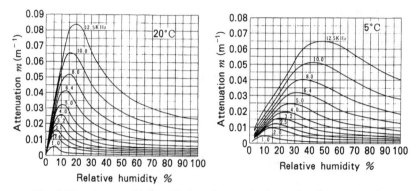

Fig. 3.10.   Attenuation coefficient due to air absorption (C.M.Harris).

c. Reverberation Formula including Air Absorption

When sound waves travel through the air the sound energy decreases owing to air absorption. If a plane wave whose intensity I_0 travels x metres the intensity becomes

$$I = I_0 e^{-mx} \tag{3.31}$$

where m is the energy attenuation constant/metre.

Putting x equal to the distance ct which the sound travels and E of eqn (3.30) subject to further such attenuation,

$$E = E_0 e^{(cSt/4V)\log_e(1-\bar{\alpha})} e^{-mct} = E_0 e^{\{(S\log_e(1-\bar{\alpha})/4V)-m\}ct} \tag{3.32}$$

Then the reverberation time from this expression can be derived in the following:

$$T = \frac{KV}{-S\log_e(1-\bar{\alpha}) + 4mV} \tag{3.33}$$

This is called the Eyring-Knudsen formula for reverberation time. The energy attenuation constant due to air absorption m is related to temperature and humidity as shown in Fig. 3.10 and calculated by the method of ANSI Standard (S1.26–1978). It is negligible below 1000 Hz.

D.   Validity of Reverberation Formulae

All the reverberation time formulae described above are based on the assumption of a diffuse sound field in a room. Since the decay curve can be expressed in terms of an exponential function, it becomes a straight line on the dB scale. However, when this assumption is not satisfied, the

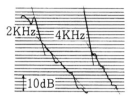

Fig. 3.11. Bending in decay curves.

decay curve does not follow a straight line and the reverberation time is difficult to define. For example, when floor and ceiling are highly absorptive but walls reflective, the reflected sounds in the vertical direction decay rapidly while the reflected sounds in the horizontal direction remain repeating reflections with slow decay, thus the decay curve bends as shown in Fig. 3.11, and the measured reverberation time, for 60 dB decay, is longer than the values calculated by any formula. Similar phenomena are observed in long tunnels, corridors and large rooms with low ceilings or coupled spaces such as audience space and stage area with different decay rates where the sound field does not act as a common diffuse space (see Section 10.8)

In such cases the calculation of reverberation formulae is no longer useful and the measured reverberation time has little meaning. Instead, it is advisable to show two different decay rates in dB/s for these cases.

3.4 SOUND ENERGY DISTRIBUTION IN ROOMS

When a pure tone from a sound source is generated in a room, the sound field is non-uniform due to standing waves produced by interference with reflected sounds. The sound pressure level distribution shows distinct peaks and troughs as shown by the solid line in Fig. 3.12 from measurements at various distances from the sound source. The peak-trough pattern varies with frequency. However, in the case of white noise which includes all frequencies the sound pressure attenuates smoothly as shown by the dotted line in the figure. Many of the peaks and troughs made by an infinite number of frequencies overlap each other and smooth out the irregularity of the distribution. Consequently, we need not consider the wave motion.

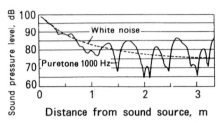

Fig. 3.12. Sound pressure level distribution in a room (Knudson & Harris).

A. Non-Directional Sound Source

The energy density under steady-state conditions from a sound source of power W is given by eqn (3.20) which is the average value for the entire room. However, in reality this density must vary depending on the distance from the source. To obtain this distribution, first the energy density due to the direct sound E_d must be obtained. Assuming the sound source is non-directional and the distance to the receiving point is r,

$$E_d = \frac{W}{4\pi r^2 c} \qquad (3.34)$$

After this direct sound is reflected at the wall, the energy is assumed to be uniformly distributed in the room as the diffused sound. The energy density is E_s, from which the total diffused sound energy $E_s V$ in the room whose volume is V loses an amount $E_s V \bar{\alpha}$ at every reflection, therefore, every second $E_s V \bar{\alpha} cS/4V$ will be lost due to $cS/4V$ reflections in a second. On the other hand, the energy supply becomes $W(1 - \bar{\alpha})$ after the first reflection from the wall. Since this energy is equal to the lost energy in the steady state,

$$E_s = \frac{4W}{cS\bar{\alpha}}(1 - \bar{\alpha}) \qquad (3.35)$$

Hence,

$$E_0 = E_d + E_s = \frac{w}{c}\left(\frac{1}{4\pi r^2} + \frac{4(1 - \bar{\alpha})}{S\bar{\alpha}}\right) \qquad (3.36)$$

where, $S\bar{\alpha}/(1 - \bar{\alpha}) = R$, is sometimes called 'room constant'.

The relationship between the energy density and the sound pressure is shown by eqn (1.16) as follows:

$$E = \frac{p^2}{\rho c^2} \qquad (3.37)$$

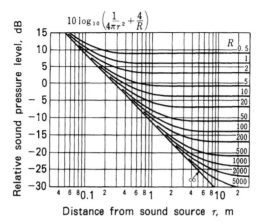

Fig. 3.13. Calculation diagram of diffuse sound field in rooms.

Substituting this relation into eqn (3.36), the sound pressure level L_p at the point under normal conditions reduces to

$$L_p = L_w + 10\log_{10}\left(\frac{1}{4\pi r^2} + \frac{4}{R}\right) \quad (dB) \qquad (3.38)$$

where, L_w is the power level defined as

$$L_w = 10\log_{10}\frac{W}{10^{-12}} \quad (dB)$$

The second term expresses the distribution due to distance from the source as shown in Fig. 3.13 for various values of R. When $R \to \infty$, this means complete absorption, which corresponds to open air.

B. Directional Sound Source
When the sound source has a directivity factor Q (see Section 10.13) to the sound receiving points, the direct sound energy density is

$$E_d = \frac{QW}{4\pi r^2 c} \qquad (3.39)$$

Therefore, in place of eqn (3.36) the energy density under steady state becomes

$$E_0 = \frac{W}{c}\left(\frac{Q}{4\pi r^2} + \frac{4(1-\bar{\alpha})}{S\bar{\alpha}}\right) \qquad (3.40)$$

The sound pressure level, similar to eqn (3.38) can be expressed as follows:

$$L_p = L_w + 10\log_{10}\left(\frac{Q}{4\pi r^2} + \frac{4}{R}\right) \quad (\text{dB}) \tag{3.41}$$

In order to carry out further detailed analysis, not only the direct sound E_d but the first reflected sounds are extracted as significant from within the diffused sound, and are counted and superimposed as follows:

$$E_0 = E_d + \Sigma ER_1 + E_{s'} \tag{3.42}$$

where $E_{s'}$ is the diffused energy density due to the second and following reflections. The second term is the total summation of the first reflected sounds from ceiling and walls.

However, for the above assumption of mirror image reflection the reflecting plane must be sufficiently large compared with the wavelength. If the wall is irregularly modelled or curved, the reflection characteristics need further investigation.

3.5   ECHO AND OTHER SINGULAR PHENOMENA

A.   Echo

After the direct sound is heard, if a reflected sound is heard separately, it is called an 'echo' which must be distinguished from reverberation. When echoes occur, speech articulation decreases considerably since speech sounds consist of successive short sounds, and the performance of music becomes difficult because the rhythm is no longer easy to follow. Thus echos damage room acoustics quite seriously. However, if the time delay is short, the reflected sound whose intensity may be even 10 dB higher than the direct sound will not be heard separately but will effectively reinforce the direct sound which is all to the good. Generally a reflected sound delayed by more than 30–50 ms after the direct sound is recognised as an echo.

The relationship between the time delay of reflected sounds after a direct sound and the relative intensity level and their influence on the degree of damage produced is contained in an index called '%-disturbance' proposed by Bolt & Doak (1950) as shown in Fig. 3.14. The figure shows what percentage of listeners are disturbed (see Lit. B13). However, the concept did not include the effect of receiving direction nor frequency spectrum change which add major complications—still further research is required.

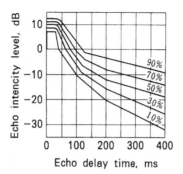

Fig. 3.14. Percentage disturbance by echos (Bolt & Doak).

B. Flutter Echo
Between a pair of parallel walls or ceiling and floor a 'flutter echo' can often occur when they are made of rigid materials. A single impulsive sound such as hand clap or footstep produces a multiple echo and is heard as a very peculiar tone such as 'put put put...' or 'pururuuru...'. This kind of echo consists of multiple repetition. The Honchido of Toshogu shrine in Nikko Japan is famous for this phenomenon of flutter echo, produced by clapping, which sounds as if the painted dragon on the ceiling is neighing, so people call it the 'neighing dragon'.

C. Colouration
When the time delay of reflected sounds from a direct sound is short, i.e. from several to a few 10 ms the timbre of the sound is changed, to some extent, by phase interference. Sometimes this phenomenon is called colouration.

D. Whispering Gallery
If a rigid wall is formed by a large concave surface, a sound moves along the surface with many repeated reflections at grazing incidence, especially at high frequency. A whisper directed to the surface can be heard distinctly at a distance as great as 60 m. The gallery of the main dome of St Paul's Cathedral in London is famous for this phenomenon.

E. Sound Focus and Dead Spot
As with light, when a sound wave is reflected by a concave surface, large compared with the wavelength, it concentrates the sound on a spot

where the sound pressure rises excessively. This is called a 'sound focus' which makes the sound field distribution irregular in the room. This means it also produces particular spots at other localities where the sounds are weak and inaudible, called 'dead spots'.

Since the above described phenomena show that the sound fields are not diffuse, those reverberation formulae and sound field calculations based on the assumption of a diffuse field become invalid. Therefore such singular conditions must be avoided as much as possible for good room acoustics. This leads to the necessity for a substantial investigation of room shapes and absorption treatment in designing rooms for good acoustics.

3.6   MEASUREMENT AND EVALUATION OF ROOM ACOUSTICS

The purpose of measuring the acoustics of a room is to determine the sound field accurately and hence to evaluate it. The evaluation of the sound field means a psychological subjective judgement based on the use of real ears.

The measurement method necessary for evaluation can only be precisely determined when it is understood what particular physical condition of the acoustics of the room corresponds to what psychological effect is produced. In this regard there has been much research, though any conclusive views are not yet recognised. In what follows the author presents the state of the art.

3.6.1   Sound Field at a Receiving Point in a Room

After a direct sound has reached a receiving point, it is then followed by reflected sounds from surrounding boundaries (i.e. walls and ceiling, etc). Further successive reflected sound waves produce reverberation. Therefore, when an impulse is emitted from a sound source, time sequential signals are observed as shown in Fig. 3.15, which is referred to as an 'impulse response'. Applying the concept of 'Fourier Transformation' (see Section 10.3), the 'transfer function' from the sound source to the receiver is obtained, which expresses the transmission frequency characteristics between the points.

Such an evaluation method based on measurement of time sequential signals was initiated by Sabine (see Lit. B2) who measured the reverberation time with an organ pipe and a stop watch. Even now reverberation

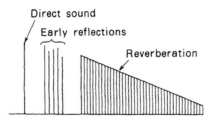

Fig. 3.15.   Schematic diagram of time sequential signals at an observing point.

measurement is still the most substantial topic in the general subject of room acoustical measurements.

3.6.2   Measurement of Reverberation

A.   Fluctuation of Decay Curve

Since the reverberation time formula was derived on the assumption of a diffuse sound field, the state of decay shows a typical logarithmic form so that the reverberation curve becomes a straight line on the dB scale. The actual measured curve, however, indicates an irregular pattern so it is necessary to consider the reverberation phenomenon as a wave motion in order to explain it.

A room space is a vibrating system which has many natural frequencies so that a sound of a particular frequency emitted from a source creates a forced vibration. When the sound source stops and a transient period starts, the source frequency rapidly vanishes, and the vibrational energy shifts to the natural vibrations causing reverberation where the frequencies are close to the source frequency. In the reverberation process those naturally excited vibrations mutually interfere so that the decay curve has an amplitude fluctuation caused by the beating of different natural frequencies one with another. Each natural vibration has its own decay rate and those of smaller decay rate remain to produce a bending of the decay curve, resulting in a deviation from the logarithmic attenuation.

If a pure tone is used as a source when measuring reverberation only a few natural vibrations in the reverberation are excited and their interference produces more distinct peaks and troughs, and bending of the decay curve as shown in Fig. 3.16(a), therefore a single decay rate can not be determined. On the other hand, with a warble-tone or broad

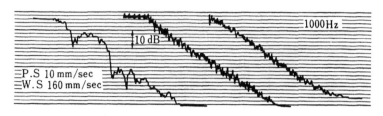

(a) Pure tone (b) Warble tone (c) ⅓ Oct. Band Noise

Fig. 3.16. Reverberation curves recorded by a high speed level recorder for different sources.

band noise, many natural frequencies are excited so that superposition of more interferences and bendings occurs, resulting in a smoothing out of the fluctuation in the decay process so that the decay curve appears to be a straight line.

At low frequencies where the number of natural vibrations is small, even where warble-tone or band noise is used, fluctuation or bending may be apparent. At high frequencies the decay curve is a straight line because of the large number and high density of natural vibrations, therefore it is clear that the assumption of a diffuse sound field in geometrical acoustics (see Section 3.3A) is justified.

B.   Choice of Sound Source

In reverberation measurement as described above, a sound source which can excite many natural vibrations in the measuring frequency range is used. The following are the most commonly used sources in practice.

- (a) *Band noise:* it is usual to filter a white noise source into octave or 1/3 octave bands in order to obtain greater sound power around the measuring frequency with a given loudspeaker. It is widely used because it is easier to handle than warble-tone.
- (b) *Warble-tone:* the frequency is varied with a modulation frequency α within a band width of $\pm\Delta f$ at the mid-frequency f. Its spectrum is not continuous but has discrete lines with a frequency spacing α mainly inside the band width.
- (c) *Short tone or AC-pulse:* speech and music are time sequential signals consisting of short sounds, by which the room characteristics are often measured in the following ways.

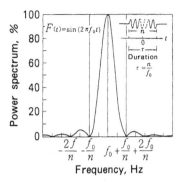

Fig. 3.17. Power spectrum of a pure tone burst.

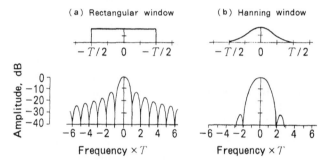

Fig. 3.18. Difference of spectrums owing to time windows.

1) *Tone-burst or pulsed-tone:* these are generated by slicing a pure tone into a few to several tens of waves. The spectrum has its own width around the original frequency f_0 and contains most of the power within the frequency range $\pm f_0/n$ as shown in Fig. 3.17. When natural vibrations in the range of $\pm 10\%$ of the measuring frequency are to be excited, 5–6 waves are found to be required. This corresponds to a rectangular time window as shown in Fig. 3.18(a), while the other windows can be used to further concentrate the power into the original frequency as an example shown in Fig. 3.18(b).

2) *Noise-burst:* breaking white noise or band noise into a few to several tens of milliseconds. In the measurement system it is

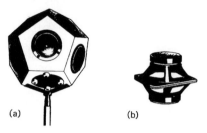

Fig. 3.19. Omni-directional speakers for measurement: (a) dodecahedron type speaker; and (b) confronting speaker.

usual to use a band filter which has its mid-frequency at the frequency of interest.

(d) *Shock wave or DC-pulse:* since an ideal impulse has a uniform continuous spectrum over all frequencies (see Section 10.3), this is used in the same way as white noise. In the laboratory the spark due to an electric discharge from a condenser (8–10 μF and 0.5–10 kV) is often used, on the other hand, because of easy control and repeatability DC-pulses emitted from a loudspeaker energised with electrical rectangular signals having widths from several to scores of microseconds generated by a signal generator are often used. However, since the intensity is small, it is necessary to practice synchronous summation for measurement. A signal pistol shot used as a source has sufficient power so that the S:N ratio is high except in the lowest frequency range, and its ease of use makes it popular in field measurements.

Except for the electrical discharge and the pistol shot, electrical signals described above are amplified and the source sound generated from an omni-directional loudspeaker. Figure 3.19(a) shows a dodechedron type speaker which has 12 transducers producing sufficient power overall. When a point source is necessary using a DC-pulse, an arrangement with two loudspeakers, as shown in Fig 3.19(b), is used.

C. Sound Receiving and Observation

For sound reception, an omni-directional sound pressure sensitive microphone is used. The amplified signal is then fed through a 1/3 octave band filter to improve the S:N ratio, and a level recorder or C.R.T. (cathode ray tube) etc used to record the measurement. For measurement *in situ*, it is convenient, for example, when using pistol shots to receive them via a sound level meter and record the decay with a tape-recorder on the spot. The signals can then be reproduced later and analysed in the laboratory. When using this technique it is important to confirm the linearity and the dynamic range of the microphone and tape-recorder system, i.e. to be sure that the same signal as the original can be faithfully reproduced.

(a) *High speed level recorder:* This apparatus records the varying sound pressure level automatically on a moving roll of paper. The pen's writing speed can be varied arbitrarily up to 1000 dB/s and the paper speed can also be varied over a wide range. This means that high speed level recorders can be used for many acoustic measurements. However, because of an automatic balancing mechanism with a moving mass the peak values of impulse sounds may not be accurately reproduced and the pen speed is limited.

When measuring the reverberation time T, the pen speed α must satisfy the relation $\alpha \geq 120/T$ (dB/s) in order to follow the decay exactly. Therefore even with the highest speed the measurement of $T < 0 \cdot 12$ cannot be achieved. Although the reverberation time is defined as the time required for the sound decay by 60 dB, it is often difficult to observe such a decay range owing to background noise level, therefore in practice, the slope of the curve down to around 30 dB is extrapolated to obtain the reverberation time.

(b) *CRT oscilloscope:* The reverberation process of logarithmic decay can be seen as an oscillogram of the direct signal. When the signal is rectified and displayed on a logarithmic scale with adequate time constant, the same decay curve as shown by the level recorder can be produced. Since a faster response speed is available as there is no moving mass, shorter reverberation times can be measured.

(c) *Instruments with digital technology:* Recently digital signal processing technology has progressed so far that not only reverberation times but other various measures can be automatically analysed. Available on the market are instruments which can show digital numbers and the wave form on the screen and also print out a hard copy of the same figure on paper, though it is necessary to understand the theoretical background described in this book in order to profit from this new equipment.

D. Measurement Method

Strictly speaking, the assumption of a complete diffuse sound field may not be satisfied, therefore as many measuring points as possible (as many as 3–10 points) should be used. The measurements should be repeated several times at each point. The average value of all measurements is then used to describe the reverberation time of the room. At low frequencies since fluctuations might be large, the number of measurements should be increased. Although ideally the measuring frequencies should be taken from 60 to 8000 Hz with 1/3 octave band spacing, sometimes simplification is possible and it is only necessary to use measuring frequencies from 125 to 4000 Hz with 1 octave band spacing.

3.6.3   Evaluation of Reverberation Characteristics

Reverberation time is considered as a quantity which can be used to control room acoustics and so over many years many researchers have proposed optimum conditions based on reverberation characteristics.

A. Optimum Reverberation Time

Reverberation gives sound a rich sonority so that it is preferable to have a fairly long reverberation time for the performance of music while for speech and lecturing articulation improves as the reverberation time gets shorter. So, depending upon the particular use of the room the optimum value of the reverberation time has to be varied.

With a shorter reverberation time a higher articulation is obtained. On the other hand, when the reverberation time is short the total absorption in the room is large, therefore the sound energy density in the room is low. When the speech level is lowered the % articulation (P.A.) tends to be lowered. These factors can be clearly understood with the aid of Fig. 1.19. As a result of two conflicting factors there is a certain value of reverberation time which may produce the highest value of P.A.

Figure 3.20 shows that the peak of the curve indicating the relationship between the reverberation time and P.A. varies as a function of room volume. If the room becomes larger, the reverberation time is preferably slightly longer (see Lit. B4).

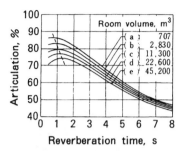

Fig. 3.20. Percentage articulation vs reverberation time of different room volume (V.O. Knudsen).

In the past many researchers have raised various proposals concerning the functional relationship between the optimum reverberation time and the room volume, both empirically and theoretically. A representative relationship is shown in Fig 3.21.

Proposals by Beranek (see Lit. B13a), Bruel (see Lit. B10) and Knudsen (see Lit. A1) are compared in Fig. 3.22 and it can be seen that there are fairly wide differences between them, which indicates that the evaluation of the auditory environment is reflected in local and traditional preferences.

Recently Ando (Lit. B33) conducted a series of psychological experiments based on computer simulation in an anechoic chamber from

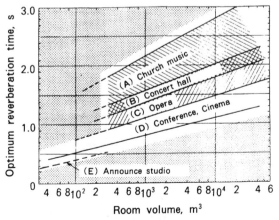

Fig. 3.21. Optimum reverberation time at 500 Hz for different types of rooms.

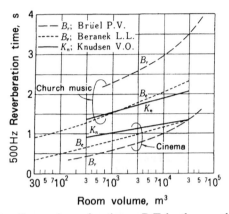

Fig. 3.22. Comparison of optimum R.T. by three authorities.

which was derived the preference scale by a paired comparison test, and the correlation with the ACF (auto correlation function) (see Section 10.3) of the sound source signal obtained. The ACF may be considered a similar property to reverberation inherent in the source signal itself. Then defining the effective duration τ_e as the time decay required for its envelope to attenuate to $1/10$ of its initial value, the optimum reverberation time may be described as that value which is about 23 times τ_e (Fig. 3.23).

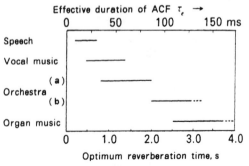

Fig. 3.23. Effective duration of ACF and optimum R.T. for several sound sources.

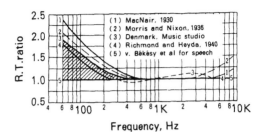

Fig. 3.24. Recommended reverberation frequency characteristics curves, generally curve 4: for music, and 5: for speech, and shaded area: tolerance for multi-purpose.

B. Frequency Characteristics of Reverberation Time

The human perception of reverberation depends not only on the reverberation time at 500 Hz but also on the variation in reverberation over the entire frequency range. The importance of this perception of reverberation has attracted the attention of many researchers who have made various recommendations regarding optimum characteristics as shown in Fig. 3.24

From the point of view of auditory sensation, in order for the loudness level to attenuate uniformly over the entire frequency range, at both low and high frequencies the reverberation time must be long. However, it becomes short at high frequencies because of air absorption, a condition under which sounds are normally heard. Therefore, if the reverberation at high frequencies is made long, the acoustic environment feels unnatural. Also in order not to reduce the percentage articulation of speech, a shorter reverberation at low frequencies rather than mid frequencies is preferred. This is particularly true when microphones for amplification and broadcasting are used.

Therefore, the frequency characteristics of reverberation must be flat over the entire frequency range. It may be noted that for music, as shown in Fig. 3.24, reverberation should be slightly raised within the shaded area. Although the permissible range might be fairly wide, as seen in Fig. 3.22, sharp variations in reverberation with frequency must be avoided because of the possibility of peculiar effects on timbre.

For example, when the natural frequency of the room predominates or degenerates at low frequencies and absorption is insufficient, not only do sharp peaks occur in the transmission characteristics but also the reverberation time becomes abnormally long at this frequency. In such cases the voice sounds 'boomy' which is unpleasant, drastically reducing the percentage articulation.

C. Indices for Assessing Feeling of Reverberance

Even in a room which satisfies the requirement of optimum reverberation time, reverberance depends on the hearing location. Even if two rooms have the same volume and same reverberation time we often experience quite different reactions to their acoustics. These facts show that reverberation time is not enough to describe the acoustics of the room completely, though it is an important factor.

The reverberation time has been determined so far with no reference to many other factors affecting the hearing sensation, such as the distribution of absorbents and the positions of sound source and receiver. Therefore it is necessary to introduce some indices which will supplement the optimum reverberation time in order to specify the acoustics of the room more satisfactorily. Since many researchers have made various proposals, some representative ones are included in the following:

(1) Jordan (see Lit. B31) suggested that since the sensation of reverberance seems to correlate well with the early slope of the decay curve, the time required for a 10 dB-decay multiplied by six might be more useful. This is called 'EDT' (Early Decay Time). In addition to this early 10 dB, the time required for 15 dB or 20 dB decay has also been proposed by other workers.

(2) Generally, a room is called 'live' when a preponderance of reflected sounds produce a reverberant feeling. On the other hand, if direct sounds are dominant and there are too few reflected sounds, it is called 'dead' or 'dry'. Attempts have been made to express liveness as the ratio of the direct sound energy density E_d, (eqn (3.34)) to the total energy density E_0 (eqn (3.20)) in the steady state. Cremer called the distance from the source where this ratio becomes unity 'Hallradius' or 'reverberation radius'. There is another proposal using the diffuse sound E_s (eqn (3.35)) in place of E_0. In either case, when the distance increases from the source, the direct sound gets less, thus the ratio becomes large.

On the other hand, recent psychological measurements show some examples where the reverberant feeling becomes a maximum immediately in front of the stage in a hall. This is due to

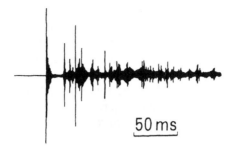

Fig. 3.25. Echo time pattern.

the time delay of reflected sounds from the rear wall, though they might be considered as echoes, resulting in the reverberant feeling. The problem seems to lie not in the steady state but to be latent in the time-sequential signals.

3.6.4 Time Sequential Signals: Measurement and Evaluation

The basis of time sequential signals is an impulse response, and ideally speaking it should include all the acoustic information in it. In addition to the direct measurement of DC-pulses, as described previously, the correlation method with white noise as source and the high speed process with M-sequential signals using a digital computer have also been used for analysis. Though it is an approximation, the DC-pulse response is useful for the evaluation of the hearing sensation, and is called 'echo time pattern' (fig. 3.25). The delay time of individual early reflected sounds following the direct sound corresponds to the transmission distance. The effects of the intensities, densities and the delay times of them on the sensation are being investigated. When a certain time (> 100 or 200 ms) elapses, many reflected sounds overlap to form the reverberation curve. Therefore the true information is assumed to be included not in the reverberation time, but in the echo's fine structure of up to 100–200 ms after the direct sound reaches us, thus more detailed analysis can be made.

A. Evaluation on Time Axis

Kuhl (1957) noticed that the larger the initial time delay gap Δt between the direct sound and the first reflected sound, the larger the spatial impression which might be obtained and suggested that about 30 ms delay would be desirable (see Lit. B29), while Beranek stated that it would be better if it were less than 20 ms (see Lit. A4). However, Ando from the results of hearing tests using a single reflection in an anechoic chamber on music and speech, discovered that the optimum time ought to be equal to the time required for the ACF envelope of the signals (Fig. 4 in Section 10.3) to attenuate to 0.1 A where A is the total reflected sound amplitude when the direct sound amplitude is unity. Therefore, when A is equal to the direct sound amplitude τ_e, in Fig. 3.23, becomes the optimum value. Here, it must be noted that the ACF depends on the type of the sound source.

B. Evaluation using Integrated Square Value of Sound Pressure

In order to evaluate the pattern of time fluctuation of energy density, Thiele (1953) introduced an index named 'Deutlichkeit'—distinctness as given in eqn (3.43) which presumes that the square of the instantaneous sound pressure within the first 50 ms is effective in reinforcing the direct sound.

$$D = \frac{\int_0^{50\,ms} p(t)^2 \, dt}{\int_0^\infty p(t)^2 \, dt} \qquad (3.43)$$

Thus, it was stated that the larger the value of D the more the distinctness of speech. Beranek et al. (1965) have extended the concept of the D value by using the level difference between the diffused sounds and the initial sound as follows:

$$R = 10\log_{10}\left(\frac{1-D}{D}\right) dB \qquad (3.44)$$

which is called 'reverberation index'.

Reichardt (1972) has developed the principle for music by modifying the integration range to 80 ms, separating the initial sounds from the diffused ones as follows,

$$C = 10\log_{10}\frac{\int_0^{80\,ms} p(t)^2 \, dt}{\int_{80}^\infty p(t)^2 \, dt} \qquad (3.45)$$

which is designated 'Klarheitmass' or 'clarity'.

In addition, there are various proposals taking into account the integration range of the ratio (see Lit. B29a,b).

C. Time Weighting of Energy Method

Cremer proposed an index with time weighting for the evaluation of the decay curve as follows.

$$t_s = \frac{\int_0^\infty t p^2(t)\, dt}{\int_0^\infty p^2(t)\, dt} \tag{3.46}$$

which is called 'Schwerpunktzeit' or 'Point of gravity time' and/or 'centre-time'. Kürer (1969) has shown that syllable articulation has good correlation with the t_s values (see Lit. B29).

When the sound field in a room is completely diffuse and the reverberation has an exponential decay, the indices of eqns (3.43)–(3.46) have perfect correlations with the reverberation time, so that no new information is provided. Only when the actual sound field is not completely diffuse do the indices provide new meanings.

3.6.5 Measurements related to Transmission Characteristics

It is very important that the sound generated by a sound source is transmitted to the listener with high fidelity. The transmission frequency characteristics measured with pure tone as shown in Fig. 3.6, however, are used to detect the natural frequencies but are not suitable for measuring the performance of the room considered as an acoustic transmission system. Methods for providing this information are described below.

A. Transfer Function

Applying the Fourier transformation (see Section 10.3) to the impulse response in the time domain enables a transfer function in the frequency domain to be obtained in which the real part expresses the amplitudes and the imaginary part the phases. Recently FFT (Fast Fourier Transform) analysers have become available by which the analog signals are converted into digital form by an A–D converter, the fast Fourier transformation carried out and a transfer function displayed almost in real time.

B. Measurement of Transmission Characteristics with Noise Signal

For coordination and performance testing of electro-acoustic systems, a method of analysing the microphone output in 1/3 octave bands at the receiving point during the steady emission of white noise is used. The white noise has a constant spectrum in which the band level of constant ratio band width tends to rise with a slope of 3 dB/oct as shown in [Ex. 1.9], therefore, if the sound source emits so-called 'pink noise' with a filter which has the reverse slope, the entire measuring system has a flat characteristic. So that the measured results immediately indicate the characteristics of the transmission system with a real time analyser.

C. Measurement of MTF (Modulation Transfer Function)

Distortion in speech signals caused by reverberation, echoes and noise in their transmission path to the listener reduce speech intelligibility. Since speech is composed of a series of pulses whose amplitudes fluctuate sharply on the time axis, reverberation and noise fill these sharp dips, thus distortion occurs. When modelling the above phenomena, using amplitude modulated noise, the modulation-reduction factor m for 100% modulation at the sound source is measured at the observer. Houtgast & Steeneken (1980) propose to measure the m-values at 14 modulation frequencies of 1/3 oct spaced 0.63–12.5 Hz

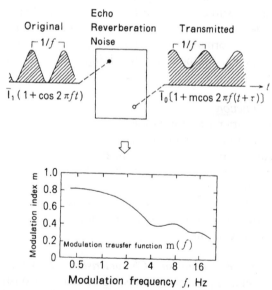

Fig. 3.26. Principle of measuring MTF in a room as a function of modulation frequency. Typically, the carrier is 1 octave-band noise (Houtgast *et al.*).

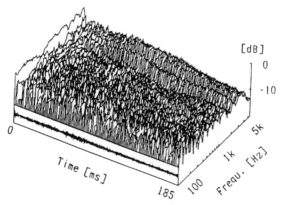

Fig. 3.27. Time-frequency display of impulse response in the Grosser Musikvereinssaal with the Wigner distribution. The integral value on the frequency-axis corresponds to the impulse response and the integral value on the time-axis becomes the power spectrum (Yamasaki).

whilst modelling the amplitude fluctuation pattern of speech using 7 octave bands of noise from 125 Hz to 8 kHz. The MTF curves are constructed from 98 measured m values as shown in Fig.3.26. A STI (Speech Transmission Index) is proposed using the same calculation method as that employed in deriving the Articulation Index. Furthermore, in order to simplify the measuring procedure the RASTI (Rapid STI) method is proposed. These methods have more merit due to objective and physical measurement compared to a direct measurement of the percentage articulation using human voices and auditory sensation. It is now probable that the standardisation of STI may become necessary for practical application.

3.6.6 Display of Time Varying Frequency Spectrum
At the transient stage the momentary changes of transmission frequency characteristics can be displayed by the Wigner distribution which is the result of the signal processing of an impulse response, an example of which is shown in Fig 3.27. It shows the time sequential change of the frequency spectrum of total reflected sounds. The technique may become useful for the evaluation of the acoustics of rooms as it parallels its use in investigating hearing sensations.

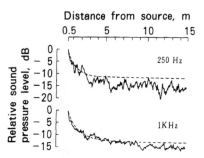

Fig. 3.28. Sound pressure level distribution in a room in steady state.

3.6.7   Measurement of Spatial Information and Evaluation

A.   Measurement of Sound Pressure Distribution

While generating a steady octave band noise from a sound source (Fig. 3.19(a)) the changes in sound pressure level with distance are continuously recorded with a moving microphone as shown in Fig. 3.28, where the dotted line indicates the calculated values from eqn (3.41) assuming a completely diffuse field. In practice, a pink noise source is used, the signal received by the moving microphone is recorded and then analysed in the laboratory, or a direct measurement is performed at several selected points in the hall. In the latter method if the power level of the source is properly calibrated, the absolute values of the sound pressure levels are obtained in the hall so that they can be compared with values measured in other halls.

B.   Evaluation of Diffusivity of Sound Field

Although geometrical acoustics based on the assumption of a complete diffuse sound-field provides a powerful tool for solving practical problems, there might be some problems based on dissatisfaction with the assumption that, for instance, complete diffusion may not be considered the best acoustic condition in all rooms. It is an interesting and unknown problem as to what degree of diffusion exists in an actual room and how much diffusivity is to be expected in a particular room.

(1)   *Evaluation with reverberation time and sound pressure distribution:* the irregular bending of the reverberation curve, the scattering of measured values of reverberation time and the deviation from the theoretical value of sound pressure distribution (Fig. 3.28)

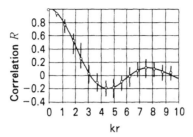

Fig. 3.29. Sound pressure correlation values between 2 points measured in a well diffused room and the theoretical curve (Cook *et al.*)

are considered to express poor diffusion although evaluation has not been normalised yet.

(2) *Evaluation due to correlation of sound pressures between two points:* the correlation R of sound pressures between two points in a completely diffuse sound field is proved theoretically to be $R = \sin kr/kr$ where r is the distance between the two points and $k = 2\pi/\lambda$. Cook *et al.* (1955) carried out a series of measurements on correlation between the outputs of two omni-directional microphones whilst changing the distance r between them in a reverberation room which appeared to be sufficiently diffuse, and observed good agreement with the theoretical curve as shown in Fig. 3.29. When the measured values are close to the theoretical ones, diffusion is considered good and the deviation might be considered a measure of that diffusion.

C. Evaluation due to Lateral Energy

Although the sound field is a spatial event, nevertheless the physical behaviour of sound waves at one point has been considered, and an omni-directional microphone is used for measurements. However, a person hears speech and music with both ears which produce a binaural effect (see Section 1.12). With this effect one can not only localise the sound source but can gain a spatial impression.

Spatial impression is a very important factor in the evaluation of room acoustics. The greatest contributors to this factor are the lateral reflections. Figure 3.30 shows an experimental result with a single reflection, the effect of a lateral sound, i.e. spatial impression is almost the same within a 10–80 ms delay. But, the more energy in the lateral

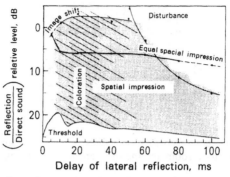

Fig. 3.30. Subjective effects of single reflection with lateral angle = 40°, of variable delay and level for music (Barron, 1971).

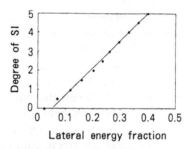

Fig. 3.31. Degree of spatial impression vs lateral energy fraction of received sound (Barron & Marshall, 1981).

reflection the greater the spatial effect obtained, as shown in Fig. 3.31. This fact is caused by dissimilarity between signals received by the two ears (see Lit. B25).

A measurement method using directional microphones has been devised in order to evaluate the binaural effect due to reflected sounds from either the left or right. Jordan (Lit. B31) proposed the concept 'room response' (RR) based on research carried out at the University of Goettingen and combined with a simplification of 'index of room impression' investigated by Reichardt *et al.* (1978).

$$RR \approx 10 \log \frac{\text{Lateral energy } (25\text{–}80) \text{ ms} + \text{total energy } (80\text{–}160)\text{ms}}{\text{early total energy } (0\text{–}80) \text{ ms}}$$

$$(3.47)$$

where the Lateral energy is measured using a 'figure of 8' directional microphone. Furthermore, and more simply 'Lateral Efficiency' (LE) has been proposed as a measure of lateral reflection as defined below, instead of a logarithmic expression.

$$\text{LE} \approx \frac{\text{early lateral energy (25–80) ms}}{\text{early total energy(0–80) ms}} \qquad (3.48)$$

D. Measurement of Directional Diffusivity

In order to show the intensity of sound incident at a receiving point in any particular direction, measurements are carried out in three dimensions using a rotating uni-directional microphone. The results are presented in the form of 'needles' the length of which are proportional to the intensity in the various directions as shown in Fig. 3.32 and resembling a 'hedgehog'. With a total number N of 'needles' each of whose length is A_i, the mean value is as follows:

$$M = \frac{1}{N} \sum_{i=1}^{N} A_i$$

The average deviation from M in every direction is

$$\Delta M = \frac{1}{N} \sum_{i=1}^{N} |A_i - M|$$

Putting $m = \Delta M / M$ and m_0, its value in free space, Meyer et al. derived the following expression

$$d = 1 - \frac{m}{m_0} \qquad (3.49)$$

which is called 'directional diffusivity'. In free space $d = 0$. In a completely diffuse sound field, $m = 0$, hence $d = 100\%$.

In practice it was measured using a parabolic microphone whose diameter is 1.2 m and narrow band 2000 Hz steady noise. The measured

Plan   **Side elevation**

Fig. 3.32. 'Hedgehog' showing directional diffusivity (Meyer *et al.*).

values of d in many halls and studios are within 20–80%, and the larger
the room volume the smaller the values of d obtained (see Lit. B17).

As described above, the diffusivity of a sound field may be directly
evaluated only in terms of its directional diffusivity. However, it has not
been a popular technique largely due to the fact that it is a difficult
measurement to make.

E. Closely Located Four–Point Microphone Method

Yamasaki *et al.* (1978–89) have recently developed a computer-aided
method using 4 omni-directional microphones where one is located at
the origin and the other three microphones are located several centimetres away from the origin along three orthogonal axes as shown in
Fig 3.33(a). With these four microphones the impulse responses at a
receiving point are measured for the DC-pulses radiated from a source
(Fig 3.19,b), then signal processing with a digital computer the arriving
sound's direction, intensity and equivalent positions of image source are
obtained. By this method the intensity of each reflected sound, the
direction from which it has come, and the time sequence of the arriving
impulses may be obtained more accurately, therefore all necessary
information can be obtained in a very short time. Figure 3.33(b,c) shows
one example of a measured result by this method. Further research
should be pursued on how to express the data corresponding to the
aural sensation from the vast amount of data contained in the four-di-
mensional information obtained by this technique.

F. Measurement of IACC (Interaural Cross Correlation)

Spatial impression is caused by dissimilarity of received sounds by two
ears as mentioned above. The dissimilarity is expressed mathematically
by the cross-correlation function (see Section 10.3). The lower the value
of cross correlation the greater the dissimilarity. Consequently, Ando
(Lit. B33) defined and adopted the IACC (see Section 10.3D) as the
important factor for evaluating concert hall acoustics (see Lit. B33).

IACC is measured using a small microphone installed at the entrance
of the outer ear of a dummy head or real head. Two channel signals are
recorded in the sound field of interest and then the signals processed by
means of a digital computer. It must be noted that the measured value
may change with the frequency spectrum of the source signal, so that
standardisation of the method of measuring IACC will be required for
wide application.

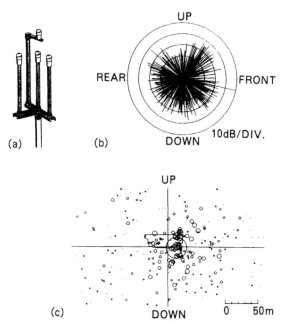

Fig. 3.33. A result measured by closely located four-point microphone method (Vienna, Grosser Musikvereinssaal, Tachibana *et al.*, 1989): (a) Closely located four microphones; (b) Directivity pattern of received sound and (c) Virtual image source distribution.

3.6.8 Total Evaluation of Concert Hall

So far we have discussed how to evaluate room acoustics by the objective measurement of various physical quantities, however, subjective evaluation of the room acoustics as perceived by the human ear cannot be avoided.

For speech a simple method of expressing comprehension by a percentage articulation test was described in Section 1.14. This is considered as an ideal evaluation method since a single numerical figure expresses the speech hearing condition as taking into account all influencing factors.

For music, on the other hand, the problem is so complicated that no definitive method has yet been established. But we can at least discuss a few proposed methods.

A. Beranek (1962) selected several evaluation factors for musical hearing. He proposed a method in which the attributes of acoustical

Table 3.1

Rating Scales for Orchestral Concerts (Beranek 1962)

Attribute	Physical quantity	Rating points	Max. point
Intimacy	Initial time delay gap (ms)	0–20 ms → 40 pts. → 70 ms → 0 pts.	40
Liveness	Reverberation time(s) at mid frequencies (500 to 1,000 Hz for fully occupied hall)	Romantic 2·2 s, Typical orchestra 1·9 s, Classical 1·7 s, Baroque 1·5 s, (either longer or shorter time than the above give lower pts.)	15
Warmth	Average of RT at 125 and 250 Hz divided by RT at mid frequency	1·2 to 1·25, (larger or smaller than this range gives lower points	15
Loudness of the direct sound	Distance from listener to conductor in ft	60 ft (beyond which every further 10 ft gives a reduction of 1 pt.)	10
Loudness of reverberant sound	$\dfrac{RT \text{ at } 500 \text{ to } 1{,}000 \text{ Hz}}{\text{room volumes ft}^3} \times 10^6$	3·0 (either larger or smaller gives lower pts.)	6
Diffusion	Wall and ceiling irregularities	If adequate	4
Balance and Blend	(Sectional balance in orchestra)	If good	6
Ensemble	Performers ability to hear each other	If easy	4

quality were categorised and the physical quantities which might govern those selected attributes measured. Each was given a rating number on a rating scale as specified in Table 3.1 and the total score used to evaluate the hall. He collected the measurement data of 54 major concert halls from all over the world and concluded that the evaluations agreed well with the judgement of most musicians and critics (see Lit. A4). However, there are still many problems relating to the particular choice of attributes and the determination of rating scales. It was most unfortunate that the New York Philharmonic Hall, built in 1962 and acoustically designed on the basis of this method, was unsatisfactory.

B. Jordan (1980) proposed an acceptable range for reverberation time RT, early decay time EDT, clarity C, eqn (3.45), and room response RR, eqn (3.47), as shown in Table 3.2, based on his experimental work over many years on the acoustical design of concert halls (see Lit. B31)

Table 3.2
Acceptable Values of Criteria Applied to
Concert Hall Assessment (Jordan 1980)

Criterion	Average	Tolerance range
RT (s)	2·1	1·4–2·8
EDT (s)	2·1	1·8–2·6
C (dB)	0	−2–+2
RR (dB)	0	−0·5–+0·5

C. Ando (Lit. B33) presented four factors identified as contributing to good acoustics in concert halls. Three of them are called 'temporal-monaural criteria' since they are closely associated with source signals which may be perceived by only one ear, i.e. total sound energy X_1, delay of early reflections X_2, and reverberation X_3. The other important factor is a 'spatial-binaural criterion' IACC X_4, which is related to the spatial impression.

These factors are normalised by each optimum value as expressed by eqn (3.50).

$$\left.\begin{aligned}
X_1 &= 20\log_{10}(P/P_{opt}) = L - L_{opt} \text{ (dB)} \\
X_2 &= \log_{10}(\Delta t/\Delta t_{opt}), \quad (3.6.3, A) \\
X_3 &= \log_{10}(T/T_{opt}), \quad (3.6.4, A) \\
X_4 &= \text{IACC} \quad (3.6.7, F)
\end{aligned}\right\} \quad (3.50)$$

The contribution of each factor to the scale value of preference is $S_i = g(X_i)$. The results of subjective tests are shown in Fig. 3.34.

If those factors can be assumed linear and independent of each other, and also their scale values have equal unit measure, the total scale value of preference may be obtained by simple addition,

$$S = S_1 + S_2 + S_3 + S_4 \qquad (3.51)$$

Each value of S_i is obtained from Fig. 3.34. They are all negative values when they deviate from the optimum value of $S_{max} = 0$.

Although he has said that the hypothesis is justified by the results of subjective preference judgement on a simulated sound field produced in an anechoic room, there is an objection on grounds of generality since it depends on personal preference (Lit. B30b). Moreover, problems still remain in the justification of many of the above assumptions.

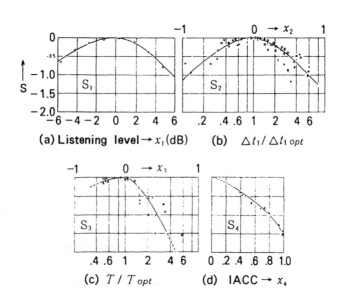

Fig. 3.34. Scale values of preferences in concert halls (Ando): (a) S_1 as a function of listening level; (b) S_2 as a function of initial time-delay gap; (c) S_3 as a function of the reverberation time; and (d) S_4 as a function of the IACC.

PROBLEMS 3

1. Enumerate the various factors which play a role in the evaluation of the acoustic environment in a room and explain the evaluation methods.
2. Describe the principal features of geometrical and wave acoustics and explain how they are applied to problems in architectural acoustics.
3. Enumerate the phenomena to be avoided in room acoustics and indicate which is the most harmful.
4. When designing a class room whose floor area is about 55 m^2 with 3 m ceiling height, explain which is acoustically preferable for the floor plan, 6 m × 9 m or 7 m × 8 m.
5. Enumerate the factors to be taken into account in selecting the optimum reverberation time.

Chapter 4

SOUND ABSORPTION—MATERIALS AND CONSTRUCTION

The absorption coefficient is a useful concept when using geometrical acoustic theory to evaluate the growth and decay of sound energy in a room. Any material absorbs sound to some extent. However, when sound is considered as a wave motion it is necessary to use the concept of acoustic impedance. In this chapter the fundamental characteristics of the terms which describe sound absorption, an outline of the performance of various absorbing materials, details of construction and their practical application in architecture are discussed.

4.1 TYPES OF SOUND ABSORPTION MECHANISMS

Absorptive materials and constructions can be divided into 3 fundamental types as shown in Fig. 4.1.

A. *Porous Absorption*
When sound waves impinge on a porous material containing capillaries or continuous airways such as are found in glasswool, rockwool and porous foam, they propagate into the interstices in which a part of the sound energy is dissipated by frictional and viscous losses within the pores and by vibration of small fibres of the material. The absorption is large at high frequencies and small at low frequencies.

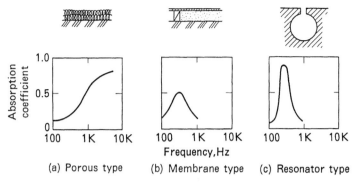

Fig. 4.1.   Absorption mechanisms and characteristics outline.

B.   Membrane Absorption

When sound strikes an air-tight material such as thin plywood or canvas panel, it excites a membrane type of vibration of the material. Part of the sound energy is then lost due to internal friction in the material. The absorption characteristic shows a peak in the low-frequency range which coincides with the resonant frequency of the membrane though the absorption coefficient is usually not so large.

C.   Resonator Absorption

Sound incident on a resonator consisting of a cavity with an opening excites large amplitude air vibrations at the opening in the resonant frequency range, dissipating the sound energy by means of viscous losses. Thus, the absorption can be very large at the resonant frequency.

In practice these 3 types, or a combination of them, are considered effective as absorptive building materials or as part of a construction.

4.2   MEASUREMENT OF ABSORPTION COEFFICIENT AND ACOUSTIC IMPEDANCE

The absorption coefficient depends on the type of sound incident on the material surface. As shown in Fig. 4.2 when a plane wave is incident normally, on the material surface, i.e. when the angle of incidence is zero, the absorption coefficient is called 'normal incidence absorption

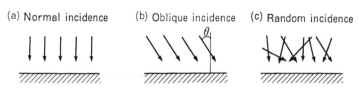

(a) Normal incidence   (b) Oblique incidence   (c) Random incidence

Fig. 4.2. Sound incidence conditions.

coefficient' and is denoted by α_0. In the case of oblique incidence the coefficient is expressed as α_θ. For sounds incident at all angles the coefficient is called 'random incidence absorption coefficient', while the calculated value of the statistical mean as a function of the angle of incidence is written α_s and the value obtained by measurement in a reverberation chamber is called 'reverberation (or reverberation room method) absorption coefficient' α_r. The latter is generally designated α and used in the practice of room acoustics and noise control. Although these absorption coefficients and acoustic impedances are defined at the surface of the material it should be noted that they may also vary according to the thickness of the material and the backing condition.

4.2.1 Normal Incidence Absorption Coefficient and Acoustic Impedance

A. Measurement of Normal Incidence Absorption Coefficient
Since a tube whose diameter is smaller than the wavelength is used in order to create a plane wave incident normal to the specimen, the method is called the 'tube method'.

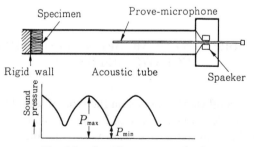

Fig. 4.3. Standing wave method.

As shown in Fig. 4.3 when the specimen is placed at the end of the tube and a pure tone is generated at the other, a standing wave is produced. The standing wave pattern has peaks and troughs alternately spaced at distances of $\lambda/4$ according to eqn (1.35). Since the reflected sound amplitude B is small compared with the incident sound amplitude A, even at the position of pressure minimum in the reverse phase, $P_{\min} = |A - B|$ never becomes zero. At the pressure maximum $P_{\max} = |A + B|$, then

$$\frac{P_{\max}}{P_{\min}} = \frac{|A + B|}{|A - B|} = n$$

the 'standing wave ratio'. Moving a microphone (or probe-microphone in case of a slender tube) in the tube and measuring n, enables the sound pressure reflection coefficient $|r_p|$ to be determined.

$$|r_p| = \left|\frac{B}{A}\right| = \frac{n-1}{n+1} \tag{4.1}$$

Therefore, the normal incidence absorption coefficient is expressed as follows:

$$\alpha_0 = 1 - |r_p|^2 = 1 - \left(\frac{n-1}{n+1}\right)^2 = \frac{4}{n + (1/n) + 2} \tag{4.2}$$

This can be obtained from Fig. 4.4 and also Table A. 1 in the Appendices.

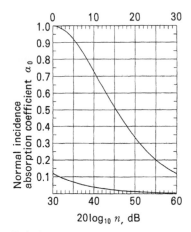

Fig. 4.4.   Relationship between $20 \log n$ (dB) and α_0.

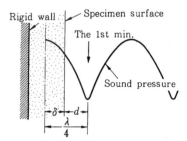

Fig. 4.5. Standing wave pattern.

B. Measurement of Acoustic Impedance

When closely observing the pattern of a standing wave produced near the material surface, as shown in Fig. 4.5, it can be seen that the distance from the material surface to the first Pressure minimum $P_{\min}$ is

$$d = \frac{\lambda}{4} \pm \delta, \tag{4.3}$$

The figure shows the case of $-\delta$. Thus the position of the first $P_{\min}$ which occurs at $\lambda/4$ in the case of perfect reflection is found to be displaced by δ. This is because the phase is shifted at the reflection point as the reflected wave is considered to start from the material surface; then the phase shift becomes

$$2k\delta, \qquad (k = 2\pi/\lambda)$$

due to reflection.

Now, expressing the sound pressure reflection coefficient of the material surface in complex form with

$$\frac{B}{A} = |r_p| e^{j\Delta}$$

it follows that

$$\Delta = 2k\delta = 4\pi \frac{\delta}{\lambda} \tag{4.4}$$

Therefore, when n and δ are measured, $|r_p| e^{j\Delta}$ can be obtained by using eqns (4.1) and (4.4).

Using Z for the acoustic impedance of the material surface from eqn (1.30) it follows that

$$|r_p|e^{j\Delta} = \frac{Z - \rho c}{Z + \rho c} = \frac{z - 1}{z + 1} \tag{4.5}$$

where z is the impedance ratio. Hence,

$$\frac{Z}{\rho c} = z = \frac{1 + |r_p|e^{j\Delta}}{1 - |r_p|e^{j\Delta}}$$

Thus Z can be calculated. The relationship between $Z/\rho c$ and α_0 is also given by eqn (1.34). In practice the acoustic impedance ratio is expressed as follows:

$$\frac{Z}{\rho c} = \frac{R}{\rho c} + j\frac{X}{\rho c} = r + jx \tag{4.6}$$

The real part r and imaginary part x can then be simply obtained by using a Smith Chart (see Section 10.11) with measured values of n and δ shown in Fig. 4.5.

Referring also to eqns (4.1) and (4.5) if $\Delta = 0$ then $n = z$. Therefore, when assuming the reflecting surface to be at the position shifted by δ from the material surface (see Fig. 4.5) the phase shift of the reflected sound becomes nil, with the result that the impedance of the assumed reflecting surface is a real number n^*.

The diameter D of the measuring tube should satisfy the condition $D < 0 \cdot 59\lambda$, otherwise the requirement for normal incidence for a plane wave will not be satisfied. Also, since P_{min} requires more than 2 measurements, the tube length needs to be larger than $3/4\lambda$. Therefore, 2 or 3 different sizes of tube are used to cover the frequency range of interest.

There is also a method of obtaining the acoustic impedance of the specimen by measuring the sharpness of the tube resonance. α_0 can also be obtained by measuring the decay of length-wise natural modes of vibration in the tube.

These tube methods have several advantages: small specimen, simple apparatus for measurement and reproducible accuracy. Therefore these methods are used for the comparison of materials and for developing

---

*Brüel names this n as 'true impedance' which must not be confused with the absolute value $|z|$ of the impedance ratio of the material surface $z = r + jx$, and also the real part r of it (see Lit. B10)

new materials but they can not be used for measuring the absorption of membrane absorbers.

4.2.2 Oblique Incidence Absorption Coefficient

A. Measuring Method
Although it is generally difficult there are several methods for determining the oblique incidence absorption coefficient. The first is an analytical method using standing wave modes in a rectangular room into which the specimen under investigation has been introduced (Hunt 1939). The second is a method based on steady-state measurements of the interference pattern caused by waves incident on and reflected from a specimen of sufficient size located in free space (Ando 1968). The third is a method of separating reflected and incident sound as follows:

(a) separation in space using the directivity of a measuring microphone,
(b) separation in the time domain with a short tone or an impulse response,
(c) separation based on an application of correlation techniques.

The new method of sound intensity measurement may also prove useful.

Figure 4.6 shows an example of the second method based on the interference pattern, where, at low frequencies, the accuracy is affected by the free-space dimension and the specimen size and at high frequen-

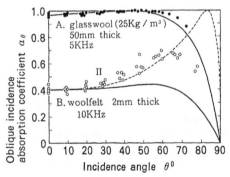

Fig. 4.6. Oblique incidence absorption coefficients comparison of values measured by the interference pattern method with theoretical values, solid line: calculated by eqn (4.9), dotted line: values assuming $x_n = 0$ in eqn (4.9).

cies by destructive interference. Also, when the angle of incidence gets close to 90°, the error increases.

B. Assumption of Locally Reacting Condition

At the boundary between two different media whose characteristic impedances are Z_1 and Z_2 the sound pressure reflection coefficient r_p can be determined against the angle of incidence θ_i as shown in Problem 1.2; therefore the absorption coefficient is expressed in a similar way to eqn (1.33) as follows,

$$a = 1 - |r_p|^2 = 1 - \left| \frac{Z_2 \cos \theta_i - Z_1 \cos \theta_t}{Z_2 \cos \theta_i + Z_1 \cos \theta_t} \right|^2 \qquad (4.7)$$

However, for further simplification, the concept of a locally reacting surface is introduced, which assumes that the component of particle velocity perpendicular to the surface depends only on the pressure at the surface and not on the angle of incidence. Hence, the 'normal acoustic impedance' Z_n of the material is defined as the ratio of the sound pressure to the particle velocity normal to the surface. Assuming that Z_n is independent of the angle of incidence, then the measured value obtained by the tube method, as described previously, can be used. Hence, substituting $\theta_t = 0$, and ρc (characteristic impedance of air) for Z_1, and Z_n (normal acoustic impedance of the material) for Z_2 and, replacing θ_i in eqn (4.7) with θ, the following is obtained:

$$\alpha_\theta = 1 - \left| \frac{Z_n \cos \theta - \rho c}{Z_n \cos \theta + \rho c} \right|^2 \qquad (4.8)$$

Then substituting for Z_n using eqn (4.6)

$$\alpha_\theta = \frac{4 r_n \cos \theta}{(r_n \cos \theta + 1)^2 + (x_n \cos \theta)^2} \qquad (4.9)$$

Thus, the oblique incidence absorption coefficient varies with the angle of incidence θ. An example using the above equation is shown by solid curves in Fig. 4.6.

4.2.3 Random Incidence Absorption Coefficient

A. Statistical Absorption Coefficient

When a plane wave is uniformly incident from all directions, averaging the coefficients in terms of the angle of incidence using Fig. 3.7, the following is obtained.

$$\alpha_s = \frac{\int_0^{\pi/2} \alpha_\theta \sin\theta \cos\theta \, d\theta}{\int_0^{\pi/2} \sin\theta \cos\theta \, d\theta} = 2\int_0^{\pi/2} \alpha_\theta \sin\theta \cos\theta \, d\theta \quad (4.10)$$

Substituting eqn (4.9) in the above, the following is obtained

$$\alpha_s = \frac{8r}{r^2 + x^2}\left[1 - \frac{r}{r^2 + x^2}\log_e\{(r+1)^2 + x^2\}\right.$$
$$\left. + \frac{r^2 - x^2}{x(r^2 + x^2)}\tan^{-1}\left(\frac{x}{r+1}\right)\right] \quad (4.11)$$

As there may be cases where the assumption of a constant value for Z_n regardless of the angle of incidence is not satisfied, the above expression is not always appropriate.

London's (1950) concept of non-directivity of the sound pressure at the point of incidence leads to a different statistical proposal as follows:

$$\alpha_s^* = \frac{\int_0^{\pi/2} \alpha_\theta \sin\theta \, d\theta}{\int_0^{\pi/2} \sin\theta \, d\theta} \quad (4.12)$$

B. Measurement of Reverberation Absorption Coefficient

In a completely diffuse sound field, sounds are incident on the wall surface from all directions. Suppose a reverberation room has a volume V (m^3) with total surface area S (m^2) and reverberation time T_1 seconds. When a specimen s (m^2) is placed in the room and a reverberation time T_2 is obtained, Sabine's formula for the reverberation time eqn (3.23) yields the following:

$$T_0 = \frac{KV}{S\bar{\alpha}}, \qquad T_m = \frac{KV}{s\alpha_r + (S-s)\bar{\alpha}},$$

where, α_r is the reverberation absorption coefficient for the specimen and $\bar{\alpha}$ is the average absorption coefficient of the room. From the above two equations the following is obtained:

$$\alpha_r = \frac{KV}{S}\left[\frac{1}{T_m} - \frac{1}{T_0}\right] + \bar{\alpha} \quad (4.13)$$

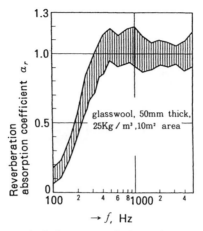

Fig. 4.7. Measurement deviation range of absorption coefficients obtained by sound-robin test in 9 different reverberation rooms in Japan for the same specimen (1966).

Therefore, when the reverberation times T_m and T_0 are measured, the absorption coefficient α_r can be obtained; $\bar{\alpha}$ is so small that it may often be neglected.

For this measurement a fairly large area (~ 10 m^2) of material is required. Since the construction detail to be employed in the laboratory should be precisely that used in the field, the absorption coefficients to be used for the estimation of reverberation time and noise control purposes must be the actual measured values. It is also important to note that absorption characteristics due to panel vibration can only be obtained by this method.

The most important condition in this technique is that the sound field in the reverberation room is completely diffuse. However, when a sample is installed in the room, the condition becomes difficult to satisfy; therefore, even the same specimen produces different results measured in different laboratories as shown in Fig. 4.7. Thus, in order to reduce the differences, ISO 354 provides the following instructions.

(1) The reverberation room should have a minimum volume of 180 m^3, preferably more than 200 m^3.

(2) The specimen should cover an area of about 10 m^2, placed on the floor so that the borders do not parallel any wall.

Fig. 4.8.   Diffusing panels hung in a reverberation room.

(3)   Diffusion is to be provided, for instance, by using many diffusing panels as shown in Fig. 4.8, or rotating paddles.

Irregular room shapes without any parallel walls are preferable. Moreover, in order to make the reverberation time of the empty room as long as possible, the inside wall surface must be of hard smooth finish using painted concrete, polished terrazzo or mosaic tiles so that $\bar{\alpha}$ is between 1 and 2%.

C.   Normal Incidence vs Random Incidence Sound Absorption Coefficients

The relationship between the normal incidence absorption coefficient α_0 and statistical absorption coefficient α_s depends upon how closely the assumption that the sample is locally reacting is satisfied. Furthermore, the relation of α_0 and α_s with the reverberation absorption coefficient α_r is affected by the diffusion characteristics provided in the reverberation room. In addition the area effect described below has to be taken into account. As an example Fig. 4.9 shows the relationship on measurements for dry sand and gravel.

The curves are obtained from eqns (4.10) and (4.12) in which the following is substituted in place of eqn (4.8).

$$\alpha_\theta = 1 - \left(\frac{n \cos \theta - 1}{n \cos \theta + 1} \right)^2$$

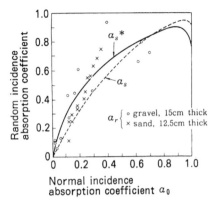

Fig. 4.9. Relationship between measured values of α_0 and α_r, and comparison with α_s.

Where n is the standing wave ratio for normal incidence.

D.   Area Effect

When measuring the reverberation absorption coefficient, it is found that the smaller the specimen area, the larger the measured value, as shown in Fig. 4.10. This is called the 'area effect' and is more pronounced in cases where the linear dimensions of the specimen are less than the sound wavelength and also for materials whose coefficients are large. As a result α_r may exceed 1 (see Fig. 4.7).

The reason may be due to incidence of reflected sound waves diffracted around the absorptive material.

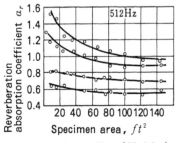

Fig. 4.10.   Area effect (Chrisler).

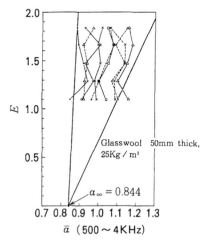

Fig. 4.11. Edge effect of sound absorption derived from the data shown in Fig. 4.7.

Kosten (1960), observing that the edge of the specimen has a larger absorption coefficient, proposed the following expression:

$$\alpha_r - \alpha_\infty + \beta E \tag{4.14}$$

where α_∞ is the absorption coefficient for an infinitely large specimen, E is the edge length per unit area of the specimen and β its multiplier. Figure 4.11 shows values of E when the area and shape of the same specimen used in Fig. 4.7 are varied in nine reverberant rooms in Japan. The statistical coefficient from eqn (4.11) is used for α_∞. β is the slope of the straight line drawn from α_∞. Since β varies for each specimen, the use of this concept is of no practical value unless β is constant for each room.

4.3 CHARACTERISTICS OF POROUS SOUND ABSORBER

A. Material Thickness and Air Space

In a porous absorber, acoustic absorption is due mainly to viscous losses as air moves within the pores. Since the viscous loss is proportional to the dynamic pressure of the moving air, porous materials can provide more absorption when they are located in positions where the particle velocity of the sound wave is large. When sound is incident on a rigid

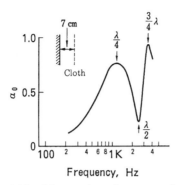

Fig. 4.12.   Measured α_0 for cotton cloth.

wall like concrete, for example, a standing wave results and the particle velocity is a maximum at a distance of $\lambda/4$, $3/4\lambda,\ldots$ from the wall as shown in Fig. 1.9. On the other hand, Fig. 4.12 shows the measured values of α_0 when cotton cloth is mounted with an air space in front of a rigid wall and shows that even a thin porous material can provide considerable absorption where the particle velocity is large. In contrast, when a porous material is directly mounted on the wall where the particle velocity is zero, unless the material thickness is equivalent to $\lambda/4$, absorption is no longer effective. Within porous materials the sound velocity is lower than in air and the wavelength becomes shorter. Therefore, generally the absorption coefficient is low at low frequencies while at high frequencies the absorption coefficient is larger and is particularly large at those frequencies where the material thickness is equivalent to $\lambda/4$. From the above discussion and as shown in Fig. 4.13a it is clear that the thicker the material the better the absorption at low frequencies and when improvement in absorption at low frequencies is required an air space should be provided as described in Fig. 4.12. An example of the latter case is given in Fig. 4.13b. The material density is proportional to the price, but it suppresses the reduction of absorption over a wide frequency range as shown in Fig. 4.14.

B.   Material Density and Flow Resistance

Regarding the density of porous materials there is an optimum value for each species and frequency. For instance, the optimum density for rockwool is larger than that of glass fibre. This is mainly determined by

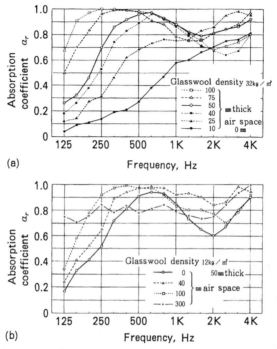

(a)

(b)

Fig. 4.13. (a) Absorption coefficients measured on glass wool with various thicknesses. (b) Absorption coefficients measured on glass wool with various air spaces.

flow resistance to air through the material. The flow resistance R_f is defined as

$$R_f = \frac{\Delta P}{u} \qquad (4.15)$$

where the pressure difference ΔP (N/m^2) between both surfaces has been measured using the apparatus as shown in Fig. 4.15 along with the flow speed, i.e. particle velocity u (m/s) produced in the material.

R_f is given in (N.s/m^3) = (kg/m^2 s) = M.K.S.rayl. Although this is analogous to direct current resistance, it is assumed applicable to a sound wave which is an alternating current and hence the term is often compared to the characteristic impedance of air ($\rho c = 415$) which is

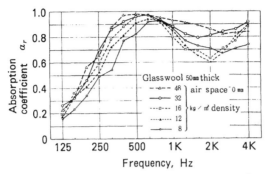

Fig. 4.14. Absorption coefficients measured on glass wool with various density.

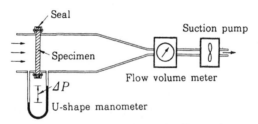

Fig. 4.15. Measuring apparatus for flow resistance.

often taken as the reference. An example is shown in Fig. 4.16 in which, generally, the larger the flow resistance, the lower the absorption coefficient except at low frequencies where the situation is reversed.

The case shown in Fig. 4.12 is confirmed by experiment, i.e. when the flow resistance equals ρc the theoretical value of the absorption coefficient is 100%.

C. Porosity and Structure Factor

Other factors governing absorptivity of porous materials are 'porosity' and 'structure factor'. Porosity P is defined as follows:

$$P = \frac{\text{volume of pores connected to external air}}{\text{total volume}} \times 100\%$$

Foamlike material, e.g. sponge, consists of different kinds of pores, i.e. connected and individual ones. While only connected pores are effective

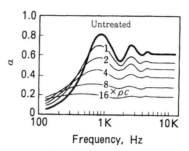

Fig. 4.16. Relationship between flow resistance and absorption coefficient of porous material (Kosten 1960). Numbers on curves show how many times the flow resistance of air units of ρ_c.

for absorption, individual ones barely absorb sound. Moreover, pore shapes and connection patterns are so varied that it may be appropriate to conceive a factor such as structure factor to account for the deviation from the theoretical derivation based on the assumption of simple parallel capillaries.

Beranek (1947) proposed a method for evaluating the absorption by introducing the concept of 'propagation constant' (see Section 10.10, A) derived theoretically from an appropriate 'structure factor' and measured 'flow resistance' and 'porosity'. This method is useful for research and the development of new materials (see Lit. B9a, B22).

D. Effect of Construction on Absorption Characteristics of Porous Materials

Since glass fibre, rockwool, etc., are not, in themselves, suitable as surface finishes but require supplementary covering materials, the absorption characteristics may vary greatly depending on the nature of the latter.

(1) Coarse and thin fabrics such as wire mesh, saran net, cheese cloth etc. are transparent to sound, therefore they have no effect.

(2) Perforated plates have little effect if thin, with many holes of small diameter and a perforation ratio more than 30%. When the perforation ratio is smaller, the absorption coefficient decreases at high frequencies. Then, depending upon the air space behind the plate, the absorber has characteristics more like those of a resonant absorber.

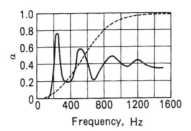

Fig. 4.17. Absorption characteristics of mat type (Kosten 1960). 30-mm thick sponge rubber, dotted line: without any treatment; solid line: with air-tight sheet.

(3) When an air-tight sheet or mat such as vinyl leather or canvas covers porous absorbents, the absorption at high frequencies decreases markedly for a hard porous material. However, the frequency curve shows distinct peaks and dips as shown in Fig. 4.17 for soft porous material such as foam or cotton wool, with the additional effect that absorption is extended to lower frequencies.

(4) Coating by oil painting blocks the pores and lowers the absorption, particularly at high frequencies. On the other hand, water paint applied so that no film is formed may be less detremental.

(5) In the case of board-like porous materials, such as acoustic-tiles, if these are installed with sufficient air space behind then this allows the tile to vibrate and increases the absorption at low frequencies.

4.4 CHARACTERISTICS OF MEMBRANE SOUND ABSORBER

An air-tight and soft material whose mass per unit area is m (kg/m^2) such as vinyl sheet or hessian with an air space L (m) and backed behind by a rigid wall, has the following resonant frequency when the material is excited into membrane type vibration with the entrapped air acting as a spring.

$$f_r = \frac{1}{2\pi}\sqrt{\frac{\rho c^2}{mL}} = \frac{1}{2\pi}\sqrt{\frac{1\cdot4 \times 10^5}{mL}} \text{ (Hz)} \qquad (4.16)$$

where ρ = air density and c = sound speed.

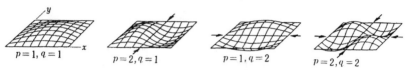

Fig. 4.18. Normal mode vibration of plates.

Further, if the material possesses elasticity and permits the propagation of bending waves, this effect has to be added and the frequency expressed as follows for a rectangular plate whose dimensions are $a \times b$ with supported edge.

$$f_r = \frac{1}{2\pi} \sqrt{\frac{\rho c^2}{mL} + \frac{\pi^4}{m}\left[\left(\frac{p}{a}\right)^2 + \left(\frac{q}{b}\right)^2\right]^2 \frac{Eh^3}{12(1-\sigma^2)}} \quad (\text{Hz}) \quad (4.17)$$

where, p, q are arbitrary positive integers, E is Young's modulus of the plate, h the thickness and σ Poisson's ratio. If the plate is thin, i.e. h and m small, the effect of the second term is reduced and particularly when L is small, the effect of the first term for the air-spring dominates so that f_r from eqn (4.16) can be used as an approximate value. If, on the other hand, h and L become large, the resonant frequency is determined by the second term of the equation. The vibration mode examples are shown in Fig. 4.18 for various p and q values. Higher modes are not significant. The original equation was derived for idealised conditions which may not be realised in practice; therefore, eqn (4.17) can be expressed as follows:

$$f = \frac{1}{2\pi} \sqrt{\frac{1 \cdot 4 \times 10^5}{mL} + \frac{K}{m}} \quad (\text{Hz}) \quad (4.18)$$

where K, the plate stiffness, should be determined by experiment. Figure 4.19 results from this method. At the resonant frequencies described above, the absorption coefficients become larger. Their measured values are illustrated in Fig. 4.20.

The following are some hints in the use of membrane type of absorption:

(1) Panels, which are thin, provide more absorption, as they can vibrate easily.

(2) The peaks of absorption coefficient are located at frequencies lower than 200 or 300 Hz and shifted towards a lower frequency

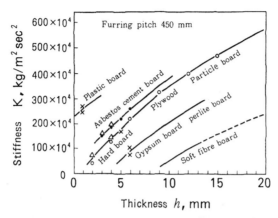

Fig. 4.19. Stiffness of board panel (S. Kimura).

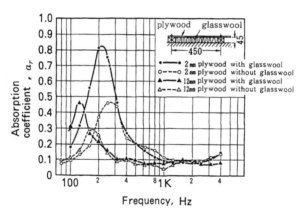

Fig. 4.20. Absorption characteristics of panel vibration (S. Kimura).

range as the material weight increases and as the air space behind the material is enlarged.

(3) If some porous material is added to the air space behind the surface material, the peak value of absorption coefficient is much enhanced.

(4) Painting of a membrane does not affect the absorption.

(5) When porous absorptive panels are used with air space behind, the absorption characteristic is a combination of porous and membrane absorption.

4.5 CHARACTERISTICS OF SINGLE RESONATOR
ABSORBER

Air in a cavity, whose dimensions are small compared with the wave-length, acts as a spring. When the cavity has a small opening to outside air, the air in the neck moves as a single mass, the mechanical analogue of which is a mass supported by a spring, thus forming a simple resonator as shown in Fig. 4.21. This is called a 'Helmholtz resonator'. The resonant frequency is given by

$$f_0 = \frac{c}{2\pi} \sqrt{\frac{G}{V}} \qquad (4.19)$$

where c = sound speed, G = air conductivity describes the ease with which the air moves in the hole and V = cavity volume (see Section 10.2D).

$$G = \frac{s}{l_e} \qquad (4.20)$$

where s = area of the opening and l_e = effective neck length. In this context, where the air in the neck moves as a single mass, not only the air plug of length l but also portions of air at the front and back of the plug called the 'adding mass' move, therefore, $l + \delta = l_e$ is used instead of the actual length l. δ is called the 'end correction'. Then

$$f_0 = \frac{c}{2\pi} \sqrt{\frac{s}{V(l + \delta)}} \quad \text{(Hz)} \qquad (4.21)$$

In the case of a circular hole whose diameter is d, $\delta \simeq 0 \cdot 8d$.

When sound at the resonant frequency strikes the resonator the air in the neck vibrates strongly, thus absorbing the sound by viscous loss.

Such a single resonator is effective only for a limited range of frequencies close to the resonant frequency at which it shows a sharp peak. However, it is not suitable for use as a general absorber but is

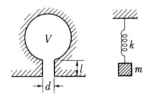

Fig. 4.21. Single resonator.

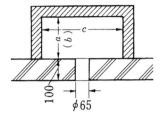

$a \times b \times c$	Resonant frequency
$150 \times 150 \times 300$	98 Hz
$200 \times 200 \times 400$	63 Hz

Fig. 4.22. An example of applied single resonator (Copenhagen Radio Hall ceiling, see Lit. B31).

useful in controlling boom, resulting from a specific low frequency due to the natural mode of vibration of the air in the room (Fig. 4.22). Although cavities can be made from timber, they are also made from tiles, bricks and ceramic jars or glass bottles and are built into the ceiling or wall, since the resonators should be both rigid and air-tight. Using pipes for the neck enables f_0 to be controlled by the neck length. In order to increase the absorption, V should be increased but any dimension of the resonator must be less than about $1/6$ of the wavelength concerned.

The resonator re-radiates sound which may not be heard because the decay rate in the resonator is greater than the room reverberation. Therefore, it functions only as absorber. However, such re-radiated sounds can be heard distinctly outdoors and it is said that some ancient Greek and Roman amphitheatres provided such resonators under the seating to produce a sensation of reverberance.

4.6 ABSORPTIVE CONSTRUCTION MADE OF PERFORATED OR SLOTTED PANELS

A. Resonant Frequency due to Perforated Panel
In order to understand the behaviour of a perforated panel separated from a rigid wall by an air space, a system of air cells should be visualised with imaginary partitioning for the air space behind each hole of the panel (as shown in Fig. 4.23) thus forming a series of Helmholtz resonators. Thus, the resonant frequency can be calculated from eqns (4.19) to (4.21). The hole opening ratio

$$P = \frac{\text{hole opening area summation}}{\text{whole panel area}}$$

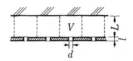

Fig. 4.23. Absorptive construction with a perforated panel.

When the panel is L (m) from the wall and has n holes of open area s per unit area,

$$P = ns \qquad \therefore \ s = \frac{P}{n}$$

The cavity volume per unit area becomes L and the volume per hole is expressed as follows:

$$V = \frac{L}{n}$$

Substituting these values into eqn (4.21), the following equation is obtained:

$$f_0 = \frac{c}{2\pi} \sqrt{\frac{P}{L(l+\delta)}} \ \ \text{(Hz)} \qquad (4.22)$$

When the hole is circular, $\delta \simeq 0 \cdot 8d$ can be used.

B. Resonant Frequency due to Slotted Panel

For a slotted panel eqn (4.22) is applicable except that in this case the value of δ is given by

$$\delta = Kb \qquad (4.23a)$$

where b is the slot width.

K is derived as follows:

(1) *Limited slot length:* with length a

$$K = \frac{1}{\pi} + \frac{2}{\pi} \log_e \frac{2a}{b} \qquad (4.23b)$$

shown also in Fig. 4.24 for values of a/b.

(2) *Infinite slot lengths:* For a construction such as 'hit and miss' boarding

$$K = \frac{2}{\pi} \log_e \left(\text{cosec} \ \frac{\pi}{2} P \right) \qquad (4.23c)$$

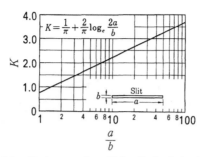

Fig. 4.24. End correction K for limited slot length.

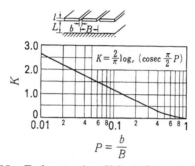

Fig. 4.25. End correction K for infinite slot length.

where, the slot opening ratio $p = b/B$ and B: slot pitch, K is obtained from Fig. 4.25. Thus the resonant frequency f_0 can be calculated from

$$f_0 = \frac{c}{2\pi} \sqrt{\frac{P}{L(l + Kb)}} \quad \text{(Hz)} \tag{4.24}$$

for both examples of slot length.

C.   Example of Large Air Space
When the air space becomes larger and an array of single resonators is assumed, the cavities are considered as tubes instead of conceived as a simple spring; therefore, the closed pipe impedance should be

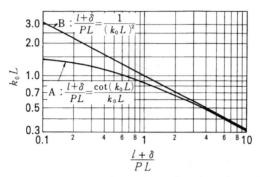

Fig. 4.26. The resonant frequency for perforated or slotted panel construction.

employed. The frequency is then obtained as follows (Ingard & Bolt 1951) with the wavelength constant at the resonant frequency

$$\frac{l+\delta}{PL} = \frac{\cot(k_0 L)}{k_0 L} \tag{4.25}$$

where

$$k_0 = \frac{\omega_0}{c} = \frac{2\pi}{c} f_0$$

After expansion of $\cot(k_0 L)^*$, only the first term is taken, eqn (4.25) becomes eqn (4.22). The difference is shown in Fig. 4.26 which is convenient for the calculation of eqn (4.25).

[Ex. 4.1] When a panel of 8 mm thickness has very long slots of 5 mm width at 50 mm pitch and the air space behind the panel is 30 mm thick, then from Fig. 4.25 where $p = 5/50 = 0·1$, $k = 1·2$ is obtained. The resonant frequency is then obtained from eqn (4.24) as follows:

$$f_0 = \frac{340}{2\pi} \sqrt{\frac{0·1}{0·03 \times 10^{-3}(8 + 1.2 \times 5)}} \approx 830 \text{ (Hz)}$$

* $\cot x = \dfrac{1}{x} - \dfrac{x}{3} - \dfrac{x^3}{45} - \cdots$.

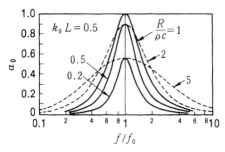

Fig. 4.27. Resonant absorption characteristics due to perforated panel when the resistance at the neck is changed.

When the air space is 300 mm thick, the left-hand side of eqn (4.25) gives

$$\frac{(8 + 1.2 \times 5)10^{-3}}{0 \cdot 1 \times 0 \cdot 3} = 0 \cdot 467$$

From Fig. 4.26, $k_0 L = 1 \cdot 1$; therefore

$$f_0 = \frac{c \times 1 \cdot 1}{2\pi L} = \frac{340 \times 1 \cdot 1}{2\pi \times 0 \cdot 3} \approx 200 \text{ Hz}$$

D.   Absorption Characteristics

(a) *Absorption characteristics due to normal incidence:* The absorptive system, which is composed of a perforated or slotted panel and air space, has an absorption coefficient which peaks at the resonant frequency obtained as in the calculation described above. The peak value and its spread is controlled by the resistance to air motion in the neck. Figure 4.27 shows the theoretical values for normal incidence and the relationship with the real part R of the impedance per unit area of the panel. When $R = \rho c$, $a_0 = 100\%$ at f_0. When $R < \rho c$, the peak value becomes lower but its spread is wider. R is proportional to the flow resistance in the neck and can be adjusted by cloth of appropriate thickness or by porous material such as glass wool behind the hole. When the resistance is optimum, the factor which controls the peak width is $k_0 L$ as shown in Fig. 4.28; thus, the larger the air space, the wider the frequency range to be absorbed.

(b) *Absorption characteristic due to random incidence:* Generally, in the case of random incidence, by adjusting the dimensions of hole opening

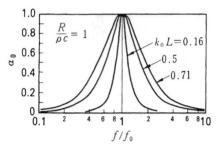

Fig. 4.28. Resonant absorption characteristics due to perforated panel when the thickness of air space is varied.

and slit, thickness of air space and the flow resistance at the neck, there is the possibility of designing any arbitrary absorption characteristic (Ingard & Bolt 1951). The difference from the case of normal incidence is that when $R/\rho c$ is between $1\cdot5$ and $1\cdot8$ the absorption at f_0 becomes the maximum. As of now, although there are still problems in designing the resistance, fairly accurate prediction is possible by reference to actual measurements of various reverberation absorption coefficients. As an example, when the air space is quite large, f_0 calculated from eqn (4.25) becomes a lower value and the statistical incidence absorption coefficients calculated from eqn (4.11) yield a series of peaks lined up in the higher frequencies as shown by dotted lines in Fig. 4.29 while the reverberation absorption coefficients, due to actual measurements, show a spectrum enveloping these peaks, thus producing a wide range absorption.

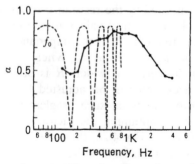

Fig. 4.29. Absorption characteristics of perforated panel (hole opening ratio 13%) with large air space (1 m thick) (S. Kimura).

4.7   COMMENTS ON COMMERCIAL PRODUCTS, DESIGN AND CONSTRUCTION

In order to make absorption effective one must understand fully the absorption mechanisms and characteristics so that appropriate designs can be developed to meet the requirements. At the same time, it is necessary to produce correct design and construction details and to have careful field supervision.

A.   Selection of Absorbent
Although, in practice, the most useful data is that provided by reverberation absorption coefficients, it varies depending not only on material itself but also critically on the chosen construction detail, therefore, unless the measured value relates directly to the construction detail, the data should be distrusted as a means of selecting and applying a particular commercial product. Some measured data are given in the attached Table A2 of Appendices.

B.   Use of Area Effect
Instead of using an absorbing material to cover the whole area, it is better to divide it into smaller areas, thus increasing the total absorption of the material as well as increasing the diffusion of reflected sound.

C.   Selection of Places for Absorptive Treatment
Even the same absorbent, if applied to places such as corners or the perimeter of the ceiling where the sound pressure is high, becomes more effective as a means of increasing the total room absorption. These remarks apply particularly to the application of single resonators, the performance of which are highly dependent on their position in a room.

D.   Comments on Installation
(1) *Porous type:* It is advantageous to have as large an air space as possible behind the material. For instance, absorptive fibre board can be set into panel vibration which enhances absorption at low frequencies. As shown in Fig. 4.30 the absorption of wood wool cement increases at middle frequencies due to penetrating interstices and hence it behaves like a perforated panel with an air space. On the other hand, such wood wool cement, when cast into concrete with its interstices filled, may lose absorption.

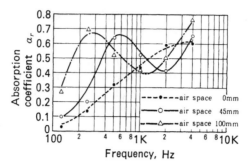

Fig. 4.30. Absorption characteristics of cemented excelsior board (15 mm thick).

(2) *Membrane vibration type:* It is important to install panels so that vibration can easily occur. In some cases resonant frequencies can be dispersed by varying the timber furring spacing and the number of nails.

(3) *Perforated panel:* When this covers a porous absorbent, the hole opening ratio should be larger than 20% and, moreover, it is advisable to have the ratio as large as possible and the panel thickness as small as possible. In the case of the resonator type, the hole size, plate thickness and air space, etc., must all be manufactured correctly as calculated. It is important to note that the inside porous material must touch the hole to produce resistance.

E. Painting, Paper and Cloth Cover

These finishes must be carefully applied in order not to destroy the absorption mechanism of the material itself or its composition. Although panel or membrane types of absorbers generally can be used without regard to the selection of paint, in the case of porous or resonator types they must obviously not be blocked by the paint or finishing materials. In the case of cloth covering, if the flow resistance is large, the material should be selected with care because it may cause a serious change in the absorption characteristics. The use of craft paper applied with paste should be avoided because air flow is greatly restricted.

Perforated panels often show dirt around the holes due to moving air depositing dust, particularly if cloth is used. This may cause serious aesthetic problems. The situation can be improved by placing a thin polyethylene film on the furring members behind the perforated panel. This reduces the deposition of dirt with little damage to the absorption because it gives little resistance to the alternating sound wave but blocks the direct flow of air.

4.8   SPECIAL SOUND ABSORPTIVE DEVICES

A.   Variable Absorbers
It is a natural desire to wish to change the reverberation time of a room to suit its purpose. Many devices have been conceived and developed over the years to provide variable absorption of walls and ceiling. However, it is difficult to maintain a complicated system and there are few technicians capable of managing such systems. Among others, draperies and movable panels, as shown in Fig. 4.31 are increasing in popularity but still limited in application to special rooms such as broadcasting studios or listening-rooms.

Reflective surface   Absorptive surface

Fig. 4.31.   Variable sound absorbing panels.

B.   Suspended Absorbers
When absorption is required for noise suppression in a factory or other situations and where it is difficult to apply absorbents to walls and ceiling because of pipes, ducts and so on, it is quite effective to hang a number of such absorbers as shown in Fig. 4.32 from the ceiling. Due to sound diffraction the apparent absorption coefficient may often become greater than 1. Another example of a suspended absorber is a system of numbers of discs made of perforated plate or wire-mesh (whose diameter is 60–200 cm) carrying porous materials on them and a deep grid composed of porous absorbent installed at ceiling height in auditoria, factory etc.

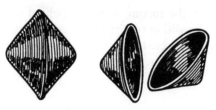

Fig. 4.32. An example of suspended absorber.

C. *Absorptive Wedge and Anechoic Room*

It is almost essential for research in acoustics to provide a room in which the sound field is equivalent to open free space. This is achieved by complete absorption on all the surrounding surfaces of the room which is then called an 'anechoic room'. An absorptive wedge of porous material is used for this purpose.

Although the standard design of an absorptive wedge unit was presented by Beranek (1946), a new, more economic design is proposed as shown in Fig. 4.33 (Maekawa & Osaki 1983). Above the cut-off frequency indicated in the ordinate, the sound pressure reflection coefficients are lower than 0.15, provided that the flow resistance of the wedge material is controlled as shown in the figure.

If only frequencies higher than 300 Hz are of interest, wedges are not necessary; only a layer of glass wool, 20 cm thick, is required for lining the anechoic room.

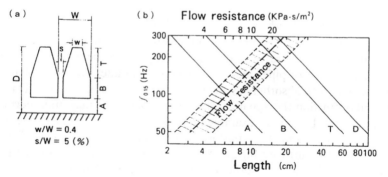

Fig. 4.33. Design chart for economic absorptive wedge.

PROBLEMS 4

1. Classify various sound absorptive materials and constructions in terms of their sound absorption mechanisms. Explain the general form of their absorption characteristics and the caution necessary in their actual application.

2. In air, when a plane wave with pressure $p = Ae^{j(\omega t - kx)}$ is incident normally on a plane whose pressure reflection coefficient is $e^{-2(a+jb)}$, show that the standing wave which results can be described as follows:

$$P(x) = 2Ae^{-(a+jb)}\cosh\{a + j(b - kx)\}e^{j\omega t}$$

and the standing wave ratio $n = \coth a$. Also show that the acoustic impedance density of the plane

$$Z = \rho c . \coth(a + jb)$$

for the above condition.

3. In a reverberation room whose volume is 150 m^3 and surface area is 190 m^2, the reverberation time at 500 Hz is 6·9 s when empty. When a specimen wall of 12 m^2 area is installed in the room, the reverberation time is 3·4 s. Find the absorption coefficient of the wall at 500 Hz.

4. The reverberation absorption coefficient of the same absorbent produces different results when measured in different laboratories. Moreover the results may exceed unity. Explain the factors which may account for this.

5. Glass wool, 50 mm thick, is mounted directly on a concrete surface. Compare the sound absorption characteristics in such an arrangement with those resulting from the introduction of a 100-mm air space behind the glass wool.

6. When 50-mm thick glass wool is mounted directly on a concrete surface, explain how the absorption characteristics will change with the following four surface finishes: (1) saran net; (2) vinyl leather; (3) 5-mm thick perforated panel with 4-mm dia. holes at 15 mm centres; (4) 5-mm thick perforated panel with 9-mm dia. holes at 15 mm centres.

Chapter 5

AIR-BORNE SOUND INSULATION

Noise control can be achieved by preventing the generation and spreading of noise. There are two ways by which noise can propagate, i.e. airborne sound which is propagated through air and structure-borne sound which is transmitted through material such as is found in building structures, etc. In this chapter the attenuation of airborne sound is discussed.

5.1 PROPAGATION AND TRANSMISSION OF AIRBORNE SOUND

A. Attenuation Due to Distance

a. Attenuation Due to Distance from a Point Source
The sound intensity I at a distance d generated from a point sound source whose acoustic power W in free field is given by

$$I = \frac{W}{4\pi d^2} \tag{5.1}$$

since the total energy which passes through a sphere of surface area $4\pi d^2$ is W.

Thus, I is inversely proportional to the square of the distance. The sound intensity/pressure level at this point can be expressed as follows:

$$L = L_w - 10 \log_{10} 4\pi - 10 \log_{10} d^2$$
$$= L_w - 11 - 20 \log_{10} d \text{ (dB)} \qquad (5.2)$$

where the sound power level of the source L_w is $10 \log_{10}(W/10^{-12})$.

If the sound source has a directivity factor Q (see Section 10.13) in the direction towards the receiving point

$$L = L_w - 11 - 20 \log_{10} d + 10 \log_{10} Q \text{ (dB)} \qquad (5.3)$$

Since this equation shows that the inverse square law is also applicable in one direction, when the sound level at distance d_1 is L_1 dB, L_2 at distance $d_2 = nd_1$, then it follows

$$L_2 = L_1 - 20 \log_{10} \frac{d_2}{d_1} = L_1 - 20 \log_{10} n \text{ (dB)} \qquad (5.4)$$

Therefore, for every doubling of distance the level is reduced by 6 dB. Also L_w can be determined from eqns (5.2) and (5.3) with measured values of L, d and/or Q.

b. Attenuation Due to Distance from a Line Source

(1) Infinite line source. When there are many sound sources in a row such as vehicles on a motorway, they can be considered as an infinite line source. It is assumed that an infinite set of incoherent point sources lies continuously on the line in random phases, where any wave behaviour can be ignored. In free field the sound waves spread in a cylindrical form around a line source which is the axis of the cylinder. When the acoustic power per unit length of the line source is W, the sound intensity I at distance d is given by eqn (5.5) since the sound energy is distributed over the cylinder surface with radius d.

$$I = \frac{W}{2\pi d} \qquad (5.5)$$

In this case I is inversely proportional to d. When the source power level is L_w per unit length then the sound intensity/pressure level is given by

$$L = L_w - 8 - 10 \log_{10} d \text{ (dB)} \qquad (5.6)$$

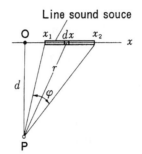

Fig. 5.1. Line sound source.

Therefore, for every doubling of distance, the level is reduced by 3 dB.

(2) Finite line source. In the case of a finite length line source, the point sources can be considered as lying continuously from x_1 to x_2 as shown in Fig. 5.1. The energy density E at the receiving point P at a distance d from the source becomes

$$E = \int_{x_1}^{x_2} \frac{Wdx}{4\pi r^2 c} = \frac{W}{4\pi c} \int_{x_1}^{x_2} \frac{dx}{(d^2 + x^2)}$$

$$= \frac{W}{4\pi c} \cdot \frac{1}{d} \left(\tan^{-1} \frac{x_2}{d} - \tan^{-1} \frac{x_1}{d} \right) = \frac{W}{4\pi c} \cdot \frac{\varphi}{d} \qquad (5.7)$$

Thus, E is proportional to the angle φ between the lines of sight from P to the respective sources x_1 and x_2 and inversely proportional to distance d.

[Ex. 5.1]   In Fig. 5.1, if the sound source length is l and $x_1 = x_2 = l/2$, the variation of sound energy density due to distance at P may be expressed with the aid of eqn (5.7) as follows:

$$E = \frac{W}{2\pi c} \cdot \frac{1}{d} \left(\tan^{-1} \frac{l}{2d} \right)$$

$$\left. \begin{array}{lll} d \ll 1; & \left(\tan^{-1} \dfrac{l}{2d} \right) \simeq \dfrac{\pi}{2} & \therefore E_{(\text{near})} = \dfrac{W}{4c} \cdot \dfrac{1}{d} \\[3mm] d \gg 1; & \left(\tan^{-1} \dfrac{l}{2d} \right) \simeq \dfrac{l}{2d} & \therefore E_{(\text{far})} = \dfrac{Wl}{4\pi c} \cdot \dfrac{1}{d^2} \end{array} \right\} \qquad (5.8)$$

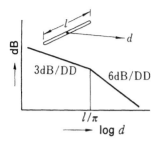

Fig. 5.2. Distance attenuation from a line source.

If both values are made equal, $d = l/\pi$. We see from Fig. 5.2 that if d is in the near distance from l/π, the sound pressure level reduces by 3 dB for every doubling of distance while in the far distance it reduces by 6 dB for every doubling of distance. This approximation is very useful for estimating the sound distribution from a line source.

c. Attenuation Due to Distance from a Plane Source

When sound propagates through a window or wall, assuming an infinite set of point sources which were used to describe the line source, the energy density E at the receiving point P, distance d from a rectangular plane source as shown in Fig. 5.3 is given by

$$E = \int_{x_1}^{x_2} \int_{y_1}^{y_2} \frac{W . dx\, dy}{2\pi r^2 c} = \frac{W}{2\pi c} \int_{x_1}^{x_2} \int_{y_1}^{y_2} \frac{dx\, dy}{\left(d^2 + x^2 + y^2\right)} \qquad (5.9)$$

where W is the sound power per unit area.

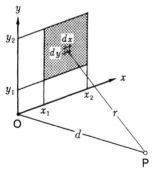

Fig. 5.3. Rectangular plane source.

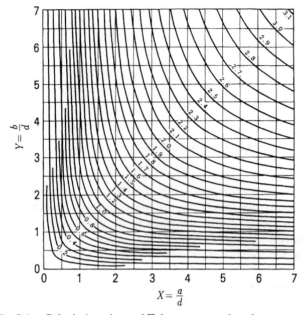

Fig. 5.4. Calculation chart of Σ for a rectangular plane source.

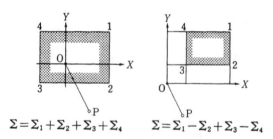

Fig. 5.5. Method for obtaining Σ in general case.

Putting $x_1 = 0$, $y_1 = 0$, $x_2 = a$, $y_2 = b$ for simplification, the integral for unit distance d is derived as follows:

$$\Sigma = \int_0^{a/d} \int_0^{b/d} \frac{dX\, dY}{1 + X^2 + Y^2} \tag{5.10}$$

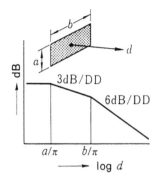

Fig. 5.6. Distance attenuation from a plane source.

The result of the numerical integration is shown in Fig. 5.4. Hence the sound intensity/pressure level at the receiving point P is

$$L = L_w - 8 + 10 \log_{10} \Sigma \text{ (dB)} \tag{5.11}$$

Generally Σ can be obtained as shown in Fig. 5.5.

As in Fig. 5.2, the distance attenuation can be approximated as shown in Fig. 5.6, i.e. when d is less than a/π no attenuation occurs, while in the range $a/\pi < d < b/\pi$ attenuation may be approximated by 3 dB/DD, and in the range $d > b/\pi$ by 6 dB/DD.

B. Effect of Reflecting Surface

When a sound wave impinges on a smooth hard large surface there is a mirror-like reflection as shown in Fig. 1.6 (Chap. 1).

a. Single Reflecting Surface

The reflected sound which is generated by the image source behind the reflecting surface is added to the direct sound at the receiving point. In the case of pure tones their phases and hence the interference pattern have to be taken into consideration, whereas, in the general case of noise, only the energy densities need to be considered. In Fig. 5.7 the direct sound energy density at the receiver P is

$$E_0 = \frac{W}{4\pi r_0^2 c} \tag{5.12}$$

and the reflected sound energy density,

$$E_1 = \frac{W(1 - \alpha)}{4\pi r_1^2 c} \tag{5.13}$$

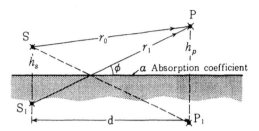

Fig. 5.7. Sound reflection by a plane surface.

added together it follows that

$$E = E_0 + E_1 = E_0 \left\{ 1 + \left(\frac{r_0}{r_1} \right)^2 (1 - \alpha) \right\} \qquad (5.14)$$

Alternatively, after obtaining each dB value for E_0 and E_1, the energy summation can be carried out using Fig. 1.4. Another way would be to consider the reflected sound as propagating to the image P_1 of the receiving point from the sound source S, which produces the same result. This method is valid only when the reflecting surface is sufficiently large compared with the sound wavelength.

b. Many Reflecting Surfaces

(1) The image sources. When there are many reflecting surfaces each has not only an image source of 1st order but a 2nd order image for a 2nd reflection and also many higher order images corresponding to multiple reflections as shown in Fig. 5.8. The energy density at the receiving point is obtained by integrating the energy densities from all images using the same principle as in eqn (5.14). Figure 5.8 shows an example of two parallel reflecting walls producing multiple reflections.

(2) Source close to a reflecting surface. When a point source whose power is known is located close to one or more large reflecting planes, the following simplified method can be used as shown in Fig. 5.9.

1) In the case of one reflecting surface the directivity factor is $Q = 2$, (see eqn 5.3) because the energy spreads only within a hemisphere; therefore the energy density is multiplied by 2.
2) Similarly, when the sound source is located close to the orthogonal intersection of two reflecting surfaces, $Q = 4$.

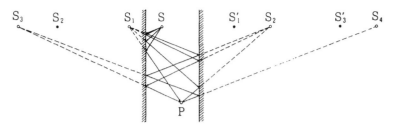

Fig. 5.8. Multiple reflections between two parallel planes, from the image source of 1st order at the left hand side plane only are shown with sound-rays.

3) When the sound source is located close to the corner where three reflecting surfaces intersect orthogonally, $Q = 8$.

[Ex. 5.2] When an air conditioning outlet is located on a ceiling the difference in noise radiation between the centre and the corner locations can be found by using eqn (5.3). At the centre $Q = 2$ whereas at the corner $Q = 8$; therefore the difference is $10\log(2/8) = -6$ (dB), i.e. the noise level is reduced by 6 dB at the ceiling centre location.

C. Excess Attenuation
Sound attenuation with distance influenced by geometrical spreading and reflection as described above is valid close to the source. At a distance of more than several tens of metres, the effects of the intervening medium meteorology and boundary conditions of the ground, etc., produce an excess attenuation greater than expected on the basis of the above formulae.

a. Attenuation Due to Air Absorption
Sound waves attenuate during propagation in air because the energy is absorbed by the medium. When a plane wave whose intensity is I

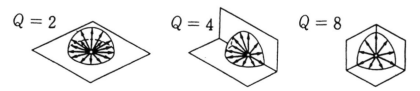

Fig. 5.9. Directivity factors due to orthogonal intersection of reflecting planes.

propagates a distance of x metres, the intensity I is given by

$$I_x = I_0 e^{-mx} \tag{5.15}$$

where m is the attenuation constant/meter. Expressing this in dB, the attenuation per metre becomes

$$10 \log_{10}(I_0/I_1) = m10 \log_{10} e = 4.34m \text{ (dB)} \tag{5.16}$$

The value of m in air is given in Fig. 3.10 (or ANSI SI.26, 1978).

The attenuation varies with humidity as well as temperature. However, at low frequencies the attenuation is so little that it can be neglected.

b. Attenuation Due to Meteorological Conditions

So far we have discussed the propagation of sound in stationary air. However, atmospheric air neither stands still nor is homogeneous. Meteorological conditions have a major influence on the propagation of sound in the open air.

Although 'fog' or precipitation such as 'rain' or 'snow' have so little effect on sound propagation that they can be ignored, the profiles of air temperature and wind have a much greater influence.

(1) Effect of temperature profile. When the weather is fine during the day, the air is heated near the earth's surface by solar radiation but gets cooler towards the upper sky, called 'lapse'. At night or in cloudy weather the temperature profile takes the form of an 'inversion'. Since the sound velocity is greater when the temperature is higher according to eqn (1.7), the sound rays bend as shown in Fig. 5.10. Therefore, during the day, a 'shadow zone' occurs beyond a certain distance from the sound source near the ground where sound is almost inaudible, while in the case of a higher temperature in the upper air the sound can easily return to earth at quite large distances from the source.

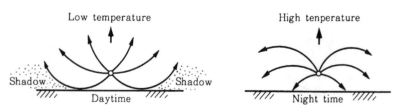

Fig. 5.10. Sound refraction by temperature profile.

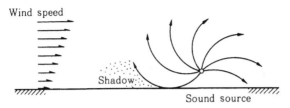

Fig. 5.11. Sound refraction by wind speed profile.

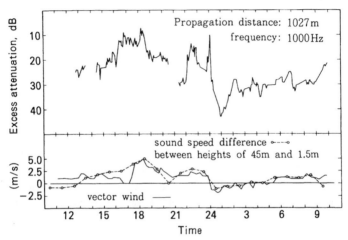

Fig. 5.12. Measured fluctuation of receiving sound pressure level and vector wind (K. Konishi).

(2) Effect of wind. Generally the profile of wind speed is faster at high altitude than close to the earth. Since the sound propagation is controlled by the vector summation of wind and sound speed, the sound rays bend as shown in Fig 5.11. Therefore, in the upwind direction shadow zones may occur while downwind sound reaches into the far distance. Figure 5.12 illustrates this phenomenon showing an abrupt change at midnight.

(3) Fluctuation of received sound level. When sound propagates through the open air there is a wide fluctuation in sound level due to varying meteorological conditions with time at the receiving point as shown in Fig. 5.12. Furthermore, the natural wind blows so erratically with many

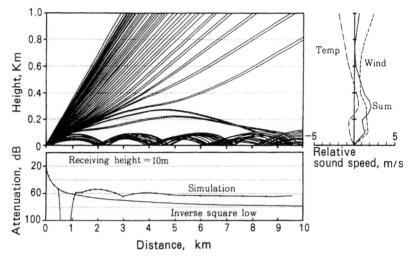

Fig. 5.13. Sound ray simulation of long range propagation (Takagi *et al.* 1985).

irregular eddies that sound waves are forced to bend whenever striking eddies, thus leading to an absence of stable sound rays connecting source and receiver. Therefore, the received sound level shows violent variation from a very short duration to several minutes by 10 dB or more.

(4) Simulation of long range sound propagation. Sound propagation can be simulated by sound ray tracing with the aid of a computer assuming steady meteorological conditions with constant profiles of temperature and wind between source and receiver. An example is shown in Fig. 5.13 (see West *et al.* 1991).

c. Attenuation due to Ground Effect

The excess attenuation of sound propagating near the ground is caused by the reflecting property of the ground. The reflection characteristic of the ground for a spherical sound wave is not defined by the reflection coefficient for a plane wave, (see Section 1.5C) but is also accompanied by a complicated mathematical function containing the distance from S to P, the grazing angle φ, and also the surface impedance Z as shown in Fig. 5.7.

The curves in Fig. 5.14 show excess attenuation for propagation over mown grass calculated by Piercy *et al.* (see Lit. B34). These results show

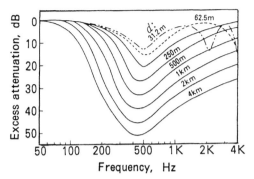

Fig. 5.14. Excess attenuation due to ground covered by mown grass for $h_s = 1.8$ m, $h_p = 1.5$ m in Fig. 5.7. The values are relative to that for the point source placed on a perfectly hard surface (Piercy *et al.*).

good agreement with field measurements. The excess attenuation increases remarkably with distance at mid frequencies and depends on the surface impedance.

D. Sound Transmission Between Rooms and Between Inside and Outside

a. Sound Transmission Between Adjoining Rooms

The case where noise transmits from the source room to the receiving room through a partition whose transmission coefficient is τ and area F is discussed. In Fig. 5.15 when the energy density in the source room is E_1, the energy incident on the partition is $(c/4)E_1F$ from eqn (3.18), so the energy transmitted into the adjoining room will be $(c/4)E_1F\tau$. If

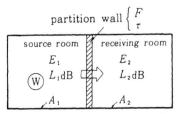

Fig. 5.15. Sound transmission between adjoining rooms.

the energy density is E_2 in the receiving room whose surface area is S, the energy incident on the whole surface is $(c/4)E_2S$ and the absorbed energy $(c/4)E_2S\bar{\alpha}$, where $\bar{\alpha}$ is the average absorption coefficient. Since the total absorption $A_2 = S\bar{\alpha}$, in the steady state eqn (5.17) we obtain

$$\frac{c}{4}E_1F\tau = \frac{c}{4}E_2A_2 \qquad \therefore \quad \frac{E_1}{E_2} = \frac{1}{\tau}\frac{A_2}{F} \qquad (5.17)$$

When the sound pressure levels in source and receiving rooms are L_1 and L_2 respectively, the level difference between rooms is

$$L_1 - L_2 = 10\log_{10}\frac{E_1}{E_2} = 10\log_{10}\frac{1}{\tau} + 10\log_{10}\frac{A_2}{F}$$

$$\therefore \quad L_1 - L_2 = R + 10\log_{10}\frac{A_2}{F} \text{ dB} \qquad (5.18)$$

If the sound source power is W in the source room with sound absorption A_1, the expression (3.20) holds. From the definition of eqn (1.17) for L_w it follows that

$$L_1 = L_w + 6 - 10\log_{10} A_1 \qquad (5.19)$$

Then, substituting into eqn (5.18)

$$L_2 = L_w + 6 - R - 10\log_{10}\frac{A_1A_2}{F} \text{ (dB)} \qquad (5.20)$$

Thus, not only the value of R of the partition wall but also the sound absorption provided in both rooms is found to be important.

b.   Sound Transmission from Outside to Inside

Assuming that the incident sound on the outside wall is a plane wave whose intensity is I and the wall area is F, the incident energy is IF. In Fig. 5.16, when the receiving room condition is the same as in Fig. 5.15

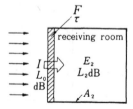

Fig. 5.16.   Sound transmission from outside to inside.

with the incident sound level L_0, the difference in sound pressure level is

$$L_0 - L_2 = R_0 - 6 + 10\log_{10}\frac{A_2}{F} \text{ (dB)} \qquad (5.21)$$

where L_0 must not include the reflection by the wall. Also R_0 should be the value for normal incidence (see Section 5.3).

c. Sound Transmission from Inside to Outside
When sound intensity I is radiated through the wall to the outside as shown in Fig. 5.17, the radiated energy is IF. If the source room has the same condition as in Fig. 5.15 and the sound level at the outside of the wall is L_0,

$$L_1 - L_0 = R + 6 \text{ (dB)} \qquad (5.22)$$

substituting eqn (5.19) into eqn (5.22),

$$L_0 = L_w - 10\log_{10} A_1 - R \text{ (dB)} \qquad (5.23)$$

where this L_0 value is at the outside surface of the wall and is equivalent to L_w in eqn (5.11). As the sound leaves the vicinity of the wall it spreads outwards.

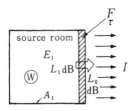

Fig. 5.17. Sound transmission from a source room to outside.

d. Composite Transmission Loss
In actual buildings walls are rarely constructed from a single material but contain windows and doors as well, thus, a wall often includes several components which have different R values. From eqn (1.25) the composite transmission loss denoted by $\bar{R}$ is expressed by,

$$\bar{R} = 10\log_{10}\frac{1}{\bar{\tau}} \qquad (5.24)$$

where $\bar{\tau}$ is the average transmission coefficient which can be obtained from the transmission coefficients τ_i for the area F_i

$$\bar{\tau} = \frac{\Sigma F_i \tau_i}{\Sigma F_i} = \frac{\Sigma F_i \tau_i}{F} \qquad (5.25)$$

The transmission coefficient τ_i for the wall whose transmission loss R_i is given by

$$R_i = 10 \log_{10} \frac{1}{\tau_i} \qquad \therefore \quad \tau_i = 10^{-R_i/10} \qquad (5.26)$$

Therefore, if each component transmission loss R_i is known, using the above three equations, the composite transmission loss can be calculated.

[Ex. 5.3]   An exterior wall constructed from reinforced concrete has an area 30 m² in which there is a glass window of 10 m² and the materials R's are 50 dB and 20 dB, respectively. Then the composite transmission loss of the wall is calculated as follows:

Wall: $\tau_1 = 10^{-(50/10)} = 0 \cdot 00001$,   Window: $\tau_2 = 10^{-(20/10)} = 0 \cdot 01$

$$\bar{\tau} = \frac{(30 - 10) \times 0 \cdot 00001 + 10 \times 0 \cdot 01}{30} = \frac{0 \cdot 1002}{30} \approx \frac{1}{300}$$

$$\bar{R} = 10 \log_{10} 300 = 24 \cdot 8 \text{ (dB)}$$

[Ex. 5.4]   When 1 m² of the window is open in the above wall, the composite transmission loss will be

$$\bar{R} = 10 \log \frac{30}{20 \times 0 \cdot 00001 + 9 + 0 \cdot 01 + 1 \times 1} \approx 10 \log \frac{30}{1 \cdot 1} = 14 \cdot 4 \text{ (dB)}$$

5.2   MEASUREMENT AND RATING OF AIRBORNE SOUND INSULATION

A.   Measurement of Sound Transmission Loss: Reduction Index

The test specimen is inserted in an opening between two adjacent reverberation rooms as shown in Fig. 5.18. The sound is generated in one room, and the sound pressure levels L_1 and L_2 in both rooms measured in the steady state. Then the sound transmission loss R is

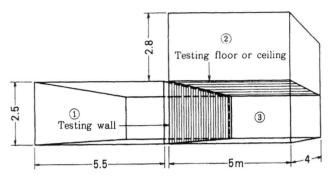

Fig. 5.18. Reverberation rooms for measuring sound insulation, minimum dimensions recommended by ISO 140. ① Source room for test wall (≈ 10 m²); ② Source room for test floor and ceiling ($10 \sim 20$ m²); ③ Receiving room > 50 m³.

obtained from eqn (5.27) derived from eqn (5.18)

$$R = L_1 - L_2 - 10\log_{10}\frac{A_2}{F}\,(\mathrm{dB}) \qquad (5.27)$$

where F is the area of the specimen, and A_2 is the absorbing area in the receiving room. For this purpose, sufficient structural isolation between source and receiving room is essential in order to be able to neglect the sound transmitted via any indirect path.

ISO140 provides the following instructions:

(1) The volumes and shapes of the two test rooms should not be exactly the same. The volumes should be at least 50 m³ and there should be at least 10% difference between them, in order not to have the same natural frequencies in both rooms. The room dimensions should be chosen so that the natural frequency should not degenerate in the low-frequency range as shown in Fig. 3.5. Further diffusion is to be provided, if possible, by using diffusing elements as shown in Fig. 4.8.

(2) The reverberation time should be modified by not more than 2 s especially at low frequencies, in order for the measured value not to depend on the reverberation time.

(3) The test opening should be approximately 10 m² for walls and 10–20 m² for floors, with the shorter edge length not less than 2.3 m. The specimen should be installed in a manner as similar as possible to the actual construction.

(4) Sound transmission via flanking paths should be negligibly small.
(5) Sound pressure levels in both rooms should be measured at many points; then the average level L is obtained with the aid of eqn (1.22). White noise is used and the sound pressure level measured in 1/3 octave bands. The frequency range should be at least from 100 to 3150 Hz, preferably 4000 Hz.
(6) The sound absorption area A_2 is obtained from the measured reverberation time using eqn (3.23)

Figure 5.18 shows the minimum size of measuring rooms according to the above specification.

B. Measured Data of Sound Transmission Loss
There have been many measured data already published on various materials and construction details. See Appendices Table A.3. These values are used in practical calculations of noise reduction. If you cannot get measured data for a particular material then you can estimate the R value by choosing the R value of a similar material in Table A.3 taking note of the comments in this chapter.

C. Field Measurement of Airborne Sound Insulation
When measuring airborne sound insulation in an actual building there are flanking sound transmission paths as well as the direct path through the partition as shown in Fig. 5.19. Therefore, even if the measurement is carried out in the same way as in the laboratory, the value should be called the 'apparent sound reduction index R'''.

$$R' = L_1 - L_2 - 10\log_{10}(A_2/F) \ (\text{dB}) \qquad (5.28)$$

This value may be used for comparison with the laboratory measured value of R.

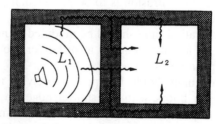

Fig. 5.19. Sound transmission paths through walls between adjoining rooms.

In order to evaluate the airborne sound insulation between rooms in the field, the level difference

$$D = L_2 - L_2 \text{ (dB)} \tag{5.29}$$

is used.

However, the receiving sound pressure level is inversely proportional to the sound absorption area in the receiving room. So that the normalised level difference, with reference absorption 10 m^2 is given by

$$D_{n,10} = L_1 - L_2 - 10\log_{10}(A/10) \text{ (dB)} \tag{5.30}$$

Alternatively, normalizing the measured reverberation time T in the receiving room to a reference value of $0 \cdot 5$ s, which is typical of domestic rooms,

$$D_{n,0\cdot5} = L_1 - L_2 + 10\log_{10}(T/0\cdot5) \text{ (dB)} \tag{5.31}$$

Equation (5.31) is adopted and called 'standardised level difference' by the International Standards Organisation.

D. Single Number Rating of Airborne Sound Insulation

Generally the value of R depends on frequency. However, it is often desirable to convert the information into a single number rating of acoustical performance. ISO 717 provides a method as follows:

(1) The measured curve of R (or R') values is compared with a reference curve shown in Fig. 5.20.
(2) The reference curve is shifted towards the measured curve until the mean unfavourable deviation is as large as possible but not more than $2 \cdot 0$ dB.

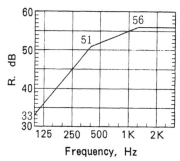

Fig. 5.20.   Curve of reference values for airborne sound (ISO 717/1).

(3)   The value of the reference curve at 500 Hz, R_w (or $R'w$) is called the 'weighted sound reduction index' (or 'weighted apparent sound reduction index').

(4)   Also, the maximum unfavourable deviation shall be reported if it exceeds 8 dB.

(5)   The same procedure is also applied to the value of D and $D_{n,0.5}$, then D_w and $D_{n,0.5w}$ are called 'weighted level difference' and 'weighted standardised level difference' respectively.

Unfortunately, many countries have their own standards or codes with different criteria, although most systems are similar in principle. Some of them are shown in Section 10.12.

5.3   MASS LAW FOR SOUND INSULATION OF A SINGLE WALL

A.   Normal Incidence Mass Law

When a plane wave whose angular frequency in $\omega = 2\pi f$ is incident normally on an infinitely wide thin wall some is reflected and some transmitted. Let the sound pressures of the incident, reflected and transmitted sounds be denoted by p_i, p_r and p_t, respectively, as shown in Fig. 5.21(a). The wall is excited by the sound pressure difference between the two surfaces of the wall and the equation of motion is

$$(p_i + p_r) - p_t = m\frac{dv}{dt} \tag{5.32}$$

where m is the surface mass of the wall, and v is its velocity.

In the case of simple harmonic motion, $d/dt = j\omega$ can be used (see Problem 1.1),

$$(p_i + p_r) - p_t = P = j\omega m v \tag{5.33}$$

$$\therefore \quad j\omega m = \frac{P}{v} \tag{5.34}$$

This is the impedance per unit area of the wall. Since it is assumed that the particle velocity of the air adjacent to both wall surfaces is equal to v,

$$\frac{p_i}{\rho c} - \frac{p_r}{\rho c} = \frac{p_t}{\rho c} = v$$

$$\therefore \quad p_i - p_r = p_t = \rho c v \tag{5.35}$$

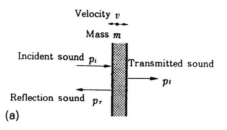

(a)

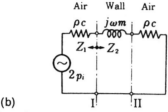

(b)

Fig. 5.21.   (a) Sound insulation of single wall and (b) its analogous circuit.

From eqns (5.33) and (5.35)

$$\frac{p_i}{p_t} = 1 + \frac{j\omega m}{2\rho c} \tag{5.36}$$

Therefore the transmission loss is

$$R_0 = 10\log_{10}\frac{1}{\tau} = 10\log_{10}\left|\frac{p_i}{p_t}\right|^2$$

$$= 10\log_{10}\left\{1 + \left(\frac{\omega m}{2\rho c}\right)^2\right\} \tag{5.37}$$

Generally, $(\omega m)^2 \gg (2\rho c)^2$; hence

$$R_0 \approx 10\log_{10}\left(\frac{\omega m}{2\rho c}\right)^2$$

$$= 20\log_{10} f \cdot m - 43 \text{ (dB)} \tag{5.38}$$

which is proportional both to frequency and the surface mass m of the wall. This is called the 'mass law' for airborne sound insulation. Doubling the weight of the wall or the frequency gives an increase of 6 dB in R_0.

This wall motion may be expressed by an analogous electrical circuit as shown in Fig. 5.21(b) (see Section 10.2). In this circuit, if no wall

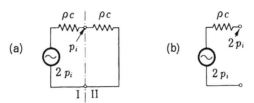

Fig. 5.22.   Analogous circuit: (a) Open air and (b) Rigid wall.

exists, it becomes as shown in Fig. 5.22(a) and at the wall surface the sound pressure is p_i. When the wall is completely rigid in which the velocity becomes zero, the current is zero, thus the circuit is open as shown in Fig. 5.22(b), and at the wall surfaces

$$p_i + p_r = 2p_i, \qquad \therefore \quad p_r = p_i$$

In Fig. 5.21(b), at the junction I of the circuit, the impedances to the left and the right are denoted by Z_1 and Z_2 respectively. Since there is no internal absorption, the transmission coefficient τ can be expressed by eqn (1.32), where $Z_1 = \rho c$, $Z_2 = j\omega m + \rho c$, then eqn (5.37) is obtained.

B.   Random Incidence Mass Law
When the incident angle is θ, eqn (5.39) can be derived as follows:

$$R_\theta = 10\log_{10}\frac{1}{\tau_\theta} = 10\log_{10}\left\{1 + \left(\frac{\omega m\cos\theta}{2\rho c}\right)^2\right\} \qquad (5.39)$$

If we are calculating the average value in the range $\theta = 0 \sim 90°$, eqn (5.40) is obtained as the 'random incidence mass law'

$$R_{\text{random}} = R_0 - 10\log_{10}(0\cdot23R_0) \qquad (5.40)$$

However, in an actual sound field using the range of $\theta = 0 \sim 78°$, is more realistic and the following approximate formula is obtained:

$$R_{\text{field}} = R_0 - 5 \text{ dB} \qquad (5.41)$$

which is recognised as closer to reality and called the 'field incidence mass law'. Figure 5.23 shows these theoretical curves (see Lit. B16, B22).

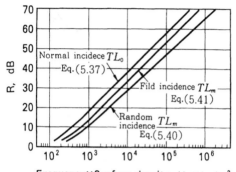

Fig. 5.23. Mass law curves for transmission loss (Beranek).

5.4 COINCIDENCE EFFECT ON SOUND TRANSMISSION

Mass law has been derived on the assumption that the walls are set in uniform piston motions. However, flat plates are accompanied by bending vibrations which cause significant decrease in R values.

As shown in Fig. 5.24 when a plane wave whose wavelength λ is incident on a wall at angle θ, a pattern of alternating sound pressure moves along the wall with a wavelength of

$$\lambda_B = \frac{\lambda}{\sin \theta} \tag{5.42}$$

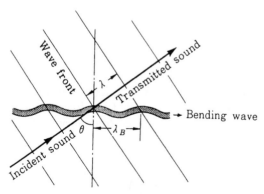

Fig. 5.24. Coincidence effect.

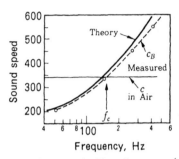

Fig. 5.25. Propagation speed of bending wave (see Lit. B16).

Therefore, the wall is excited into bending vibration which produces a bending wave which propagates along the wall surface.

On the other hand, the propagation speed c_B of the bending wave of a plate whose thickness is h can be derived from the theory of bending vibration of a bar.

$$c_B = \left(2\pi h f \sqrt{\frac{E}{12\rho(1-\sigma^2)}} \right)^{1/2} \tag{5.43}$$

where ρ is the density of the plate, E is the Young's Modulus of the plate material and σ Poisson's ratio. c_B can be seen to increase with frequency (see Lit. B6, B19). In Fig. 5.25 we can find the condition where the value of c_B satisfies eqn (5.44),

$$c_B = \frac{c}{\sin\theta} \tag{5.44}$$

At this frequency the bending vibration is such that its amplitude may become comparable to the incident sound wave, resulting in a serious decrease in sound insulation. This frequency is called the 'coincidence frequency'. This phenomenon is called the 'coincidence effect' as distinct from resonance. The coincidence frequency is obtained from eqns (5.43) and (5.44) as follows:

$$f_{(\theta)} = \frac{c^2}{2\pi h \sin^2\theta} \sqrt{\frac{12\rho(1-\sigma^2)}{E}} \tag{5.45}$$

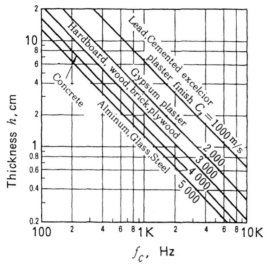

Fig. 5.26. Critical frequencies vs material thickness.

The lowest coincidence frequency when $\theta = 90°$ is given by

$$f_c \approx \frac{c^2}{2\pi h} \sqrt{\frac{12\rho}{E}} \approx \frac{c^2}{1 \cdot 8hc_s} \tag{5.46}$$

where $\sigma \approx 0 \cdot 3$ (leading to an approximation $(1 - \sigma^2) \approx 1$) and c_s is the sound speed in the solid material as shown in eqn (1.8).

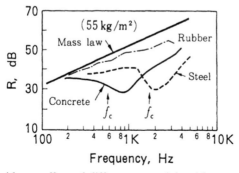

Fig. 5.27. Coincidence effect of different materials with same surface density (Goesele).

f_c is called the 'critical frequency'. Any lower frequency than this yields $c_B < c$ resulting in an absence of coincidence while at any higher frequency than f_c coincidence will occur.

In Fig. 5.26 the relationship between the material thickness h and f_c for various materials is shown. The higher f_c with smaller h the less the effect, but with larger h f_c decreases to the middle or lower frequency range essential for good sound insulation and so the transmission loss is seriously decreased. Fig. 5.27 shows an example where f_c is different depending upon the wall material even where the walls have the same surface density.

The decrease of R by coincidence is very complicated as it is also related to the loss factor due to the material's internal friction.

Fig. 5.28 is a practical design chart from a theoretical and experimental study, which gives good approximation for large panels. The length

	Surface density kg/m²/cm	Plateau height dB	Plateau breadth f_3/f_2
Aluminum	26.6	29	11
Concrete, dense	22.8	38	4.5
Glass	24.7	27	10
Lead	112	56	4
Plaster, sand	17.1	30	8
Plywood,fir	5.7	19	6.5
Steel	76	40	11
Brick	21	37	4.5
Cinder block	11.4	30	6.5

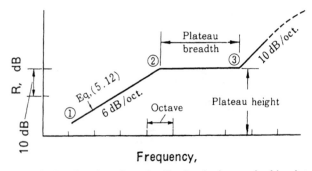

Fig. 5.28. Practical estimation chart for R of a single panel taking into account coincidence (Watters 1959).

and width of the panel should be at least 20 times the panel thickness (Watters 1959). The straight line portion ①–② is drawn from the field incidence mass law eqn (5.41). The plateau height and breadth ②–③ are determined from the table. The part above ③ is an extrapolation (see Lit. B22).

5.5 FREQUENCY CHARACTERISTICS OF A SINGLE WALL

We have considered the infinitely-wide wall for the mass law and the effect of coincidence on the sound transmission. This may be a reasonable approximation for middle and high frequencies on a wall of finite size. In the low frequency range, however, a finite wall has its own resonances, as shown by eqn (4.17) and Fig. 4.18 under the condition of a supported edge. So that the frequency characteristics of the airborne sound transmission loss might be as shown in Fig. 5.29, although, if the real wall were rigidly clamped at the boundaries, the lowest resonance frequency f_{rl}, would be twice as high and all others would be higher than those obtained from eqn (4.17).

In region I in Fig. 5.29, below f_{rl}, the wall is generally controlled by its stiffness and edge condition. In the 2nd region higher resonances are

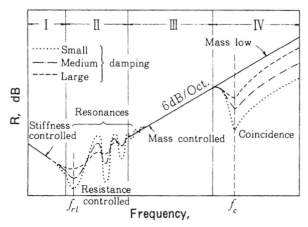

Fig. 5.29. Frequency characteristics of the airborne sound insulation of a single wall.

controlled not only by the mass but also by internal energy losses and losses at the boundaries. At frequencies two to three times f_{rl} up to and near the critical frequency, f_c is the mass controlled region. In region IV is multi-coincidence which is controlled by both stiffness and resistance. It is very difficult to estimate the sound transmission in the lowest frequency region I, but easier to make approximations in the higher frequency regions as mentioned above (Fig. 5.28).

5.6   SOUND INSULATION OF DOUBLE LEAF WALLS

A.   Construction of Double Leaf Walls
According to the mass law the transmission loss of a single wall increases by only 6 dB for a doubling of the wall thickness, i.e. twice the mass (Fig. 5.23). Also, when the thickness increases, the coincidence effect may cause undesirable results. This suggests that sound insulation of a single wall has its limitations. However, if the wall is made up of two leaves, each of which is an isolated single wall, the total transmission loss must be the sum of the transmission loss of each leaf.

For example, if R is 48 dB for a 15-cm reinforced concrete wall, the double leaf wall with sufficient air space can give an R as much as 96 dB; on the other hand, if the wall thickness is doubled, i.e. to 30 cm, only 54 dB is obtained even if there is no coincidence effect. Therefore a double leaf construction has considerable advantage over the single wall.

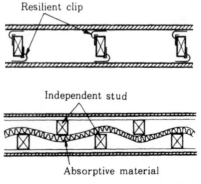

Fig. 5.30.   Typical double-leaf walls.

In practice, as it is very difficult to make the two leaves completely detached, so that sound is transmitted via (1) the structural coupling and (2) the acoustic coupling due to the air between the two leaves. At some frequencies the sound insulation may become inferior to that of a single wall due to resonance. Therefore, to approach an ideal condition for optimum sound insulation it is necessary to find out how to reduce the coupling through the structure and air.

In order to isolate the structural coupling, the leaves should be mounted on staggered studding with a resilient connection between stud and leaf. Also, in order to reduce the acoustic coupling, through the air, the airspace should be increased as much as possible and absorptive treatment introduced into the cavity between the leaves. Two typical examples are shown in Fig. 5.30.

In the case of a fixed double- or triple-glazed window, since absorptive treatment in the air space is limited to the reveals as shown in Fig. 5.31, it is recommended that the air space should be enlarged to increase the absorptive area and its absorption characteristic tuned to the resonance frequency of the air space. There are also techniques for reducing the effects of coincidence by using different thicknesses of glass for the two panes and attenuating well-defined resonances by slanting one pane with respect to the other. Ideally the panes should be mounted in resilient gaskets, completely isolated from the base structure, which consists of a double leaf wall.

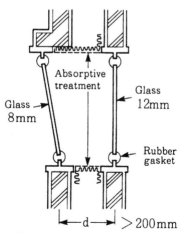

Fig. 5.31. Double-glazed window.

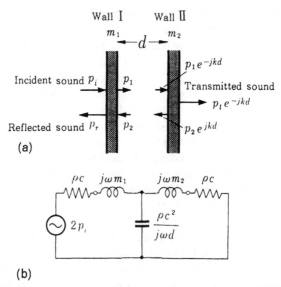

Fig. 5.32. Sound insulation and analogous circuit for a double-leaf wall.

B. Theory of Double Leaf Walls

Let us consider the sound insulation when a plane wave is incident normally on two parallel thin infinite walls separated by a distance d. As shown in Fig. 5.32(a) the sound wave in the reverse direction in the air space must be taken into account. For wall I the equation of motion can be written

$$(p_i + p_r) - (p_1 + p_2) = Z_{w1}\left(\frac{(p_i - p_r)}{\rho c}\right) \qquad (5.47a)$$

where Z_{w1} is the impedance per unit area of wall I.

Since there is continuity of particle velocity we can also write

$$\frac{(p_i - p_r)}{\rho c} - \frac{(p_1 - p_2)}{\rho c} = 0$$

$$\therefore \quad (p_i - p_r) - (p_1 - p_2) = 0 \qquad (5.47b)$$

At wall II there is a phase change due to the distance d which leads to the following equation:

$$\left(p_1 e^{-jkd} + p_2 e^{jkd}\right) - p_t e^{-jkd} = Z_{w2}\frac{p_t e^{-jkd}}{\rho c} \qquad (5.48a)$$

and

$$\frac{\left(p_1 e^{-jkd} - p_2 e^{jkd}\right)}{\rho c} - \frac{p_t e^{-jkd}}{\rho c} = 0$$

$$\therefore \quad \left(p_1 e^{-jkd} - p_2 e^{jkd}\right) - p_t e^{-jkd} = 0 \qquad (5.48b)$$

where $k = \omega/c = 2\pi/\lambda$ and Z_{w2} is the impedance per unit area of wall II.

From the above four equations the following can be derived

$$\frac{p_i}{p_t} = 1 + \frac{Z_{w1} + Z_{w2}}{2\rho c} + \frac{Z_{w1} \cdot Z_{w2}}{(2\rho c)^2} (1 - e^{-2jkd}) \qquad (5.49)$$

Then, assuming that both walls have the same mass m per unit area for simplification, the impedance can be expressed from eqn (5.34) as

$$Z_{w1} = Z_{w2} = j\omega m$$

Substituting this into eqn (5.49), the transmission loss of the double leaf wall becomes:

$$R_{02} = 10 \log_{10} \left| \frac{p_i}{p_t} \right|^2$$

$$= 10 \log_{10} \left[1 + 4 \left(\frac{\omega m}{2\rho c} \right)^2 \left\{ \cos kd - \left(\frac{\omega m}{2\rho c} \right) \sin kd \right\}^2 \right] \qquad (5.50)$$

When $d = 0$,

$$R_{02} = 10 \log_{10} \left[1 + \frac{(2\omega m)^2}{(2\rho c)^2} \right] \qquad (5.51)$$

which is the transmission loss of a wall of twice the mass of the single wall referred to in eqn (5.37). Also, when the expression

$$\left\{ \cos kd - \left(\frac{\omega m}{2\rho c} \right) \sin kd \right\}^2 \qquad (5.52)$$

becomes zero then $R_{02} = 0$, i.e. there is no insulation. At low frequencies if the wavelength λ is sufficiently large compared with air space d, kd becomes small, hence

$$\frac{2\rho c}{\omega m} = \tan kd \approx kd = \frac{\omega}{c} d$$

$$\therefore \quad f_{rm} = \frac{1}{2\pi} \sqrt{\frac{2\rho c^2}{md}} \qquad (5.53)$$

which means that at this frequency f_{rm} the sound insulation is zero.

f_{rm} can be thought of as the resonant frequency of a mechanical vibration system consisting of an air spring between two masses m. This can be represented by an analogous electrical circuit as shown in Fig. 5.32(b) consisting of inductance resistance and capacitance.

At high frequencies the expression (5.52) also becomes zero, i.e.

$$\frac{2\rho c}{\omega m} = \tan \frac{\omega}{c} d \tag{5.54}$$

for certain values of ω and under these conditions $R_{02} = 0$. Although it is difficult to obtain this frequency f_{rd} analytically, it can be obtained graphically or numerically.

On the other hand, when

$$k_n d = (2n - 1)\frac{\pi}{2} \quad (n = 1, 2, 3, \ldots) \tag{5.55}$$

then expression (5.52) becomes

$$\left\{ \cos kd - \left(\frac{\omega m}{2\rho c} \right) \sin kd \right\}^2 = \left(\frac{\omega m}{2\rho c} \right)^2$$

and R_{02} is a maximum value at frequencies given by

$$f'_{rd} = \frac{(2n - 1)}{4} \cdot \frac{c}{d} \quad (n = 1, 2, 3, \ldots) \tag{5.56}$$

Hence, eqn (5.50) can be written,

$$R_{02} \approx 40 \log_{10}\left(\frac{\omega m}{2\rho c} \right) + 6 \tag{5.57}$$

Thus, the R_{02} curve has many peaks and troughs as shown in Fig. 5.33. The C line shows the following approximation derived from the analogous circuit in the frequency range between f_{rm} and f_{rd}

$$R_{02} = 10 \log_{10}\left(\frac{\omega^3 m^2 d}{2\rho^2 c^3} \right)^2 = 2R_{01} + 20 \log_{10} 2kd \tag{5.58}$$

where R_{01} is the transmission loss of a single wall given by eqn (5.38).

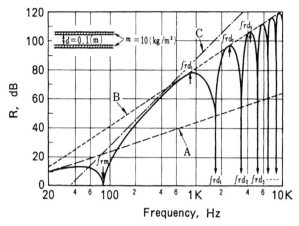

Fig. 5.33. Theoretical values of double-leaf wall transmission loss. A: eqn (5.51), B: eqn (5.57), C: eqn (5.58).

C. Practical Sound Insulation of Double Leaf Walls

Some examples of the measured transmission loss of light weight partitions whose outer skins consist of thin panels are shown in Fig. 5.34. A dip may occur in the R curve around the resonance frequency f_{rm} (as given by eqn 5.53), beyond which the curve slopes up by about 10 dB/oct to higher frequencies. The peaks and dips due to f_{rd} in eqn (5.54) and due to f'_{rd} in eqn (5.56) may not appear distinctly, but the fall at 4 kHz coincides with the critical frequency f_c of a single plywood wall. Therefore, sometimes different panel thicknesses are employed so that the values of f_c for each panel are different.

There are two ways of increasing the R of this type of wall as shown in the figure. One is by inserting absorbing material into the air space and the other is by underlining the outer skin with plaster board. It can be seen that in (a) the effect of glass fibre is larger in the case of a lightweight partition while in (b) inadequate application of plaster board does not work so well.

D. Sandwich Panels

As an application of the above mentioned double-leaf wall construction, filling the air space with other materials, thus creating a sort of

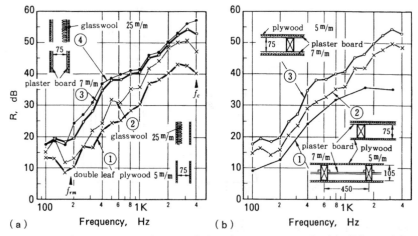

Fig. 5.34. Improvement of transmission losses measured with light weight partition walls.

triple-layer wall, can be considered in order to increase thermal insulation or for other purposes. Theoretically, in place of the air spring previously discussed, the core material is thought of as acting as an elastic spring or resistance in the analogous electrical circuit. If the core material is glass fibre, for example, it acts as a resistance which improves the sound insulation while an elastic material such as sponge or foamed plastic may produce more peaks and troughs in the frequency characteristics, thus decreasing sound insulation. Therefore careful selection of material with reference to measured data is essential.

5.7 EFFECT OF OPENINGS AND CRACKS

A. Sound Transmission through Openings and Cracks

(a) So far the wall is assumed to be air-tight, but when a porous material or one with cracks is used, the transmission loss may be greatly reduced from the value estimated on the basis of the mass law because sounds leak through the pores or cracks. For instance, a 10 cm thick bare concrete block whose surface density is 160 kg/m^2 has an average $R = 28$ dB, but when both faces are coated with oil paint the R increases by as much as 13 dB up to 41 dB due to air tightness.

(b) If a fairly large opening is provided, the composite transmission loss (see Section 5.1D,d) should be calculated using a transmission coefficient $\tau = 1$ ($R = 0$ dB) for the opening area.

(c) Where a small opening exists, diffraction may occur. There is a complicated relationship between the wall thickness and the sound wavelength and in some cases $\tau > 1$ at the resonance frequency. Therefore, even with a tiny opening there might be an unexpectedly large sound transmission so that insulation may be seriously decreased. Thus, there must be careful detailing and construction in order to achieve sufficient air-tightness at the partition panel joints and the perimeter around doors and windows.

Wilson and Soroka (1965) derived an approximate expression for the sound radiating from a circular hole in a wall. They assumed that sound incident on a cylindrical pipe of radius a and length l propagates as a plane wave inside the pipe and radiates sound from both ends which vibrate like massless pistons. Figure 5.35 shows the result for $l = 30$ cm and $a = 5$ cm compared with experimental values. At many resonance

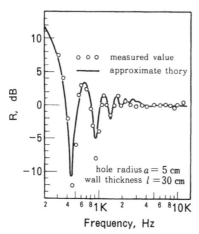

Fig. 5.35. Example of transmission loss for circular hole (Wilson & Soroka 1965).

frequencies determined by the tube length (wall thickness), R becomes negative, which means $\tau > 1$. Gomperts (1964) has derived another approximate formula by a different method. The resonance frequency is obtained when the condition $l + 2\delta = n\lambda/2$ ($n = 1, 2, 3 \ldots$) is satisfied, where δ is the end correction and λ the wavelength. The maximum transmission coefficient $\tau_{max} = 2/(ka)^2$ where $k = 2\pi/\lambda$ at the resonance frequency. When $ka > \sqrt{2}$ $R = 0$ is valid within ± 1 dB.

Gomperts has also derived an approximate solution for a wall with slits and shows the results compare with measured values (Fig. 5.36). Theoretical values for an 11-mm wide slit in a wall are plotted between the measured values of 8 mm and 16 mm wide slits. Also at the resonance frequency it is found that $\tau > 1$ for the slit. The reason why peaks and troughs do not appear in the measured values is because measurements were made over wide frequency bands.

B. Sound Insulation of Windows and Doors

The sound insulation of windows and doors depends not only on the insulation of the fittings but also upon the sealing around their perimeters.

The sound insulation of fittings is evaluated in the same way as for a single- or double-leaf wall also taking into effect small cracks as

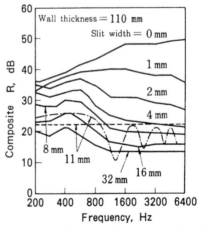

Fig. 5.36. Example of measured composite transmission losses of walls with slits; wall size: 1.9 m × 1.9 m, slit located at centre; slit length: 1.9 m; solid line: measured value by 1/2 octave band; broken line: calculated value assuming slit $R = 0$; dash-dotted line: theoretical value of pure tone (Gomperts 1964).

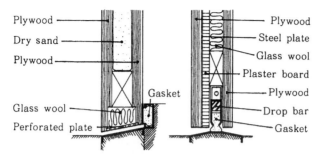

Fig. 5.37. Examples of sound-insulating doors.

discussed above. Generally, the insulation is governed by the latter so that detailing and accuracy of construction may produce very variable results. Thus, even though the R value of the door panel is increased, the insulation may not improve unless the gaps at the perimeter are minimised. Figure 5.37 shows two examples of details for the gap between door and floor, which is the weakest point. Type A has not only a gasket for sealing the edge of the door, but also absorptive treatment at the perimeter. It is essential to minimise the gap. Type B has a drop-bar which automatically seals the gap when the door is in a closed position. This is very useful where a flat floor is required even under the door. In some cases doors are weighted with dry sand or consist of dense boards and porous materials.

When an R value of more than 30 dB is required it may be advantageous to employ a double-door arrangement with absorbent lining to the walls and ceiling between the doors as a sound-lock (see Section 5.6A).

5.8 NOISE REDUCTION BY BARRIERS

A. Calculation of Noise Reduction by a Barrier Using a Design Chart

When a sufficiently large solid screen is erected between a noise source and receiver, although, on the source side, the noise level is raised due to reflection, on the receiving side a finite noise reduction can be expected because of the acoustic shadow. In order to obtain the sound-pressure level in the shadow zone, the approximate diffraction

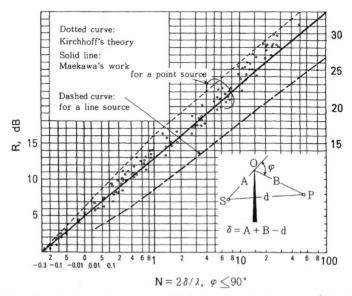

Fig. 5.38. Sound attenuation by a semi-infinite screen in free space (Maekawa).

theory of optics can be applied though there are some discrepancies. Figure 5.38 shows the calculated and measured attenuations as well as experimental curves for a design chart (Maekawa 1968). This chart is derived on the basis of a semi-infinite screen in free space located between an omni-directional sound source and a receiving point. The attenuation value indicates the difference between the situation with and without a screen. The abscissa in the figure shows the Fresnel Number N which divides the sound path difference with and without the screen into multiples of a half wavelength and is adjusted so that the experimental values make a straight line. When $N = 0$, SOP is a straight line and when $N < 0$, the receiver is in the illuminated region; even so, there is a little attenuation, too. In the region $N > 1$ the attenuation can be expressed by $10 \log(20 N)$.

When a real screen is erected on the ground, the reflections from the ground and other objects must be considered. In practice, if the sound-pressure level including the reflections is actually measured at the top O of the screen as reference, this approximates reasonably well to the sound level on the source side. On the receiving side the calculation for the image P' of the receiving point P is performed as shown in Fig.

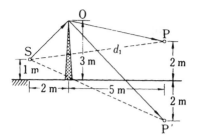

Fig. 5.39. Example of noise reduction by a screen.

5.39 and the energy summates, neglecting their phases as they are both noise signals.

[Ex. 5.5] When a 3-m high screen is erected between the sound source S and the receiving point P, as shown in Fig. 5.39, the noise reduction can be obtained as follows: the path difference is

$$\delta_1 = \overline{SO} + \overline{OP} - d_1 = \sqrt{2^2 + 2^2} + \sqrt{1 + 5^2} - \sqrt{1 + 7^2} = 0 \cdot 86 \text{ (m)}$$

The ground reflection is from path SOP'

$$\delta_2 = \sqrt{2^2 + 2^2} + \sqrt{5^2 + 5^2} - \sqrt{3^2 + 7^2} = 2 \cdot 28 \text{ (m)}$$

Hence, N_1 for δ_1 is calculated, and the attenuation L is obtained from Fig. 5.38. Similarly the attenuation L_2 is obtained from δ_2. Then, combining them, L_3 (dB) is obtained as shown in the following table. This is the noise reduction of an omni-directional sound source. At higher frequencies, when N is greater than one it is clear that the attenuation increases by 3 dB/oct.

$f(c/s)$	125	500	2000
λ (m)	2·72	0·68	0·17
$N_1 = \delta_1 . 2/\lambda$	0·63	2·52	10·10
$-L_1$ (dB)	$-11 \cdot 5$	$-17 \cdot 0$	$-23 \cdot 0$
$N_2 = \delta_2 . 2/\lambda$	1·68	6·70	26·80
$-L_2$ (dB)	$-15 \cdot 0$	$-21 \cdot 0$	$-27 \cdot 0$
$-L_3$ (dB)	$-9 \cdot 8$	$-15 \cdot 5$	$-21 \cdot 5$

When the sound source is not omni-directional and the sound-pressure level measured at the top of the screen is L_0 then the sound pressure level at P is

$$L_p = \left(L_0 - 20 \log_{10} \frac{d_1}{\overline{SO}} \right) - L_3 \text{ (dB)} \qquad (5.59)$$

Also in the case of a line source such as a traffic stream on a motorway the sound pressure level is approximated by

$$L'_p = \left(L_0 - 10 \log_{10} \frac{d_1}{\overline{SO}} \right) - L'_3 \text{ (dB)} \qquad (5.60)$$

where L'_3 is the value calculated by the same method shown in Fig. 5.39, except using the dashed curve in place of the solid line in Fig. 5.38.

By these methods the sound pressure level at any point in the shadow zone of the screen can be calculated with good approximation, provided that

(1) The sound pressure level distribution along the vertical line above the screen decays gradually away from the top O.
(2) The wall length is several times larger than the wall height to either side of the receiver.

In order to fulfil condition (1), before erecting the screen, the vertical sound-pressure level distribution should be measured upwards as high as possible and the position of O set higher than the maximum sound-level position. In some particular cases, where the sound level increases as we progress upward, a noise reduction may not be expected. When condition (2) is not satisfied, diffraction not only in the vertical direction but also laterally has to be taken into account using Fig. 5.38 (see Section 10.14).

B. Approximation for Thick Barriers

Until now it has been assumed that the screen has zero thickness. Barriers, however, like earth banks and buildings have solidity. As a first approximation, in order to calculate the noise reduction, by using the chart of Fig. 5.38 with values of the path difference, as shown in Fig. 5.40:

$$\delta = \overline{SP} + \overline{OP} - \overline{SP}, \quad \text{or} \quad \delta = \overline{SX} + \overline{XY} + \overline{YP} - \overline{SP}$$

This is the simplest way though there are more accurate methods as described in Section 10.14.

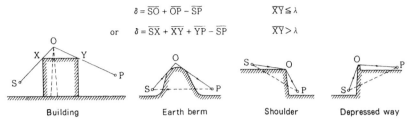

$$\delta = \overline{SO} + \overline{OP} - \overline{SP} \qquad \overline{XY} \leqq \lambda$$

$$\text{or} \quad \delta = \overline{SX} + \overline{XY} + \overline{YP} - \overline{SP} \qquad \overline{XY} > \lambda$$

Building   Earth berm   Shoulder   Depressed way

Fig. 5.40. Approximation for thick barriers.

C. Barrier Effects of Trees and Forests

Although tree-plantings and forests furnish some attenuation due to absorption and dispersion, unless there is a substantial dense planting of considerable thickness (several tens of metres) there is very little attenuation. A quickset hedge, for example, has little to offer. However, tree-plantings are still absorptive compared with hard concrete or brick surfaces and they do make both a visual and psychological contribution to the environment; the leaves, moreover, provide masking noise due to the wind; therefore, trees and shrubs can be considered as important elements in the control of noise.

5.9   NOISE REDUCTION IN AIR DUCTS

Ducts convey not only air but also noise efficiently. Noise reduction means the prevention of sound transmission whilst conveying air. We must start by analysing sound transmission through ducts.

A.   Natural Attenuation of Sound Waves in Tubes

When a plane wave propagates along a tube whose cross sectional area is S, from eqns (1.10) and (1.12) the acoustic impedance Z_A is

$$Z_A = \frac{p}{Sv} = \frac{\rho c}{S} \qquad (5.61)$$

Since Sv is the volume velocity, Z_A in this case is called the 'volume impedance' and is inversely proportional to the cross sectional area.

a.   Attenuation Due to Change in Cross Section

When an acoustic tube section abruptly changes as shown in Fig. 5.41, since the impedance also changes the plane wave propagating in the

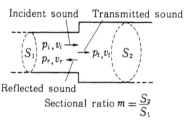

Sectional ratio $m = \dfrac{S_2}{S_1}$

Fig. 5.41. Sectional area change in acoustic tube.

tube loses a portion of its energy by reflection in the same way as sound loses its energy at the boundary plane between two media in Fig. 1.8. Both result in sound attenuation. Equations (1.28)–(1.32) are used to calculate the attenuation but with 'volume impedances' in place of the characteristic impedance

$$\text{i.e.} \quad Z_1 = \frac{\rho c}{S_1}, \qquad Z_2 = \frac{\rho c}{S_2}$$

Hence introducing the cross sectional ratio $m = S_1/S_2$,

$$R = 10 \log_{10} \frac{|p_i|^2 S_1}{|p_t|^2 S_2} = 10 \log_{10} \left(\frac{S_1 + S_2}{2S_1} \right)^2 \frac{S_1}{S_2}$$

$$= 10 \log_{10} \frac{1}{4} \left(m + \frac{1}{m} + 2 \right) \text{ (dB)} \tag{5.62}$$

This value is valid when both tubes are infinitely long, i.e. they have non-reflective ends. Actually, at the junction, the attenuation may be more complicated depending on the connecting impedances, but it is generally considered that attenuation occurs at any discontinuous sections.

b. Attenuation Due to Reflection at Duct Open End

An open end of a duct such as an air outlet or inlet is such an abrupt change of cross section that the attenuation is large. The sound waves outside the open end may be thought of as radiated by an imaginary piston vibrating at the open end of the duct instead of as plane waves. The results from the theoretical derivation of the 'radiation impedance*' of the piston are shown in Fig. 5.42 while the measured values were

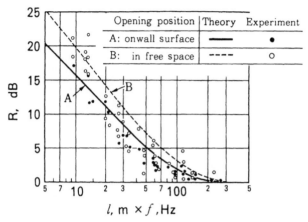

Fig. 5.42. Attenuation due to reflection at duct open ends (open-end area l^2).

obtained by experiments which arranged for the duct to have an open end in a reverberant room (Maekawa *et al.*).

c. Attenuation Due to Duct Bends

If the duct has a radius of curvature at a bend, attenuation may be small, but at a right-angled bend the attenuation is obtained as shown in Fig. 5.43 because of phase differences between inner and outer paths. When it is necessary to avoid increasing the air flow resistance, the internal side should be curved while the external side should be right-angled.

The application of an absorptive lining to the inside of a bend is very effective for noise reduction, where an additional attenuation can be

---

*Radiation impedance: when a vibrating plate radiates a sound wave with vibrating velocity v, the ratio of it to the reaction F_r of the vibrating plate is given by

$$Z_r = \frac{v}{F_r}$$

Z_r is called the 'radiation impedance'. F_r is obtained by integration of the reactions of all portions of the vibrating plate (see Lit. B7).

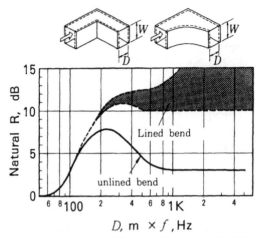

Fig. 5.43. Natural attenuation in right-angled duct bend, lining length should be at least $2D$ to $4D$ beyond the bend. W is arbitrary.

expected by an amount shown by the dotted line in Fig. 5.43, except the attenuation caused by the lining calculated by eqn (5.63) in the next section.

B. Attenuation Devices in Ducts

There are two types of device to increase noise reduction in ducts; one device is dissipative which dissipates sound energy by absorption while the other is reactive which reflects sound back to the source due to an abrupt change in impedance. Figure 5.44 shows their conceptual designs.

C. Lined Ducts

The energy flowing in a duct is proportional to the cross-sectional area S (m^2) and the amount absorbed is proportional to the perimeter P (m). Therefore, the attenuation R is approximately given by

$$R = K \cdot \frac{P}{S} \ (\text{dB/m}) \tag{5.63}$$

where K is a constant which is determined by the absorption coefficient of the lining material, as shown in Fig. 5.45.

Equation (5.63) is valid up to the frequency at which the wavelength is equal to the diameter or the short-side width of the duct, beyond

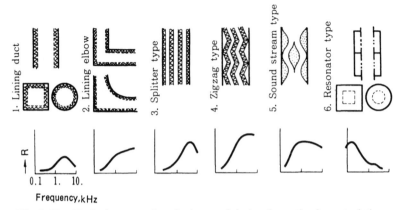

Fig. 5.44. Typical attenuation devices and their schematic characteristics.

which the sound wave becomes a beam flowing along the centre of the duct, in which case the attenuation decreases.

Figure 5.46 shows an example of a multi-cell duct which has in it many small sections so as to increase P/S without reducing the volume of air flow. The figure shows that measured values decrease at frequencies above 3000 Hz at which point the wavelength is equal to the internal size of the cell.

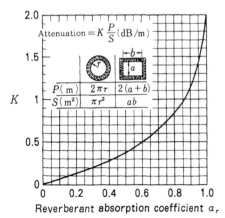

Fig. 5.45. Values of K in eqn (5.63) for absorption coefficient of lining material.

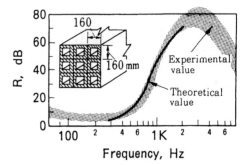

Fig. 5.46.   Example of a cell type lined duct: rock wool lining (180–200 kg/m³), 25 mm thick; solid line: calculated value by eqn (5.63).

These characteristics of lined ducts can be fully analysed with the aid of wave theory in closed spaces (see Lit. B6, B7). However, these discussions seem to be too complicated for practical application.

The parallel baffle type 3 of Fig. 5.44 which is a variation of the lined duct has the same disadvantage as described above, although the zigzag type 4 can improve it but the resistance to air flow becomes larger. In order to reduce such resistance the sound stream type 5 has been devised. They are available on the market, ready fabricated in various sizes.

In the high-frequency range the simplest method of increasing effective attenuation is to line the right-angled bends, in such a way as to increase the number of lined elbows until sufficient attenuation is obtained using Fig. 5.43 and eqn (5.63).

D.   Expansion Type Mufflers
When the cross section of a portion of a duct is expanded to form a cavity, as shown in Fig. 5.47, the latter becomes an acoustic filter due to the cross-sectional changes at two places. The attenuation for plane wave propagation may be derived by the same principle used in Fig. 5.41 and Fig. 5.32. In the simplest case when $S_1 = S_3$, with $m = S_2/S_1$ and $k = 2\pi/\lambda$,

$$R = 10\log_{10}\left\{1 + \frac{1}{4}\left(m + \frac{1}{m}\right)^2 \sin^2 kl\right\} \text{ (dB)} \qquad (5.64)$$

is obtained (see Lit. B14a).

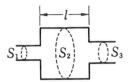

Fig. 5.47. Expansion-type muffler.

Examples are shown in Fig. 5.48. As m is increased, the peak of the attenuation becomes higher and when l is smaller, the number of troughs is reduced, thus, improving the performance. Although eqn (5.64) shows the attenuation characteristics, it should be noted that every dimension of the cavity should be smaller than a wavelength in order to satisfy the condition of plane wave propagation in the duct. If the frequency becomes higher this condition may not hold.

E. Sound Absorbing Chambers

When an air chamber is provided at the junction of ducts or at the base of outlets, it acts as an expansion muffler. However, at any frequency for which the wavelength is smaller than the dimension of the chamber eqn (5.64) does not apply. In practice, absorptive treatment is required inside the chamber so that geometrical acoustics may have to be used. Hence, referring to Fig. 5.49, eqn (5.65) is obtained:

$$R = 10 \log_{10} \cfrac{1}{S \left[\cfrac{\cos \theta}{2\pi d^2} + \cfrac{1 - \alpha}{A} \right]} \text{ (dB)} \qquad (5.65)$$

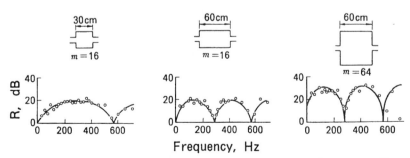

Fig. 5.48. Examples of attenuation characteristics of expansion-type mufflers (D.D. Davis).

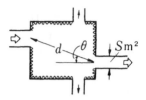

Fig. 5.49. Sound-absorbing chamber.

where S = outlet area from chamber (m²); d = distance from inlet to outlet (m); θ = the angle between d and the normal to the outlet surface; A = total absorption in chamber (m²); and α = absorption coefficient of lining material.

The first term of the denominator of the equation gives the direct sound energy from inlet to outlet while the second term gives the diffused sound to the outlet. If some baffles are provided inside so that the direct sound cannot reach the outlet, the following approximation may be used:

$$R = 10\log_{10}\frac{A}{S(1-\alpha)} \text{ (dB)} \qquad (5.66)$$

Since in the derivation of these equations, a diffuse sound field is assumed, the approximation can hold well into the higher frequency ranges where the wavelength is smaller than the chamber dimension.

F. Resonator Type Mufflers

The attenuators so far discussed, particularly the dissipative type, are generally effective at high frequencies, but poor at low frequencies. In order to improve the attenuation at low frequencies, resonator attenuators are often used. These consist of N perforations and an exterior air-tight cavity as shown in Fig. 5.50. Hence, the resonance frequency from eqn (4.19) is

$$f_r = \frac{c}{2\pi}\sqrt{\frac{NG}{V}} \text{ (Hz)} \qquad (5.67)$$

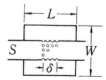

Fig. 5.50. Resonator-type muffler.

where G = conductivity/1 hole of perforation, i.e. $G = s/(l + 0 \cdot 8d)$; l = wall thickness; d = hole diameter, and s = a hole area. Then, the attenuation is given by

$$R = 10 \log_{10}\left[1 + \left\{\frac{\sqrt{NGV}/2S}{(f/f_r) - (f_r/f)}\right\}^2\right] \text{(dB)} \qquad (5.68)$$

thus, it shows very large attenuation around the frequency f_r. However, since the octave band attenuation should be taken into account for rating with noise criteria, f_r should be taken as the centre frequency, then

$$\text{octave band attenuation} = 10 \log_{10}\left[1 + \frac{NGV}{2S^2}\right]$$

$$= 10 \log_{10}[1 + 2K^2] \text{ (dB)} \qquad (5.69)$$

where

$$K = \frac{\sqrt{NGV}}{2S} \qquad (5.70)$$

For this calculation Fig. 5.51 is very useful (Maekawa 1959).

[Ex. 5.6]   Let us design a resonator-type attenuator of which the octave band attenuation at the mid-frequency 70 Hz must be 10 dB in a duct of diameter 180 mm.

From Fig. 5.51, $K = 2$ and duct cross-sectional area

$$S = 90^2 \pi = 25 \cdot 4 \times 10^3$$

From eqn (5.70)

$$\sqrt{NGV} = 2 \times 2S = 102 \times 10^3$$

From eqn (5.67)

$$\sqrt{\frac{NG}{V}} = 70 \times 2\pi/(340 \times 10^3) = 1 \cdot 31 \times 10^{-3}$$

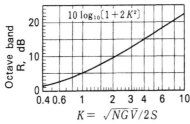

Fig. 5.51.   Octave-band attenuation of resonator type muffler.

Hence,

$$V = \sqrt{NGV} \Big/ \sqrt{\frac{NG}{V}} = 78 \times 10^6 \ (\text{mm}^3)$$

$$NG = 1 \cdot 31^2 \times 78 = 132$$

For a hole with $d = 12$ mm, $l = 0 \cdot 7$ mm, then $G = 11 \cdot 0$

$$N = 132/11 = 12 \ \text{pcs}$$

For the determination of the dimensions shown in Fig. 5.50 the following condition must be satisfied.

Condition 1: W or $L < \lambda_r/3$ where λ_r is the wavelength at the resonance frequency. Therefore, the design cannot be used for high frequencies.

Condition 2: The range of perforation $\delta < \lambda_r/12$ must be concentrated at the centre of the cavity while the pitch of holes should be some $2d$ otherwise G will be changed.

PROBLEMS 5

1. By how much does noise attenuate from the centre of a window (W:10 m, H:2 m) of a factory, when the sound level is 93 dBA at the outer surface of the window? Calculate the sound level at 6 points, 0.5 m, 1 m, 2 m, 4 m, 8 m and 16 m from the window using eqn (5.11) and compare with Fig. 5.6.
2. There is a noise source of sound power level 100 dBA between two parallel wide walls spaced 2 m apart as shown in Fig. 5.8. Calculate the sound level at a receiving point 3 m distance from the source assuming a sound absorption coefficient of $0 \cdot 8$.
3. When a plane sound wave is incident at angle θ on a single wall, as shown in Fig. 5.21, derive eqn (5.39) for the sound transmission loss. Verify eqn 5.40 for the random incidence mass law of sound transmission loss of a single wall.
4. When a plane sound wave is incident at an angle θ on a double leaf wall, shown in Fig. 5.32, derive an equation expressing the sound transmission loss of the wall.
5. Explain the basic principles necessary to improve the sound insulation of light weight walls.

6. Outline the thoughts required on architectural planning and design in order to achieve good sound insulation in a window which is required for good natural lighting.

7. A noise screen is not always effective for noise reduction. What kind of noise is reduced effectively?

8. Enumerate the principal devices for noise attenuation in the noise control design of an air conditioning system.

9. Design a muffler to provide 15 dB attenuation in the 1/3 octave band at 63 Hz in an air duct (sectional area 400×400 m). Then, sketch the frequency characteristics of the muffler's sound attenuation by theoretical calculations.

Chapter 6

ISOLATION OF STRUCTURE-BORNE NOISE AND VIBRATION

Structure-borne sound which is transmitted through solid material is essentially a vibration of the material. In this chapter the fundamentals of isolation of structure-borne sound and vibration are discussed.

6.1 PROPAGATION AND RADIATION OF STRUCTURE-BORNE SOUND

A. Generation of Structure-Borne Sound

When impacts resulting from footsteps, the slamming of doors, furniture movement etc are transferred to the building structure, there is a resulting vibration which is propagated through the structure, known as structure-borne sound.

Vibration of mechanical equipment in the building such as a pump, blower, elevator, refrigerator etc. generates structure-borne sound as steady-state sources.

Plumbing and piping for steam or water for example also generate structure-borne sounds at faucets and valves and convey those intermittent structure-borne sounds through themselves and the building structure.

Sound generated in a room excites the walls, ceiling and floor into vibration which is also propagated as sound-induced structure-borne sound.

In addition, noise and vibration generated by traffic or construction work and industry outside the building is transmitted into the building through the ground and the building foundation as structure-borne sound as shown in Fig. 6.1.

Structure-borne sound is perceived by a listener as a consequence of the air-borne sound radiated from the vibrating surfaces.

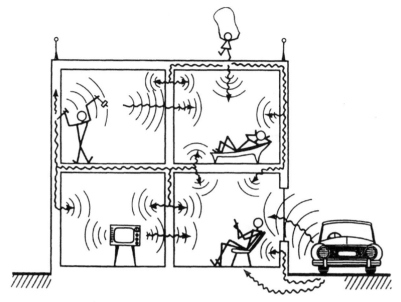

Fig. 6.1. Transmission of air-borne and structure-borne sound.

In order to quantitatively predict the generation of structure-borne sound we have to calculate the vibration velocity or acceleration which occurs in the structure from a knowledge of the exciting force of impact or driving force of vibration which causes the structure-borne sound and hence obtain the mechanical impedance at the receiving point. A design method of vibration isolation of a machinery base using an analogous electrical circuit is given in the literature (Breeuwer *et al.* 1976). Applying this method the structure-borne sound might be calculated. Unfortunately there are few quantitative data on the exciting force and other parameters which are used for the calculation and, moreover, it is not easy to measure them. Therefore, more effort is needed to obtain the necessary data so that the process of predicting structure-borne sound is the same as for air-borne sound.

B. Propagation and Measurement of Structure-borne Sound

a. Wave Types in Solids

Although sound in air is propagated only as longitudinal waves in solids it may be transmitted by several types of wave, i.e. a longitudinal

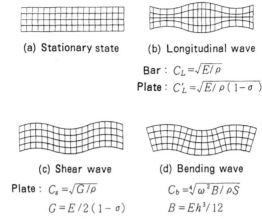

(a) Stationary state   (b) Longitudinal wave

Bar : $C_L = \sqrt{E/\rho}$

Plate : $C'_L = \sqrt{E/\rho(1-\sigma)}$

(c) Shear wave   (d) Bending wave

Plate : $C_s = \sqrt{G/\rho}$ $C_b = \sqrt[4]{\omega^2 B/\rho S}$

$G = E/2(1-\sigma)$ $B = Eh^3/12$

Fig. 6.2. Wave types and speeds of sound in solids (Beranek). E: Young's modulus; ρ_m: density of the material, kg/m^3; σ: Poisson's ratio; G: shear modulus; B: bending stiffness/unit width; h: thickness; and S: sectional area.

(compressional) wave and a transverse (shear) wave etc., since solids have not only compressional stiffness but shear stiffness as well. They often combine with each other to make a more complicated wave field, such as a bending wave or surface (Rayleigh) wave. In some cases the wave speed depends on frequency, thus giving rise to dispersion. The motion of elements of the solid material and formulae for the wave speed for the various wave types are shown in Fig. 6.2.

Generally the speed of longitudinal waves in a solid is very high, as shown in Table 1.1 in Chap. 1, and attenuation very small. The bending wave speed varies with frequency as shown in Fig. 5.25 resulting in the coincidence effect.

b. Measurement of Structure-borne Sound

A vibration pick-up as in Fig. 2.10 is mounted rigidly on a vibrating solid surface and detects the vibration perpendicular to the surface.

In order to eliminate the effect of the pick-up itself a very small and light piezoelectric type sensor is often used. The data are given in terms of the velocity level L_v, which is suitable for comparing with air-borne sound data.

$$L_v = 10\log_{10}\frac{v^2}{v_0^2} \tag{6.1}$$

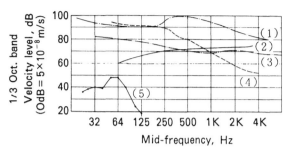

Fig. 6.3. Examples of velocity levels per 1/3 octave (M Heckl): (1) subway rail when train is passing at 60 km/h; (2) standard tapping machine acting on a 12-cm concrete floor; (3) electric motor on elastic mounts running at 1400 r.p.m.; (4) elastically mounted elevator for six persons; and (5) house wall when a street-car is passing at 45 km/h and at 13 m distance.

where v^2: mean square velocity.

$$v_0 = 5 \times 10^{-8} \, (\text{m/s}), \text{reference value}.$$

Since v is related to the acceleration $a \, (\text{m/s}^2)$ where $a = 2\pi f v$, L_v can also be related to the acceleration level L_a as follows:

$$\frac{v}{v_0} = \frac{a}{a_0} \cdot \frac{a_0}{2\pi f v_0}$$

$$\therefore \quad L_v = L_a + 20 \log_{10} \frac{a_0}{(2\pi f v_0)} \tag{6.2}$$

where a_0 is the arbitrary reference value for L_a.

Figure 6.3 shows some examples of measured velocity levels (Lit. B34).

C. Sound Radiation from a Vibrating Solid Body

a. Sound Radiation Ratio of Vibrating Piston

When an infinite plane rigid wall vibrates as a piston with velocity v, the air particles in contact with the wall surface also vibrate with velocity v, so the sound pressure is $\rho c v$ since the impedance of the air is ρc. Consequently the radiated sound power is $\rho c v^2$/unit area. Then, the sound power level is

$$L_w = 10 \log_{10} \frac{\rho c v^2}{10^{-12}} = 10 \log_{10} \frac{v^2}{v_0^2} + 10 \log_{10} \frac{\rho c v_0^2}{10^{-12}} \tag{6.3}$$

substituting $v_0 = 5 \times 10^{-8}$ the second term can be neglected, then $L_w = L_v$, the velocity level becomes the sound radiation power level itself.

When the size of the plate is less than the wavelength of the sound in air, the air particles adjacent to the plate surface move into the surroundings or to the rear side, so that pressure changes do not occur. This fact means that the sound radiation efficiency varies with the relative size of plate and wavelength. Then, the sound power W radiated from a plate of area F vibrating with velocity v, is expressed as

$$W = \sigma_{\text{rad}} \rho c v^2 F \qquad (6.4\text{a})$$

where σ_{rad} is called the 'radiation ratio'.

Logarithmically we can write

$$10 \log_{10} \sigma_{\text{rad}} = L_w - (L_v + 10 \log F) \text{dB} \qquad (6.4\text{b})$$

This is the difference between the power level and the velocity level when $F = 1 \text{ m}^2$.

As the most basic condition, the radiation ratio of a circular or rectangular piston set in a sufficiently large rigid wall corresponds to the real part of the radiation impedance (see Section 5.9A.b). Its theoretical values are shown in Fig. 6.4. At higher frequencies where the wavelength is smaller than the piston diameter the value of σ_{rad} becomes unity, and the velocity level L_v becomes equal to the power level L_w per unit area, but at lower frequencies at which the wavelength is larger than the diameter the value decreases by 6 dB/oct.

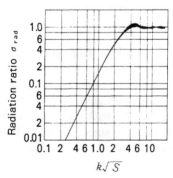

Fig. 6.4. Radiation ratio of a rectangular piston $k = 2\pi/\lambda$, S: area of a rectangular piston whose aspect ratio is less than 2, and also an approximation for a circular piston.

b. Sound Radiation Ratio in Bending Vibration

If a wide wall is set into free bending vibration by any means, as shown in Fig. 5.24, it radiates a plane wave in the direction θ which satisfies the relation

$$\sin \theta = c/c_B \qquad (6.5)$$

from eqn (5.44). Therefore when $c < c_B$, i.e. $f > f_c$ at frequencies higher than the critical frequency the radiation ratio $\sigma_{\text{rad}} = 1$.

When $f = f_c$ σ_{rad} becomes somewhat larger than one, and when $f < f_c$ the direction which satisfies eqn (6.5) does not exist, then, even if the air particles in contact with the surface are moved by bending vibration of the wall they do not create any pressure change. That is, the radiation ratio is very much decreased and its value depends on the value of f/f_c and of the internal energy losses.

In a finite wall, because it has resonant vibration modes as shown in Fig. 4.18 and eqn (4.17), the radiation behaviour is very complicated. But the approximate method of obtaining the average radiation ratio vs frequency for a rectangular panel is obtained by using the space-time

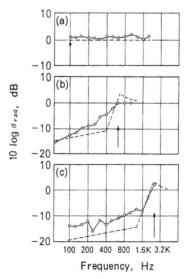

Fig. 6.5. Radiation ratios of lightly damped point-excited plates (Dashed curves are theoretical ones) (Cremer *et al*): (a) 24-cm thick brick wall of 12 m² area; (b) 7-cm thick wall of light concrete, 4 m² area; and (c) 13-mm plaster-board wall, divided into 0·8-m² panels by lath gridwork.

average mean-square velocity of the panel as quoted in the literature (see Lit. B22b, p. 294). Cremer *et al.* (Lit. B19a) presented theoretical results and compared them with experimental results as shown in Fig. 6.5 (see Lit. B.19b, p. 496).

c. Room-noise Level Resulting from the Vibration of the Enclosure
If a part of the enclosure F_i (m^2) vibrating with velocity v_i (m/s) radiates sound into the room, then when every part of the enclosure vibrates the total sound power radiates $W = \Sigma IW_i$. The sound energy density is then from eqn (3.20) and (6.4a)

$$E = \frac{4\rho c \Sigma \sigma_{\text{rad}\,i} V_i^2 F_i}{cA} \tag{6.6}$$

The value of the radiation ratio in the frequency range higher than the critical frequency can be approximated by $\sigma_{\text{rad}} = 1 \cdot 0 \sim 1 \cdot 1$, however, at lower frequencies the estimation from Fig. 6.5 proves rather difficult.

6.2   REDUCTION OF STRUCTURE-BORNE NOISE

Structure-borne sound waves are reflected and attenuated during propagation more or less at every discontinuity such as at a sudden change in cross section or material, due to change in direction at bends or branches as well as due to added masses (see Lit. B.19b, Chap. V).

A.   Reduction by Change of Cross Section
The longitudinal wave is attenuated at a sudden change of cross section as shown in Fig. 5.41, eqn (5.62) is valid in this case.

For bending waves four boundary conditions for continuity must be satisfied at $x = 0$. The point of change shown in Fig. 6.6(a) as follows,

1. velocities	$V_{y1} = V_{y2}$		(6.7a)
2. shear forces	$F_{y1} = F_{y2}$		(6.7b)
3. angular frequencies	$\omega_{z1} = \omega_{z2}$		(6.7c)
4. moments	$M_{z1} = M_{z2}$		(6.7d)

For the incident wave propagating from the left $(x < 0)$, the first boundary condition of (6.7a) leads to the simple expression at $x = 0$.

$$1 + r + rj = t + tj \tag{6.8}$$

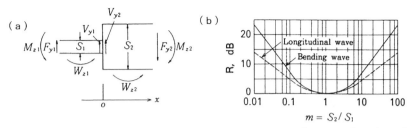

Fig. 6.6. Transmission loss at a discontinuity in cross section, as a function of the thickness ratio (Cremer *et al*).

where, r: reflection coefficient, t: transmission coefficient and rj, tj are coefficients which express the near-field vibration decaying far from $x = 0$. At $x = 0$ the four unknowns may be complex quantities to be determined from the four boundary conditions; t is of greatest interest here. Since the process is complicated, the results are only presented here as a transmission loss

$$R_B = 10 \log_{10} \left(\frac{X^{5/4} + X^{3/4}}{1 + X^2/2 + X^{1/2}} \right)^2 \text{ dB} \qquad (6.9)$$

where, $X = m + m^{-1}$, $m = S_2/S_1$.

These values are shown in Fig. 6.6(b) together with the values for the longitudinal wave. We find that a cross-sectional change does not give a large reduction of structure-borne noise in building practice.

B. Reduction by Bends and Branches at Right Angles

When a free bending wave reaches a bend or a branch at a right angle in a bar or plate, the behaviour of reflection and transmission at these junctions is complicated as some of the partial wave changes its wave

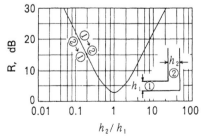

Fig. 6.7. Transmission loss for bending waves at corners (Cremer *et al*).

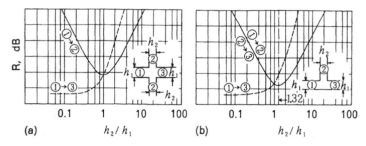

Fig. 6.8. Transmission loss for bending waves (Cremer *et al*): (a) at plate intersections; and (b) at plate branch.

type. Some examples of the results of theoretical analysis are shown in Figs. 6.7 and 6.8. Further reductions may be obtained by adding masses en route or at bends and branches such as ribs, beams or columns which are called 'blocking masses'. Also, with random incidence at the junctions a little more reduction is possible, because with oblique incidence the reduction increases with the angle of incidence.

C.   Reduction by Different Materials

a.   Reduction at the Boundary between Two Materials
The behaviour of a longitudinal wave incident normally on a boundary between two different materials, *has* already been illustrated in Fig 1.8 (Chap. 1). By using the notation of Fig 1.8, the transmission loss is

$$R = 10 \log \frac{p_i v_i}{p_t v_t} = 10 \log \frac{1}{t_p \cdot t_v} = 10 \log \frac{(Z_1 + Z_2)^2}{4 Z_1 Z_2} \text{ dB} \quad (6.10)$$

b.   Reduction by Resilient Layers
Resilient layers such as rubber, springs, etc. are efficient means of reducing structure-borne sound. Figure 6.9 shows analytical results produced by Cremer *et al*. The softer the resilient materials the more effective they are. However, when the inter-layer thickness becomes large, phase shift in the material has to be taken into account, as the total transmission may occur in the important frequency region, a phenomenon similar to that illustrated by eqn (5.64) and Fig. 5.48 (Chap. 5).

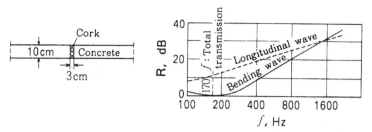

Fig. 6.9. Transmission loss of an elastic interlayer (Cremer *et al*).

As for bending waves the behaviour is complicated by deformation of the resilient material. The total transmission can be found at the particular frequency 170 Hz, in Fig. 6.9.

D.   Reduction of Structure-borne Noise in a Real Building
A real building is a complicated combination of plates and bars which form the construction of walls or floors and columns or beams, respectively. It is so difficult to deal with structure-borne noise analytically that 'Statistical Energy Analysis' is often used (see Section 10.15). However, there are still many problems left in attempting to obtain a precise estimation of structure-borne noise.

Figure 6.10 shows an example of measured structure-borne noise levels in rooms caused by the vibration excited by a concrete chipping machine in an existing hospital which has a rather simple construction

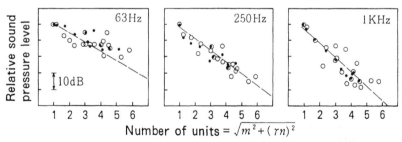

Fig. 6.10. Attenuation of structure-borne sound measured in an existing building of 10 storeys. The unit is $(6 \cdot 0 \times 5 \cdot 9)m^2 \times 2 \cdot 9$ m high, m and n are number of rooms counted horizontally and vertically respectively. γ is a proper weighting factor. The circles $\circ$ and $\bullet$ are measured on the floors above and under the excited wall respectively. Dashed lines are calculated by SEA method.

of reinforced concrete, compared with values calculated by the method of SEA (Furukawa *et al.* 1990).

6.3   MEASUREMENT AND RATING OF IMPACT SOUND INSULATION

The amount of insulation provided by building elements against structure-borne noise is only measured and classified for floors and ceilings. A standard impact machine specified by ISO 140/6 is used for this purpose as follows:

A.   Laboratory Measurement of Impact Sound Insulation of Floors

The test specimen is installed in the test opening between two reverberant rooms, No. 2 and No. 3, shown in Fig. 5.18. The space and time average sound pressure levels in the receiving room when the test floor is excited by the standard tapping machine are measured and denoted by L_i called 'impact sound pressure level'. The 'normalised impact sound level' is defined in the same way eqn (5.30).

$$L_n = L_i + 10\log_{10}(A/10)\,\text{dB} \qquad (6.11)$$

where A is the sound absorption area obtained from the measured reverberation time and with eqn (3.23).

ISO 140/6 specifies the details as follows:

(1)   The tapping machine should have 5 hammers, each of which is 0.5 kg weight, placed in line and 40 cm between both ends. The hammers are freely dropped from 4 cm high onto the specimen successively at a rate of 10 times per second.

(2)   The size of the test specimen should be between 10 m² and 20 m² with the shorter edge length not less than 2.3 m.

(3)   The tapping machine should be placed in at least four positions. In the case of an anisotropic floor construction (ribs, beams etc.) more positions are necessary. In addition, the hammer connection line should be orientated at 45° to the direction of the beams or ribs. The distance of the tapping machine from the edges of the floor should be at least 0.5 m.

(4)   The impact sound pressure level in the receiving room should be averaged using eqn (1.22) with measured values at a number of microphone positions or alternatively by means of a continuously moving microphone. It is recommended that a Type 1

sound level meter is used with time weighting 'S' as shown in Fig. 2.3.

(5) The sound pressure level should be measured using 1/3 octave or octave band filters of which the frequency range should be at least from 100 to 3150 Hz (preferably 4000 Hz) for 1/3 octave bands and from 125 to 2000 Hz for octave bands.

B. Field Measurement of Impact Sound Insulation of Floors

When the purpose of the field measurements is to determine the impact sound insulation properties of a building element, the 'normalised impact sound level' (eqn (6.11)) and the 'standardised impact sound level' normalised by a reference value of reverberation time 0.5 s, in the same manner as eqn (5.31), are used. However, in these cases they should be denoted by L'_n, and $L'_{n,0.5}$ respectively, because there is flanking transmission.

When evaluating the effect on the occupants of the buildings, it is considered that the 'impact sound pressure level', L'_i, itself without any normalisation, is appropriate, though this is in contradiction to ISO 140/7.

In Japan there is a standard according to this concept and a heavy weight impact machine simulating children's jumping is used in addition to the standard tapping machine (see Section 10.12D).

C. Single Number Rating of Impact Sound Insulation of Floors

As for airborne sound insulation, a method of single number rating for impact sound insulation of floors is formalised by ISO 717/2 as follows:

(1) The reference curve shown in Fig. 6.11 is shifted towards the measured curve of L_n (or L'_n and/or $L'_{n,0.5}$) values until the

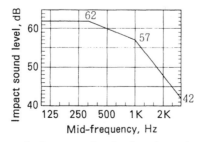

Fig. 6.11.   Curve of reference value for floor impact noise (ISO 717).

mean unfavourable deviation is as large as possible but not more than 2·0 dB.

(2) The value of the reference curve at 500 Hz, L_{nw} (or L'_{nw}), is called the 'weighted normalised impact sound pressure level' and $L'_{n, 0·5w}$ is called the 'weighted standardised impact sound pressure level'.

(3) In addition the maximum unfavourable deviation at any frequency shall be recorded if it exceeds 8 dB.

There are two problems, one is the standard tapping machine which is not adequate to simulate the impacts occurring in a dwelling, and the other is the need for too much time for field measurements specified by ISO. In Section 10.12, other methods are given which are used in many countries with their own standards or codes and criteria.

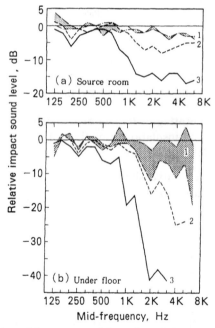

Fig. 6.12. Reduction of impact sound from floor by means of various finishes: 1: vinyl tile; 2: linoleum; and 3: vinyl sheet on foam underlay 3 mm thick; (a) reduction of impact sound pressure level in the source room; and (b) reduction of impact sound in the receiving room under the excited floor.

D. Reduction of the Impact Sound Transmission of Floors

Generally it is so difficult to block the transmission of structure-borne sound, that we must do our best to suppress the generation of the shock or vibration. For this purpose soft or resilient material should be used on the floor finish or on any other areas where impact sound may occur.

The reduction of the impact sound transmission of the floor is said to be 5–10 dB with a cork finish, and 4–20 dB with a carpet. Figure 6.12 shows examples of the effect of various finishes measured with a standard tapping machine, compared with a bare concrete floor, using the method specified in ISO 140/8. It can be seen that the softer material even if it is thin, gives more reduction at higher frequencies. Furthermore thicker materials such as Japanese tatami, or thick straw mat, give more reduction of impact sound even at low frequencies.

The effect of finishes on the impact of a heavy load is so small that the mass and stiffness of the floor slab need to be increased to deal with it. So a concrete floor should have a thickness of more than 20 cm depending on floor area.

It is essential that any impact should not be transmitted directly to the building structure, and ideally, not only the floor but also the ceiling and walls should be floated from the main structure using the principle of vibration damping discussed in the next section.

6.4 PRINCIPLE OF VIBRATION ISOLATION

In order to deal precisely with the vibration of a solid body, vibrations in each direction of a three-dimensional coordinate axis around which rotational vibrations can also take place need to be considered. This results in a requirement for analysis of 6 d.f. (degree of freedom). However, the principle of vibration damping is presented here on the basis of a simple vibration system based on 1 d.f. as shown in Fig. 6.13, which still has application in building practice.

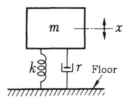

Fig. 6.13. Principles of vibration isolation.

A. Vibration of a 1 Degree of Freedom System

A body whose mass is m rests on an elastic spring which has elastic modulus k. When it is forced to vibrate in the vertical direction by an external force $P \cos \omega t$, its motion can be represented by

$$m \frac{d^2 x}{dt^2} + r \frac{dx}{dt} + kx = P \cos \omega t \tag{6.12}$$

where r is the frictional resistance factor.

If the vibrational driving force to the floor is P_t.

$$P_t = kx + r \frac{dx}{dt} \tag{6.13}$$

From eqn (6.12) and (6.13) the vibration transmissibility T is derived as follows,

$$T = \frac{|P_t|}{|P|} = \left\{ \frac{1 + \left(2 \cdot \frac{\omega}{v} \cdot \frac{r}{r_c} \right)^2}{\left(1 - \frac{\omega^2}{v^2} \right)^2 + \left(2 \cdot \frac{\omega}{v} \cdot \frac{r}{r_c} \right)^2} \right\}^{1/2} \tag{6.14}$$

where,

$$v = 2\pi f_n = \sqrt{k/m}, \quad f_n: \text{natural frequency}$$

$$r_c = 2mv = 2\sqrt{mk} \quad \text{the critical damping resistance}$$

When the resistance is zero, $r = 0$, then,

$$T = \frac{1}{\left| 1 - \left(\frac{\omega}{v} \right)^2 \right|} = \frac{1}{\left| 1 - \left(\frac{F}{f_n} \right)^2 \right|} \tag{6.15}$$

As Fig. 6.14 clearly shows, when $F/f_n < \sqrt{2}$ the force transmitted is greater than the applied force. At the point where the driving frequency and natural frequency are equal, the transmitted force theoretically becomes infinite when $r = 0$. Of course damping resistance would prevent this situation arising, though it reduces the isolation efficiency to some extent, but it illustrates the problems associated with using springs as resilient mounts. When $F/f_n = \sqrt{2}$ then the transmitted force equals the applied force. At higher frequencies we start to get isolation and for vibration isolation $F/f_n > 4$ should be the aim.

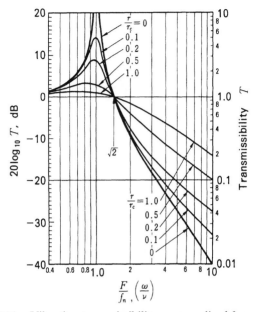

Fig. 6.14. Vibration transmissibility vs normalised frequency.

The above discussion can be applied in the reverse direction in Fig. 6.13 where vibration is transmitted from the floor to the mass m. Thus, in order to produce a quiet room which is isolated from vibration and from the transmission of structure-borne sound, the room considered as a mass m should be supported on a suitable spring system which is generally called a 'floating structure'.

B. Vibration Isolation Design

When a body whose weight is W kg is loaded on an elastic spring whose elastic modulus is k (kg/cm), the deflection δ is

$$\delta = \frac{W}{k} \text{ (cm)} \tag{6.16}$$

The natural frequency of this vibration system, ignoring resistance, is

$$f_n = \frac{1}{2\pi} \sqrt{\frac{kg}{W}}$$

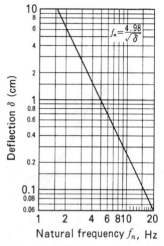

Fig. 6.15. Static deflection vs natural frequency.

where g is acceleration due to gravity and from eqn (6.16)

$$f_n = \frac{1}{2\pi} \sqrt{\frac{g}{\delta}} \approx \frac{4 \cdot 98}{\sqrt{\delta}} \qquad \text{where} \quad g \approx 980 \ (\text{cm}/s^2) \qquad (6.17)$$

Thus, the natural frequency f_n is determined by the static deflection δ. This relationship is shown in Fig. 6.15.

The design procedure is as follows:

(1) Knowing the frequency F of the vibration source, f_n is determined from Fig. 6.14 in order to secure sufficient attenuation.
(2) To realise this, the necessary deflection δ is obtained from Fig. 6.15.
(3) Select the vibration isolation material to maintain the δ while supporting the total weight W.

Since Fig. 6.15 is based on the assumption that the material is perfectly elastic, it must be noted that except for steel springs where Fig. 6.15 has direct application all other materials have a non-linear relationship between load and deflection so that dynamic deflections are smaller than static deflections. Therefore, the value of δ in Fig. 6.15 must be increased by a correction factor indicated in Table 6.1

C. Vibration Control Materials
The materials listed in Table 6.1 are briefly described below.

Table 6.1
Various Vibration Isolating Materials

	Coil Spring	Rubber Isolator	Cork	Felt
Static deflection limit	Design free	Up to 10% of max. thick	Up to 6% thick (max. 10 cm)	—
Correction factor for static deflection	1	$1 \cdot 1 \sim 1 \cdot 6$	$1 \cdot 8 \sim 5$	$9 \sim 17$
Effective frequency range	5 Hz or less	5 Hz or more	40 Hz or more	100 Hz or more
Allowable load (kg/cm^2)	Design free	$2 \sim 6$	$2 \cdot 5 \sim 4$	$0 \cdot 2 \sim 1 \cdot 5$

a. Coiled Steel Spring

Usually the design properties of steel springs are clearly stated and sufficiently large deflection can be obtained, therefore, they are indispensable for the isolation of low frequency vibration. A disadvantage, however, is their lack of damping, therefore a resistive element, such as an oil damper, must be introduced to suppress the amplitude at resonance. Also, longitudinal vibrations of the spring coil itself may occur with a resonance frequency given by

$$f_s = \frac{n}{2} \sqrt{\frac{k}{m_s}} \quad (n = 1, 2, 3, \ldots) \tag{6.18}$$

where k is the elastic modulus and m_s is the moving mass of the spring. This may negate the effect of vibration damping and is called 'surging'. As for the transmission of structure-borne sound between the spring and concrete floor, vibration isolation may not be expected due to the small difference in characteristic impedance (Table 1.1) as explained in Fig. 1.8. However, this can be overcome by using a rubber isolator in combination with the spring.

b. Rubber Isolator

This type has become popular in recent years. The reasons are:

(1) various reliable installation devices have been so developed that the selection of the appropriate isolator for the required use has become quite simple, as shown in Fig. 6.16;

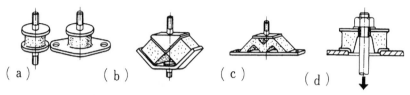

Fig. 6.16. Examples of various rubber isolators.

(2) much design data are available and there is a wide choice of elastic moduli to choose from; and

(3) rubber has intrinsic damping properties due to internal friction so that the resonance amplitude may not be excessive.

Although natural rubber has poor resistance to weather, oil and chemicals, recently synthetic rubber products which have various characteristics are available so that a type appropriate to the particular requirement can be selected.

c. Cork

The material quality may be neither constant nor homogeneous, therefore, it is difficult to carry out a precise design of isolation. Also since cork cannot handle large deflections the natural frequency may be limited to frequencies not less than 10 Hz, thus, instead of vibration control, cork may be more useful for the prevention of the transmission of structure-borne sound.

d. Felt

This material, except in lightweight systems, may not be used. The quality is so varied that comprehensive data are not available. Instead of vibration control, felt can be used to prevent the transmission of structure-borne sound, using its properties as a good packing material with low friction to maintain air-tightness.

e. Air Spring

This is often used in vehicles. Although the structure is complicated, the performance is very good. The air spring can be used as an advanced vibration damping support for machinery and in special testing laboratories.

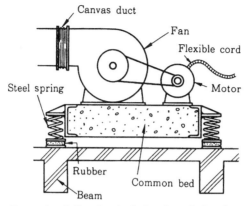

Fig. 6.17.   Example of vibration-isolation foundation for machinery.

6.5 VIBRATION CONTROL OF EQUIPMENT AND MECHANICAL SYSTEMS

A. Vibration Isolation of a Machinery Base

Vibration control in the installation of equipment and machinery in buildings is achieved by placing them together with the driving motor on a common bed, as shown in Fig. 6.17, in such a way that the bed is 2–3 times heavier than total weight of machinery in order to reduce the vibration amplitude and to satisfy the condition of 1 d.f. Referring to Fig. 6.15 for the total weight including the common bed one can select a suitable vibration damping material or mechanism to produce the required deflection. It is recommended that δ should be 2.5–7.5 cm using a system of steel coil spring with rubber pad, so that $f_n < 3$ Hz will be satisfied. If such machinery is to be installed on a high storey floor, a proper structural system should be designed to take the concentrated load of the machinery system directly on the floor beams as shown in Fig. 6.17.

B. Vibration Isolation in Plumbing

When equipment or machinery is loaded on such a vibration isolation base, as shown in Fig. 6.17, the amplitude of the machinery itself generally becomes large, therefore, all terminals of the machinery connected to ducts, plumbing and wiring etc. should be isolated from the vibration by inserting rubber pipe, canvas duct and other soft and flexible material to avoid rigid connections.

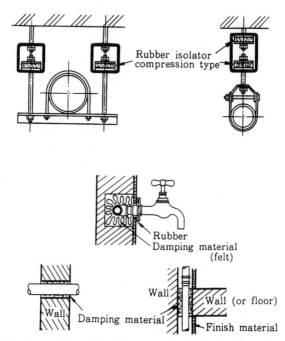

Fig. 6.18. Examples of vibration isolation in plumbing.

Apart from the machinery itself, noise and vibration are also generated by flowing fluid (air, water or their mixture) in pipes. Many
portions of a plumbing system such as right angled bends, sectional
changes, volume control dampers, valves, water flushing devices and
other faucets, air inlets and outlets create resistance to flow and cause
eddies which always produce noise and vibration. Also, an abrupt
change of pressure in a water pipe can generate the well known 'water
hammer' effect. Of course these noises should be minimised but it is
difficult to eliminate them completely, so all plumbing fixtures should be
isolated from the building structure with resilient mounts. Some examples are shown in Fig. 6.18.

6.6 FLOATING CONSTRUCTION

A. Floating Floor and Ceiling
In order not to transmit the structure-borne noises caused by footsteps
or from other sources, a discontinuous floating construction is recom-

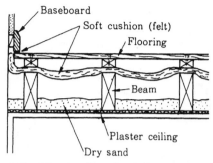

Fig. 6.19.   Floating floor for timber construction.

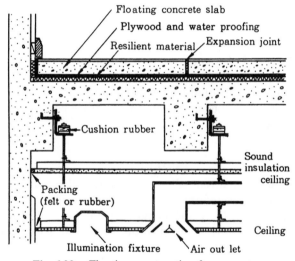

Fig. 6.20.   Floating construction for concrete.

mended, as shown in Figs. 6.19 and 6.20. Although dense glass fibre mats are used as a resilient layer, rubber cushions may be more effective.

Figure 6.20 shows that the ceiling is also floated on rubber springs, but it should be noted that there may be no advantage unless the floor is floated.

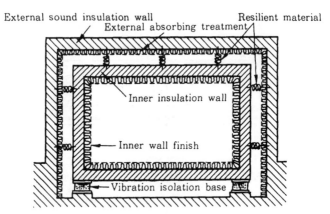

External sound insulation wall   Resilient material
                External absorbing treatment

Inner insulation wall

Inner wall finish

Vibration isolation base

Fig. 6.21. Complete floating construction concept. It is ideal to omit the resilent material connecting both inner and external insulation walls.

B.   Complete Floating Construction

When a high level of sound insulation is required, such as required for an acoustics laboratory, broadcasting or recording studios, it is essential that not only the floor and ceiling but also the room itself should be completely discontinuous and floated from other parts of the construction, as shown in Fig. 6.21.

PROBLEMS 6

1. When a wide rigid wall vibrates in a piston-like manner, show that the velocity level, referred to 5×10^{-8} m/s, of the wall equals the intensity level of the plane sound wave radiated from the wall.

2. Enumerate the devices effective in reducing structure-borne sound in a residential building.

3. Determine the single number rating of impact sound insulation of a floor using the ISO 717 method with measured data; 125 Hz: 62 dB; 250 Hz: 63 dB; 500 Hz: 57 dB; 1 kHz: 45 dB; and 2 kHz: 27 dB.

4. Explain the basic requirements needed to prevent vibration or structure-borne noise transmission when using rubber as an isolator.

5. Design a vibration damping foundation for a ventilation fan which is 110 kg weight, rotating at 617 r.p.m. and driven by an electric motor of 120 kg weight rotating at 1800 r.p.m. What is the weight needed for the common bed and what should be the deflection of the resilient support?

Chapter 7

NOISE AND VIBRATION CONTROL IN THE ENVIRONMENT

In daily life outdoors we encounter noise and vibration generated by, for example, aircraft, road and rail traffic, and indoor noise and vibration sources such as mechanical ventilation systems, elevators and other items of equipment. It is against all such sources that countermeasures are sought. Even in residential accommodation there are many kinds of electrical appliances: dishwashers, food processors, washing machines, which are on the increase and give rise to annoyance.

In principle there is no different approach for noise reduction outdoors and indoors. Therefore, we shall discuss procedures for noise and vibration control which are common to both environments.

7.1 BASIC STRATEGY

In solving environmental noise problems we need to consider the following: (1) the sources of noise and vibration; (2) the propagation paths; and (3) immission to the receivers. Countermeasures should be taken to deal with each of the above in a step-by-step logical sequence.

Suppose a fraction of the energy W generated by a noise or vibration source produces a sound level L_0 (dB) at a receiving point depending on the acoustic nature of the spaces in which source and receiver exist. Assume that the sound level is reduced by R (dB) along the propagation path as described in Chaps 5 and 6, then we have:

$$L_w - R = L_0 \text{ (dB)} \tag{7.1}$$

where L_w is the power level of the source, eqn (1.17b).

On the other hand, at the receiving point if L (dB) is the level necessary to satisfy this required environmental condition and $L_0 < L$, then there is no problem, but if $L_0 > L$ complaints might be expected. Therefore, the required noise reduction R_r is given by

$$L_0 - L = R_r \text{ (dB)}$$

When there are many sources, then the energy from each source must be added together at the receiving point as shown in Fig. 7.1.

When considering a transmission path in which barriers or attenuators are in series each with their individual reduction R_i so that $R_r = \Sigma R_i$ is the total reduction in the path, then it is only necessary to add together sufficient reducing elements to meet the requirement.

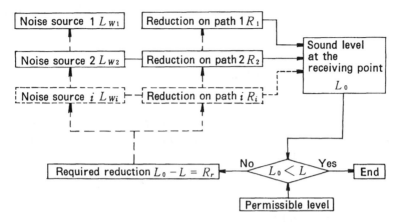

Fig. 7.1. Flow chart of noise and vibration control.

When there are many sources in parallel, after calculating the attenuation in each path, the value of L_0 is again obtained. This is a basic procedure for noise reduction by the 'energy flow method' described in Fig. 7.1 as a flow chart.

It is noted that in the process of calculating dB values it is not necessary to show the sound pressure level at individual points but to show the acoustic energy ratios. Therefore, even though a complicated phenomenon peculiar to wave motion such as interference due to reflected sound may occur locally, it is of no concern and only the energy decay need be relevant. As discussed in Chaps 5 and 6 the energy attenuation can be analysed and controlled by using wave acoustics. With fundamental knowledge properly applied, however, effective noise control measures can be executed using simple geometrical acoustic calculations. This is because noise is seldom a pure tone in nature but in most cases has a continuous spectrum with random amplitudes and phases, although, when dealing with pure tone noise, its reduction needs to take account of wave acoustics.

7.2   DETERMINATION OF REQUIRED REDUCTION

In this section we discuss the procedure for determining the required reduction R_r to be added to the existing reduction R which is calculated or measured. The value of L_w in eqn (7.1) needs to be precisely defined and the permissible level L should be suitably selected. This procedure plays an important role in the assessment of noise pollution and in the estimation of the quality and magnitude of noise control in a new project.

A. Locating Noise and Vibration Sources

a. Source Extraction
Where there are several noise sources, which together give rise to a problem, a decision has to be made as to which is the most serious and action taken to reduce it.

During the process of measurement and analysis of the noise, the various sources must be switched off one by one until the principal source is found against which control measures are to be taken. The other sources should then be investigated in a similar manner, always reducing the noise from the most prominent source. If it is not possible to carry out actual acoustic measurements then judgement must be used with the aid of existing data as to which source is the largest contributor to the noise problem, otherwise any sources which are missed can give rise to trouble later on.

b. Noise Source Quantification
If the power level in every octave band along with the directivity of every sound source is obtained, one can proceed to plan and design to reduce the noise. If, after acquiring the relevant published data, they are still insufficient, actual measurements are highly desirable.

When the sound source is pinpointed by means of measurement and analysis following the procedure described above, the frequency characteristics of the equivalent power level of the source can be found.

Generally the required frequency characteristics are presented as octave band levels. If the values are obtained from other forms of analysis then they should be converted to octave band widths (see Section 2.1B).

[Ex. 7.1] A basic noise survey was carried out in a large factory in order to plan the noise control strategy. The measured noise levels in a frequency band when the operating machines $M_1, M_2, M_3, \ldots$ were stopped one by one, are as follows:

Machine stopped	None	M_1	M_2	M_3
Band level (dB)	100	93	99·5	99·7

From this data the source producing the maximum noise level is seen to be M_1 which therefore needs to be reduced. Further, after stopping the machines one after the other, the following results were obtained.

Machine stopped	M_1	$M_1 M_2$	M_1, M_2, M_3
Band level (dB)	93	90	86

From the above, the noise level produced by each one of the three machines can be estimated as follows:

Machine	M_1	M_2	M_3	All other sources together
Band level (dB)	99	90	88	86

B. Locating the Transmission Path (Calculation of Existing Attenuation)

It is now necessary to understand the nature of the noise transmission path and to calculate the existing reduction R in eqn (7.1) along the path. When there is only one path, for example, in an air-conditioning duct, the natural attenuation can be calculated precisely. Where paths exist in parallel, the reduction in each path should be calculated and summed at the receiving point.

At the actual point where the noise is of concern the reduction R can be obtained from the difference of the measured values between two points, one close to the sound source and the other at the receiving point. However, it is generally difficult to determine the sound paths, e.g. air-borne or structure-borne. Also there are more complicated situations such as in the following example, which require special experimental approaches or techniques. Otherwise the appropriate noise reduction procedure cannot be determined.

[Ex. 7.2]   In a conference room within a municipal office building the noise from the plant room adjacent to the conference room became intrusive. In this case the noise transmission can be associated with the following paths, (a) air-borne noise transmitted through the partition wall; (b) air flow in the duct; and (c) structure-borne noise from the plant foundations. Hence, measurements of sound pressure levels were obtained, derived from spectrum analysis as shown in Table 7.1.

From the results (a) it is clear that the air-borne sound insulation is sufficient. As regards (b) and (c) after proper attenuation in the duct

Table 7.1

Experimental results for separating the airborne and the
structure-borne noise

	Sound pressure level (dB)		
Experiment	Plant Room	Conference Room	Difference
(1) Noise analysis in both rooms during normal plant operation	87	62	25 dB
(2) While plant stopped, measurements in both rooms with white noise generated by a loudspeaker in the plant room	105	46	59 dB

was determined by calculation, and localisation of the noise source in
the conference room checked by ear and confirmation that the air
outlets from the ducts were not the noise sources, the main source of
noise was judged to be due to (c) because of inadequate vibration
damping of the air conditioning plant.

C. Determination of Permissible Noise Level

The permissible values at the receiving point can be determined by the
evaluation method discussed in Chap. 2.2, NCB-curves (Fig. 2.7, Table
2.6) for steady noises, and Fig. 2.13 and Table 2.9 for vibration should
be applied.

When there are two or more noise sources or transmission paths,
each individual permissible level should be determined so that the total
value will satisfy the criteria as outlined in the flow diagram of Fig. 7.1.

For example, in a situation where noise from several sources, i.e. (1)
outdoor noise; (2) air-conditioning noise; and (3) adjacent-room noise
are transmitted then, if they are all meaningless noises, the ratio of
noise energy from each path can be determined in the usual way
depending on the ease of control. If, however, an intermittent noise is
included its peak value must be used, or, if it is an impact noise with a
large statistical fluctuation, it should be handled separately. When
meaningful noises such as speech or music are included, it is desirable
that each energy contribution is 5–10 dB lower than the other meaningless noise energy.

D. Calculation of Required Reduction

As shown in Fig. 7.1, the additional reduction required R_r in each path should be calculated in each octave band in the appropriate frequency range according to the methods described above.

7.3   ORGANISATION OF NOISE AND VIBRATION CONTROL

In order to realise the required reduction obtained with the aid of the above procedures, the measures should be planned according to the flow chart shown in Fig. 7.2. If the sequence is followed in the wrong order then all efforts may result in failure and may incur more expense and waste of time.

A. Dealing with Noise and Vibration Sources

Noise and vibration problems never occur if sources do not exist. Generation of noise and vibration should be eliminated wherever possible at source when selecting equipment and machinery for installation in a building or factory. When equipping a building or factory those versions of equipment which generate unacceptable levels of noise and vibration should be avoided by referring to the manufacturers' data. Machine specification and noise and vibration criteria should be determined from the standpoint of environmental planning.

Also, noise and vibration nuisance produced by traffic and industry should be controlled by proper land use zoning and road planning as an important strategy of city and regional planning. Figure 7.3 shows a good sample of car noise control in a residential area by means of planning layout (see Lit. A6).

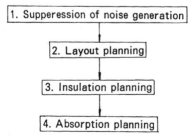

Fig. 7.2.   Sequential order for planning of noise and vibration control.

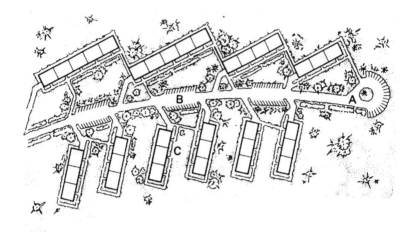

Fig. 7.3. Layout of residential street for vehicle-noise control. A: end loop of the street; B: external car parking areas; and C: pedestrian access to the buildings. (Doelle)

B. Planning Layout

All noises are reduced more or less with distance. Therefore, city and architectural planning may have, as their basis, zoning and site selection associated with effective layout of roads, buildings and rooms with noise reduction as a prime aim. In principle, zones and those rooms which need to be quiet should be located as far as possible from the offending noise sources. This also applies to indoor sources such as mechanical services.

As shown in Fig. 7.4, it is advantageous to locate buildings and rooms which are not sensitive to noise, such as storeroom or workshop, so that they will act as noise barriers in the transmission path from the source so that natural reduction can be greatly increased. If the basic planning is given sufficient thought, R in eqn (7.1) may be sufficiently large to satisfy required criteria without any other artifice. In contrast, if the layout does not reflect any acoustical planning then complaints may occur at a later date and, in fact, there have been many cases where satisfaction has not been achieved even with vast expenditure in an attempt to correct previous planning errors.

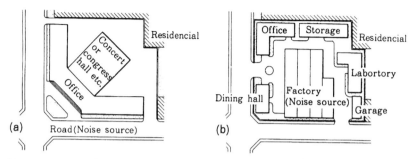

Fig. 7.4. Examples of design layout for noise control: (a) preventing street noise for quiet facilities; and (b) preventing factory noise nuisance.

C. Noise Insulation Planning

After reducing the noise at source as much as possible and transmission paths to the receiver have been identified, effective sound insulation by means of, for example, noise barriers, silencers and vibration isolation devices should be planned using the methods described in Chaps 5 and 6.

As discussed before, when identifying the transmission path, serious consideration must be given to the following:

(1) In the open air, when the diffraction attenuation by a barrier is to be calculated, it is necessary to make sure that there is no other reflection path at the same time.

(2) When calculating the transmission loss of an exterior wall, any opening such as that provided for ventilation must be taken into account.

(3) In the case of partitioning, whether or not it extends to the soffit of the floor above must be checked. Also, the transmission path, due to the ventilation or air-conditioning duct above the suspended ceiling, should be investigated.

(4) The insulating capability of doors facing the corridor, which represent a sound transmission path, should be considered. Particularly air vents in the form of louvres should be examined.

(5) Since any openings offer little in the way of sound insulation compared with a wall, their location must be very carefully considered and so, for example, a corridor or anteroom should

be treated with sound absorbent to create a sound lock if necessary.

D.   Sound Absorption Treatment

In the spaces such as those of source room and receiving room, or the corridor which is a transmission path, if the sound energy is absorbed by applying absorptive treatment, the noise level L_0 in eqn (7.1) is reduced according to eqns (5.18)–(5.20) in Chap. 5. Then the amount of sound insulation required becomes less. Moreover, in noisy factories, the subjective noisiness experienced by the employee is much reduced due to the more rapid decay of reflected and diffused sounds. This is a fact that cannot be related to the small difference in calculated or measured noise level.

The effect of absorptive treatment depends upon the amount of absorption present before treatment since the noise level is reduced by $10 \log_{10}(A_1/A_0)$ dB where only the term related to absorption needs to be considered in eqn. (5.19), where A_0, A_1 are the total absorption in the room before and after treatment, respectively.

[Ex. 7.3]   In a machine room where the average absorption coefficient $a_0 = 0 \cdot 05$ is changed to $a_1 = 0 \cdot 3$ by the absorptive treatment, the effect is a noise reduction of $10 \log_{10}(A_1/A_0) = 10 \log 6 = 8$ dB. If more absorption is added up to $a_2 = 0 \cdot 5$, the effect is increased by only $10 \log_{10}(0 \cdot 5/0 \cdot 3) = 2$ dB.

It should also be noted that the cost required for the latter $(0 \cdot 3 – 0 \cdot 5)$ is generally more than the step from $(0 \cdot 05$ to $0 \cdot 3)$.

E.   Electro-Acoustic Devices

a.   Active Absorber

There is a device, which uses a microphone and speaker system in order to cancel the noise by generating sound in antiphase, called an active absorber. Although this method has become effective with digital techniques for localised spaces such as air-conditioning ducts and is expected to have wider application, reliability, durability and maintenance cost of equipment, etc. need to be carefully assessed.

b.   Masking Noise Generator

Meaningful noises such as speech can be masked by meaningless noise which has a continuous spectrum like white noise. There is electro-acoustical equipment for generating noise in the room where the masking of undesired speech from a neighbour in an office or a hotel is needed. Air-conditioning noise is effective for this purpose, so that determination of an appropriate noise level (see Section 7.2C) needs to be taken into account.

c. Background Music
Background music is proposed for masking the noise and reducing annoyance caused by it. Although this idea may work to some extent, when the noise level becomes high, the background music itself becomes annoying. Of course, 'environmental music' can be used for purposes other than noise control to proper effect, so background music itself may not be considered an adequate means of noise control in the environment.

7.4   EXAMPLES OF NOISE CONTROL PLANNING

A.   Outdoor Noise Control
Taking as an example a hotel intended for a site alongside a busy road which has, in addition, street cars as well as road traffic, as shown in Fig. 7.5. Actual measurement of noise was carried out and the required reduction for noise control investigated as shown in Table 7.2 and Fig. 7.6. Since the required permissible level is specified as NCB-30, the required reduction is 45 dB at 500 Hz. This is found from the left-hand side of eqn (5.18); therefore, the composite transmission loss of the facade is given by the first term on the right-hand side of the equation.

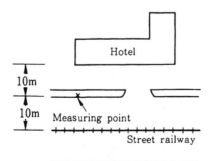

Fig. 7.5. Situation of a hotel building in order to control traffic noise (see Table 7.2 and Fig. 7.6).

Table 7.2
Example of outdoor noise preventing calculation (Figs 7.5 and 7.6)

Octave band mid-frequency	63	125	250	500	1 K	2 K	4 K (Hz)
(1) max. value from noise measurement analysis (dB)	89·0	84·5	79·5	83·0	74·5	69·5	65·5
(2) (1) − 3 dB = noise level at outside surface of wall (dB)	86·0	81·5	76·5	80·0	71·5	66·5	62·5
(3) permissible noise level in rooms (dB)	55·0	46·5	40·0	35·0	32·0	38·0	25·0
(4) (2)–(3) = required reduction (dB)	31·0	35·0	36·5	45·0	39·5	38·5	37·5

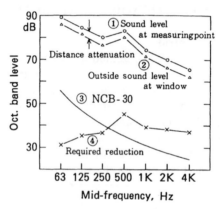

Fig. 7.6.   Calculation of traffic noise control (see Fig. 7.5 and Table 7.2).

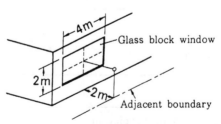

Fig. 7.7.   Geometry of noise generating window in a factory.

B. Factory Noise Control by Means of the Building Envelope

Since the noise source is inside the building, the exterior wall has to provide sufficient insulation against transmitted noise in order not to cause any annoyance to neighbours. In Fig. 7.7, a glassblock window in a heavy concrete wall is shown located at 2 m from the site boundary. Assuming a permissible level of NCB-40, the required attenuation calculation is shown in Fig. 7.8.

In this example, the source is a diesel engine whose total power is 3365 hp, and the noise power is assumed to be proportional to the hp value obtained from measurement on a similar engine. The power-level curve is labelled ① in the figure. Using eqn (5.23), the room total absorption $10 \log_{10} A_1$ and TL of the glassblock can be deduced, then curve ③ is the resultant noise power level radiated to outside from the window. Attenuation due to distance to the site boundary is found to be $-6 \cdot 5$ dB from eqn (5.11) and Figs. 5.4–5.5, thus curve ④ is obtained. Referring to the permissible level ⑤ the required attenuation ⑥ is obtained. A fixed-glass window, in addition to the glassblock, resulting in a double window configuration, outlined in Section 5.6, may satisfy the requirements. In a room which, as in the above example, is made air tight, installation of air conditioning is inevitable; therefore attenuation of noise transmitted though air ducts must also be carefully controlled as will be described later.

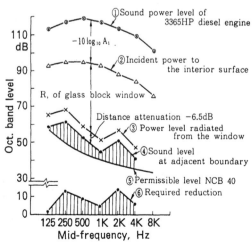

Fig. 7.8.   Calculation of noise nuisance control from a factory (see Fig 7.7).

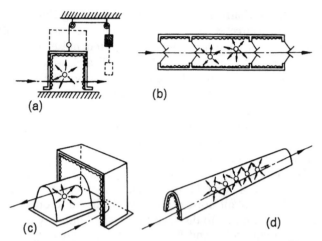

Fig. 7.9. Barriers and enclosures for noise generating sources: (a) closed and movable arrangement; (b) anteroom arrangement; (c) directional absorbing arrangement; and (d) absorbing tunnel.

C. Noise Control of Indoor Noise Sources

After control of the source noise, as discussed above, the acoustic energy still remaining or generated indoors should be dealt with by enclosing the equipment using a cover, hood or barrier. Figure 7.9 shows examples which are effective for noise generated during machine operation in factories. While the materials used for them should have adequate TL, it is absolutely necessary that they are lined with absorbent as shown in Fig. 7.10. It is also important that isolating partitions divide the shop floor into smaller sections in which there is ample absorption, in order to improve the workers' auditory environment in

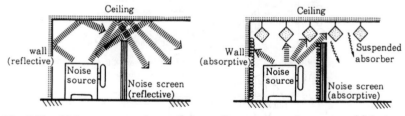

Fig. 7.10. Noise screen and sound absorption treatment in a room: (a) before treatment; and (b) after treatment.

the sense that he or she was more likely to be annoyed by noise other than that from his own machine.

D. Application of Scale Model and Computer Model Studies

The most essential task in the flow diagram of noise control planning shown in Fig. 7.1, is the finding of reduction R in the transmission paths. In the above examples A and B it is easy to find R but in case C it is rather difficult to predict R by calculation. Also, in the open air where there is a very complicated configuration such as arises when barriers are in a complicated terrain, and when the source is distributed such as in the case of a highway, or is moving, e.g. train or aircraft, it is necessary to analyse with methods described in Chaps 5 and 6. The

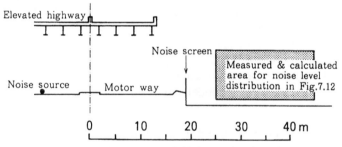

Fig. 7.11. Cross-section of an elevated highway showing the area of model measurement and computer simulation for noise propagation.

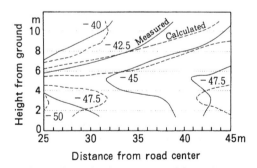

Fig. 7.12. Comparison of results between model measurements (solid lines) and computer simulation (dotted lines) for noise propagation from the highway shown in Fig. 7.11. Levels show relative (dB) values referred to the level at the point 1 m from the source. (Fukushima et al.)

Fig. 7.13. Scale model for acoustic measurement of the elevated highway shown in Fig. 7.11.

analysis may need the use of a scale model or a mathematical model closely approximating to the actual situation, the former for acoustic measurements and the latter for computer simulation. This can be used to assess the noise propagation and attenuation.

Figure 5.13 in Chap. 5 is an example of computer simulation. Figures 7.11 and 7.12 are examples of comparison between the results obtained by computer and acoustic model shown in Fig. 7.13.

E. Noise Control of Air-Conditioning Ducts

a. Noise Generated at the Air Grill
Both air outlets and inlets generate noise in the same way, independent of air flow direction, by impinging air flow on the grill or diffusers. The power level/1 m^2 of the duct neck section is empirically proportional to about the 6th power of the wind speed v (m/s) at the louver surface. This can be expressed mathematically as follows:

$$L_w \simeq 30 + 60 \log_{10} v \; (\text{dB/m}^2) \qquad (7.2)$$

This noise can be reduced only by decreasing the wind speed. Therefore, calculating sound level in the room using eqns (5.19) and (3.41), the wind speed should be decreased so that the generated noise level becomes lower than the permissible value.

b. Air Flow Noise in Ducts
At bends, junctions and dampers eddy currents occur and generate noise whose level is also proportional to the 5th or 6th power of the air speed. Although it, too, can be reduced by lowering the speed, since the

demand for high-speed ducting is common in current practice, the noise reduction of air flow becomes a significant problem. In a building which requires more strict noise control, low-speed ducting (wind speed 5–10 m/s) should be adopted with the air flow as smooth as possible and with a duct wall which, with careful design and construction, does not vibrate at low frequencies.

c. Noise Transmitted through Duct Wall
The duct wall should have adequate TL depending upon the duct location, so that noise may neither be transmitted into the duct nor emitted externally. Special attention is needed when using glassfibre ducting, which has extremely low transmission loss.

d. Cross Talk between Rooms through Common Duct
When there are outlets in nearby rooms in a common duct, sounds can be heard from one room to the other via the duct. To avoid this cross talk the distance between the outlets should be kept sufficiently large by means of a tortuous route or separate ducts should be provided. Silencers or mufflers should also be installed between the outlets.

e. Fan Noise
This is the main source of noise in low-velocity ducting. The power level of the generated noise is proportional to the nominal power K_w of the driving motor as follows,

$$L_w = 89 + 10 \log_{10} K_w + 10 \log_{10} \left(\frac{P}{25} \right) \ (dB) \qquad (7.3)$$

where P = static pressure mmAq. Although there is another formula which takes into consideration the type of vane and flow volume of the fan (see Lit. A7), eqn (7.3) gives sufficient approximation for our purpose. The relative values of the octave band level can be estimated from Fig. 7.14. After calculating the natural reduction of this noise level by the duct system, silencers or mufflers may be added if the reduction is insufficient.

The procedures are enumerated as follows with the illustrated example shown in Figs 7.15.

① It is recommended that noise generated by a centrifugal fan is obtained using data supplied by the manufacturer. When there is no data, eqn (7.3) and Fig. 7.14 can be used for estimation.

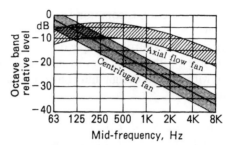

Fig. 7.14. Frequency characteristics of generated noise power from fans in a duct.

② Reduction of a duct system shown in Fig. 7.16, when it has only an absorbing chamber. Power level at a point just before the branch Ⓐ is obtained from eqn (5.65).

③ Reduction at the branch is calculated by means of the section area ratio of the ducts. 2.4 dB is obtained at point Ⓐ.

④ Reduction at the open end, where the noise power is radiated from 4 grills G into the room, is obtained from Fig. 5.42.

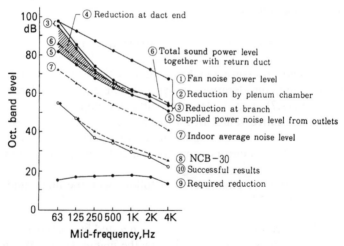

Fig. 7.15. Determination of noise control in the air-conditioning system shown in Fig. 7.16.

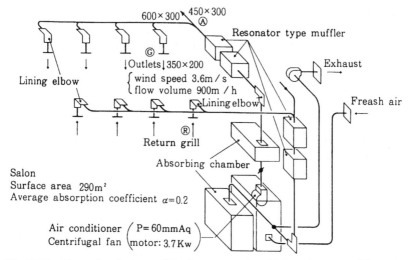

Fig. 7.16. Example of air-conditioning system in which noise control is to be determined by calculation.

⑤ The power level from outlets was obtained by the above calculation.

⑥ Adding the noise power R radiated from return grills calculated by the same method described above, the total sound power level supplied to the room can be determined.

⑦ The average noise level in the room can be obtained by eqn (5.19).

⑧ Shows the permissible level NCB-30.

⑨ The difference between values of ⑦ and the permissible level NCB-30 becomes the required reduction. Then, the bend lining for high frequencies and resonator type mufflers for low frequencies shown in Fig. 5.44 are added with the aid of proper design (see Section 5.9B–F) as shown in Fig. 7.16.

⑩ Shows successful results of this design procedure where an average noise level is produced by the air-conditioning system to the room.

When a silencer or muffler is to be added, though it is rather easy at high frequencies, it is very difficult to find sufficient space for a silencer capable of attenuating the low frequencies unless thought has been given to the problem right at the planning stage.

If the noise level at a point near the duct opening is of concern then the direct sound power from the opening should be added in with the calculation of attenuation with distance by using eqn (3.39).

f. Structure-Borne Noise Transmission by Ducts
In addition to the airborne noise carried by the duct, the duct wall transmits structure-borne noise and, furthermore, the duct-supports transmit noise to the building structure. Therefore, even if silencers or mufflers are installed, it is said that only a maximum of 25 dB for frequencies below 100 Hz and 50 dB for 1000 Hz or above may be attenuated by a continuous duct made from steel plate, provided that vibration damping is installed as shown in Fig. 6.18. Further noise control, canvas ducts and concrete ducts are inserted at certain places so that vibration and structure-borne sound can be isolated. It is most important that thought is given to vibration damping and structure-borne isolation in duct design in order to obtain a very quiet room.

PROBLEMS 7
1. Give your opinion on noise nuisance as an environmental problem.
2. Enumerate all possible means of reducing road traffic noise.
3. Describe your ideas on methods of avoiding noise nuisance from aircraft.
4. Enumerate the methods of controlling noise generated indoors applying the concept that the greatest noise has greatest priority.
5. In an apartment, there are complaints about the neighbour's TV which produces a measured sound level of 45 dB in the 500 Hz octave band. There is also air-conditioning noise of 42 dB in the same frequency band. How much reduction must be applied to each of the two sources to meet NCB-35 and eliminate any meaningful sound from TV?
6. A very noisy factory measuring $20 \times 30 \times 5$ m^2 has a measured noise level of 94 dB and reverberation time of 5.8 s in the 1 kHz octave band. How much absorptive treatment is needed to reduce the noise level to 86 dB in that band?

7. In the above factory what control measures should be considered before introducing absorptive treatment? Enumerate and explain, stating order of priorities.
8. Enumerate the sources of noise to be controlled in the air-conditioning system and explain how the control is achieved.
9. In Fig. 7.16, how does the noise level differ from the calculated value shown in Fig. 7.15 with direct sound from an outlet grill at a point 1 m from it and at a point 2 m from the grill?

Chapter 8

ACOUSTIC DESIGN OF ROOMS

Although any room may have an optimum acoustic environment, depending on the purpose for which it is intended, it is difficult to decide
which is the ultimate goal because the final evaluation still relies on the
subjective auditory sensation. However, with the knowledge so far
gained, one can design the space acoustically without any serious
defects. In this chapter we discuss the further research necessary to
create a better acoustic environment in a room.

8.1   DESIGN TARGET

General requirements for the acoustic design of a room are as follows:

(1)   any intrusive noise should be avoided;
(2)   speech intelligibility should be satisfactory;
(3)   music should sound pleasing and have warmth;
(4)   a uniform distribution of sound should be observed throughout
      the whole room;
(5)   there should be no defects such as echoes or flutter.

When all the above conditions are satisfied, the design can be considered successful.

Firstly, noise should be completely controlled. This is a prerequisite
necessary in room design.

Although there are much data available for speech intelligibility as
discussed in Chap. 1 (see Section 1.14), the question arises as to the
possibility of providing sonorous music at the same time. Further
research on which physical condition can produce the best music
performance in addition to the reverberation, as described in Chap. 3, is
needed (see Section 3.6).

On the other hand, present knowledge and techniques can improve
the sound field distribution, avoiding undesirable phenomena such as

echoes, foci, etc. The remaining problem is how to integrate the acoustic and visual treatment of the room into something which is aesthetically totally satisfying.

8.2   DESIGN OF ROOM SHAPE

A.   Fundamental Principles

The shape of the room is the most fundamental factor in influencing its acoustics. So a building requiring good acoustics needs to be examined at the basic planning stage with advice from a good acoustic consultant. As discussed fully in Chap. 3, depending on room size, wave acoustics should be used to assist in the design of small rooms and geometrical acoustics for larger spaces.

a.   Dimensional Ratio for Rectangular Room

In a small rectangular room, the natural frequencies given by eqn (3.13) should not degenerate and should be uniformly distributed. A simple integer ratio of the 3 edge-lengths must be avoided as shown in Fig. 3.5. The 'golden rule' $(\sqrt{5} - 1):2:(\sqrt{5} + 1)$, or its approximate ratio such as $2:3:5$ has been recommended over many years, generally it is considered appropriate to select values of $2^{n/3}$ or $5^{n/3}$. For example, $1:\sqrt[3]{5}:\sqrt[3]{25} \approx 1:1\cdot7:2\cdot9$ is a handy ratio to apply in practice.

b.   Surrounding Wall Shape and Sound Reflection

When sound is reflected from a wall surface which is dimensionally large compared to the wavelength, the reflected sound can be visualised

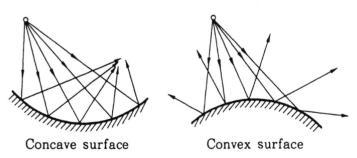

Concave surface   Convex surface

Fig. 8.1.   Reflection from a curved surface.

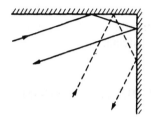

Fig. 8.2. Reflection at a corner.

in the same way as light reflected from a mirror as discussed in Chap. 1 (see Section 1.5B). So, if the wall is concave, the reflected sounds are concentrated; on the other hand, if the wall is convex, they are diffused as shown in Fig. 8.1. Therefore, in order to have good diffusion, concave surfaces which are large compared to the wavelengths should not be used. It is no exaggeration to say that almost all concave surfaces are acoustically potentially hazardous.

c. Prevention of Echo and Flutter

At a corner where two planes intercept orthogonally, either indoors or outdoors, sound waves are reflected back in the reverse direction to the incident one so echoes can arise as shown in Fig. 8.2. In order to avoid echoes completely the surface shapes must be created so as to diffuse or absorb the incident sounds as shown in Figs 8.6 and 8.7.

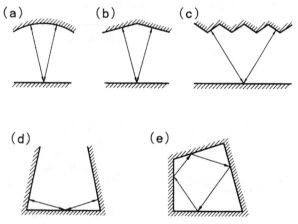

Fig. 8.3. Shape causing no flutter echo.

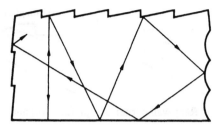

Fig. 8.4. Shapes causing flutter echo.

As mentioned in Chap. 3 (see Section 3.5B) a multiple reflection between two parallel planes may cause flutter echoes. Although it is easy to avoid them by making the two planes non-parallel or the surface undulated with dimensions close to the wavelength of sound, the shapes shown in Fig. 8.3 may cause flutter echoes when the wavelength is small compared with the pattern elements of the surfaces. Figure 8.4 shows a preferred shape. It is essential to diffuse sound waves in the frequency range above 1–2 kHz in order to prevent an audible flutter.

B. Selection of Local Shapes

a. Profiles of Sections
(1) *Ceiling*: Reflected sound from a ceiling plays a significant role in reinforcing the direct sound, particularly important for listeners in rear seats. However, a concave domed ceiling makes the sound distribution worse as shown in Fig. 8.5(a). This situation can be overcome with a combination of convex shapes as shown in Fig. 8.5(b). When the client insists on a domed ceiling the radius of curvature should be at least twice as large as the ceiling height.

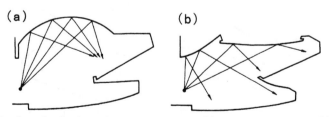

Fig. 8.5. Longitudinal sections of auditoria: (a) poor ceiling; and (b) good ceiling.

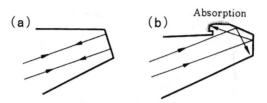

Fig. 8.6. Rear wall corner design: (a) poor; and (b) good.

Since echoes should not occur where the ceiling meets the rear wall as shown in Fig. 8.2, a tilted wall, Fig. 8.6(a), may still cause problems; therefore, a design shown in Fig. 8.6(b) is recommended.

(2) *Balcony*: When a balcony is provided in order to increase audience capacity, the acoustics under the balcony becomes generally worse because the direct sound is attenuated owing to long-distance propagation over the audience and hence the sound pressure levels decay owing to lack of effective reflection from walls and ceilings. Moreover, the reverberation time becomes shorter due to the smaller volume per audience and the weak diffused sounds. In order to improve this member of the situation the depth D of the balcony in Fig 8.7 should be as short as possible and less than twice the maximum height H, (if possible, equal to the opening height H). It is also advisable to design the seating under the balcony so that a person sitting in any seat can see as much of the main ceiling as possible.

The balcony front should be designed so that any echo or focusing may not occur either in plan or in section while the shape and material of the balcony soffit should be chosen to be an effective reflecting surface.

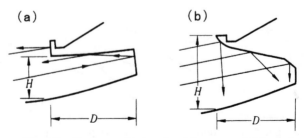

Fig. 8.7. Sections of balconies: (a) poor; and (b) good.

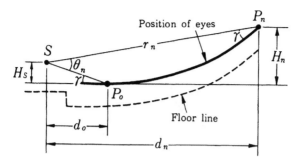

Fig. 8.8. Seating floor section (Cremer).

(3) *Floor*: Since the floor with seating has large absorption, direct sound is rapidly attenuated as it propagates over the absorbing surface because the porous-type absorption provided by chairs and audience is efficient at high frequencies. In addition, the spaces between rows of seating are found to cause resonance in the low-frequency range from 100 to 200 Hz which produces remarkable attenuation. In order to overcome the situation there is no other way but to increase the floor slope so that direct sound is not interrupted by the front seats. The method of determining the floor slope is nothing more than a problem of sight line to the stage. One means of defining this is shown in Fig. 8.8. In the figure γ is the angle of elevation of the sound source above P_0, the person sitting in the front row. With the requirement that γ is a constant, the curve so generated which starts at P_0 and continues to a receiver at P_n with distance d_n is called a 'logarithmic spiral'. Then using polar coordinates (r, θ), by definition

$$r = r_0 \exp \theta \cot \gamma \approx r_0 \exp(\theta/\gamma)$$

$$\therefore \quad \theta = \gamma \log_e(r/r_0) \approx \gamma \log_e(d/d_0) \tag{8.1}$$

Since $H_s \approx d_0\gamma$, the height H of P from P_0 is obtained

$$H = d_0\gamma + d(\theta - \gamma)$$

$$= \gamma[d.\log_e(d/d_0) - (d - d_0)] \tag{8.2}$$

where d_0 is the distance from the source to the origin P_0, the eye position. The condition where the angle γ is larger than 12–15° is said to be desirable (Cremer *et al.*, Lit. B29). The floor slope, to be equal to θ, becomes steeper as it progresses from the stage towards the remote

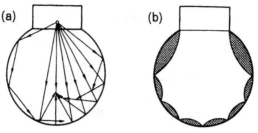

Fig. 8.9. Treatment of circular plan shape: (a) poor; and (b) good.

seating and it is possible that the result of this may conflict with the local building regulations.

b. Plan Shape

As with the ceiling profile design, it is advisable to obtain the first reflected sound from the wall nearest to the sound source, then gradually change the wall finish towards a surface which diffuses or absorbs. Concave surfaces should be avoided. Since an eliptical or circular plan, in particular, always creates serious problems, if still required, a combination of convex elements as shown in Fig. 8.9(b) should be considered.

A side-wall plan with a fan shape is often preferred by architects. However, it may produce too few lateral reflections which play an important role in the subjective acoustic impression and may also give rise to echoes from the rear wall as shown in Fig. 8.10(a). Therefore, adequate diffusion and absorption should be considered as shown in Fig. 8.10(b). Generally, a space which is irregular or asymmetrical in plan is not easy to design, but is desirable from the point of view of

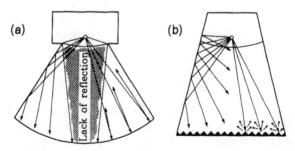

Fig. 8.10. Fan shape plan: (a) poor; and (b) good.

sound diffusion and acoustic quality; therefore, the examples in Figs 8.19(b) and (c) should be noted.

c. Sound Reflecting Panels

In multi-purpose halls, movable sound-reflecting walls and ceiling are often installed around the stage as an orchestra shell. By using them, the sound energy, which would otherwise be absorbed in the back stage space which has high absorption, is reflected back to the players, creating better ensemble, and providing improved listening conditions for the audience.

Although such reflecting panels should be as heavy as possible, a compound laminate-layer construction of plywood and damping rubber sheet has rather good reflection characteristics with less weight. The reflecting surface should consist of flat or convex units whose dimensions are comparable to the sound wavelengths (Fig. 8.11). For example, at frequencies lower than 100 Hz, the width required is more than 3·4 m.

In large halls, in order to reduce the time delay of reflected sounds, many reflecting panels are often suspended from the ceilingover the stage and audience (Figs. 8.20, 8.22). Reflection characteristics of such devices should be studied (Maekawa & Sakurai 1968; Rindel 1991).

d. Diffusion Surface or Units

For the purpose of improving sound diffusion in a room, the wall or ceiling may be given a zig-zag profile or cylindrical, spherical, pyramidal modelling or boxes of one sort or another as well as various uneven irregular-shaped units installed along the boundaries. In fact, any shape will work so long as the wavelength of interest is of the same order as the dimensions of the irregularity. Figure 8.11 may be a useful reference for designing such a unit. It is advisable to use various types and sizes so that a wide range of frequencies can be diffused. Figure 8.12 shows an example whose effectiveness has been measured by means of a scale model.

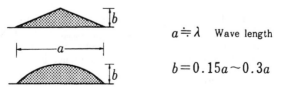

$$a \doteqdot \lambda \quad \text{Wave length}$$

$$b = 0.15a \sim 0.3a$$

Fig. 8.11. Dimensions of diffusing element.

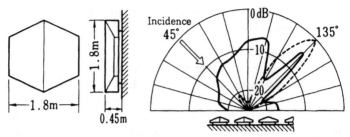

Fig. 8.12. Examples of the reflection characteristics of a diffusing element measured by a scale model: (a) actual dimensions of diffusing element; and (b) directivity of reflected sound (actual frequency 250 Hz). Dotted line shows the case without any diffusing element.

Schroeder (1979) proposed a special configuration developed from number theory, Fig. 8.13(a), and showed that it reflects diffusely for normal incident sound such as shown in Fig. 8.13(b). This idea is currently being applied to walls and ceilings, however, it must be tested

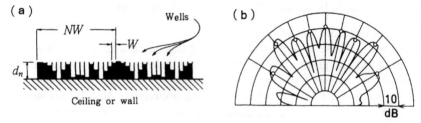

Fig. 8.13. Example of diffuse reflection surface based on quadratic residues (Schroeder 1979): (a) section of the surface; and (b) directivity of reflection, when $\lambda = \lambda_{max}/2$ where, the well width

$$W < \lambda_{min}/2,$$

the well depth

$$d_n = s_n \lambda_{min}/2$$

$s_n = n^2$ (quadratic residues; s_n are taken as the least non-negative residues with modulus N) and $n = 0, 1, 2, \ldots, N$ and $N = \lambda_{max}/\lambda_{min}$, the wavelength ratio of both ends of the diffusing frequency range, and N is an odd prime. For example, when $N = 17$, starting with $n = 0$, the sequence is

$$s_n = 0, 1, 4, 9, 16, 8, 2, 15, 13, 13, 15, 2, 8, 16, 9, 4, 1$$

so that N is the period.

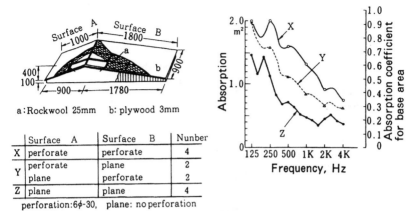

a: Rockwool 25mm   b: plywood 3mm

	Surface A	Surface B	Number
X	perforate	perforate	4
Y	perforate	plane	2
	plane	perforate	2
Z	plane	plane	4

perforation:6φ-30, plane: no perforation

Fig. 8.14. Absorption measured on 4 pieces of prismatic diffusing element.

for its absorption even if it is made from hard material (Fujiwara *et al.* 1992).

Various materials for diffusers can be considered as follows: for reflective purpose, cement and tiles are acceptable while plywood and other boards are used for absorption in the low-frequency range. Further enhanced absorption is obtained with porous materials and perforated boards which provide particular absorption characteristics. These devices are often used to modify the reverberation characteristics. Figure 8.14 shows examples of measured data.

C. Geometrical Drawing Study of Room Shape
Once a room has been designed with due reference to the components described above, the whole room shape can be developed as a functional acoustic system. There is a geometrical method of representing the behaviour of sound transmission and reflection as illustrated in Figs 8.1–8.10 and also Fig. 1.6b in Chap. 1. First, in order to distribute the first reflections uniformly to the whole audience area avoiding undesirable phenomena such as echoes, it is necessary to adjust the positions and angles of the reflecting surfaces. Further, in order to avoid the creation of long-path echoes and sound foci, etc., a trial and error method is employed to adjust the diffusive and absorptive treatment until an adequate reflected sound distribution is obtained. Figure 8.15 shows an example of the investigation of the longitudinal section of the

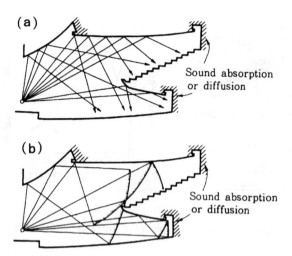

Fig. 8.15. Geometrical drawing investigations of room section profiles: (a) sound ray tracing; and (b) wave front drawing.

room: (a) with sound rays; and (b) with wave fronts. The same analysis should, of course, be applied to the floor plan.

8.3   PLANNING THE REVERBERATION

A.   Determination of Optimum Reverberation Time

a.   Room Volume and Purpose

With a knowledge of the major purpose for which the room is to be used and its volume, the optimum reverberation time and its frequency characteristics can be found from Figs 3.21 to 3.24 in Chap. 3.

In the case of a multi-purpose hall, the programme of events should be obtained and the architectural design should then be dictated by the bias towards, for example, music, or, alternatively, drama, etc.

b.   Variable Reverberation Time Facilities

In a multi-purpose room, the requirement is for the reverberation to be variable. Figure 4.31 shows an example of devices for achieving this flexibility. However, the area which can be used for such a variable surface function is often limited whether it is on the ceiling or on walls, resulting in variations up to 10–20%. Further, since the timbre or sonority is also changed by changing the frequency characteristics of absorption or is distorted for some unknown reason, it is difficult to cover the range shown in Fig. 3.21 with complete ease. A reasonable approach to the problem is to install a thick curtain with a deep air space behind it.

Currently, electro-acoustic devices are being developed which can actively control the sound field and increase the reverberation time over a wider range. Even if the reverberation time could be made totally variable, either architecturally or electro-technically, it is doubtful whether anyone could be found who would be capable of operating such a device so that it would always produce the best acoustic conditions. There is even the possibility of making them worse. In order to make best use of the facilities, a new monitoring system capable of indicating the necessary operating conditions based on objective measurements would be required.

c. Electro-Acoustic Systems

It is of fundamental importance to note whether the electro-acoustic system acts as the main facility or takes on a subsidiary supporting role. In recent years, although microphones and loudspeakers are frequently used in many places, there have been many unsuccessful applications due to improper design of the system or difficulty of operation. If an electro-acoustic system is to be given priority, then it is advisable to adopt a somewhat shorter reverberation time than the recommended value as indicated in Fig. 3.21, so as to reduce operational difficulties which can arise, because recorded sounds already contain the proper reverberation and to suppress howling and adding reverberation simply by an electronic reverberator when reinforcing stage sound (Chap. 9). At the very least the sound absorption surrounding the microphone should be increased.

B. Determination of Room Volume

The reverberation time is directly proportional to the room volume and inversely proportional to the total absorption as shown in eqn (3.23). Since an audience has a large absorption, unless the unit volume/person for the space is appropriate, the reverberation time may be inadequate. The unit-floor area/seat is about $0 \cdot 6$ m^2 including aisles, and, by adjusting the ceiling height, the unit volume should meet the value indicated in Table 8.1, which shows the recommended unit volume for a

Table 8.1
Recommended Room Volume per Seat

Concert Hall	8–10 m³
Opera, multi-purpose hall	6–8 m³
Theatre, Cinema	4–6 m³

variety of rooms. Any room in which music is performed needs a larger volume because of the need for a longer reverberation time; however, too large a volume decreases the acoustic energy density, resulting in unfavourable acoustics. On the other hand, a movie theatre requires a smaller volume hence a shorter reverberation time because the use of an electro-acoustic system is necessary. Of course the smaller the volume, the more economical the construction and the lower the running costs.

C.   Sound Absorption Design

a.   Determination of Necessary Absorption

Once the target values of reverberation time T and room volume V are determined, the necessary absorption A can be obtained from the reverberation time formulae, eqns (3.23)–(3.25), from which the absorption of the audience is subtracted. This result is then the basis for the design, construction and finishes of walls and ceilings.

b.   Effect due to Variable Audience

For an auditorium whose absorption is largely affected by the audience, the reverberation times in both the fully-occupied and empty situation should be calculated; thus, the seats should provide absorption which is close to that of full audience absorption in order to minimise the effect due to the different occupancy. However, it should be noted that the seat must not have too much absorption when a member of the audience sits on it.

c.   Location of Absorbents

Having designed the room shape, the following steps are then followed: (1) Determine the absorption required for local spot surfaces which need treatment in order to avoid echoes and flutter. (2) Apply reflective (live) treatment around the stage and absorptive (dead) treatment along the rear wall. This is called 'live end' and 'dead end' method. (3) Furnish

Table 8.2
Reverberation Time Calculation for a Concert Hall

Places	Finish materials	Area S (m²)	125 Hz α	125 Hz Sα	250 Hz α	250 Hz Sα	500 Hz α	500 Hz Sα	1 KHz α	1 KHz Sα	2 KHz α	2 KHz Sα	4 KHz α	4 KHz Sα
Floors	Vinyl chloride tile on concrete	494	0·01	5	0·02	10	0·02	10	0·02	10	0·03	15	0·04	20
	45-mm timber flooring on joists	118	0·15	18	0·10	12	0·08	10	0·07	8	0·05	6	0·05	6
Ceilings	12-mm gypsum board with large air space	431	0·25	108	0·15	65	0·10	43	0·08	34	0·06	26	0·05	22
	Diffuse and absorptive construction	92	0·30	28	0·30	28	0·30	28	0·30	28	0·30	28	0·20	18
Walls	Mortar, paint	403	0·01	4	0·02	8	0·02	8	0·03	12	0·03	12	0·03	12
	24-mm gypsum board with 150 mm air space	60	0·18	11	0·13	8	0·06	4	0·06	4	0·06	4	0·05	3
	Perforated board, 25-mm glasswool, large air space	92	0·55	51	0·80	74	0·75	69	0·48	44	0·33	30	0·15	14
	Reflecting panels on stage	321	0·15	48	0·15	48	0·10	32	0·08	26	0·07	22	0·06	19
Door	Vinyl leather with upholstery	44	0·10	4	0·15	7	0·20	9	0·25	11	0·30	13	0·30	13
Window	Glass panes	16	0·30	5	0·20	3	0·15	2	0·10	2	0·06	1	0·03	0·5
Chairs	Theatre chair upholstered	660	0·15	99	0·20	132	0·28	185	0·30	198	0·30	198	0·30	198
Persons	Adult audiences	660	0·20	132	0·25	165	0·33	218	0·40	264	0·40	264	0·40	264

Surface $S = 2071$ m²
Volume $V = 4850$ m³

Total absorption (m²)
	125 Hz	250 Hz	500 Hz	1 KHz	2 KHz	4 KHz
Unoccupied condition	380	393	399	376	355	325
With full audiences	413	426	432	442	421	391

Air absorption (4 mV)
	1 KHz	2 KHz	4 KHz
	17	43	109

Reverberation Time (s)
	125 Hz	250 Hz	500 Hz	1 KHz	2 KHz	4 KHz
Unoccupied	1·86	1·79	1·76	1·80	1·81	1·69
With full audiences	1·70	1·64	1·61	1·52	1·52	1·44

dead treatment around microphones when they are used as electro-
acoustic devices and (4) distribute the absorbents in patches of small
dimensions comparable to sound wavelengths instead of using an absorption treatment of large extended area in order to diffuse the sound
field in the room and to increase the total absorption by the area effect
(Fig. 4.10).

d. Remarks on Calculation

Following on from the above guidelines, the frequency range from 125
to 4000 Hz should be investigated and the final reverberation times
calculated using eqn (3.25), satisfying oneself that, by a process of trial
and error, the optimum values have been attained by selection from
various combinations of materials and construction details (Chap. 4 and
Table A.2). Table 8.2 shows an example of this type of calculation.

8.4 COMPUTER SIMULATION AND ACOUSTIC MODEL
ANALYSIS

A. Computer Aided Analysis of the Sound Field in a Room

a. Computer Aided Design Based on Geometrical Acoustics

Investigation of the design of the room shape by geometrical drawing
described in Section 8.2C is now carried out in three-dimensional space,
mathematically, by means of a digital computer. There are two methods; one is called 'Ray-tracing' which generates many sound rays from a
point source with equal solid angular spacing and traces the propagation path and reflections of each ray. The other is called the 'Image
method' which calculates the positions of mirror images of a source
behind reflecting surfaces, produces a drawing of sound rays by connecting the images and a receiver, and also, from the length of the sound
rays, determines the impulse response approximately at the receiver. In
the 'Ray-tracing' method, although it is convenient to show the distribution and density of the sound rays arriving at the seating area in time
sequence (Fig. 8.16(a), Krokstad et al. 1983), when the paths are
extended in time the distance between sound rays is extended so that
the probability of incidence at the receiver becomes small. This has
significance in determining the intensity at the receiver which depends
on the number of rays arriving in a defined region around the receiver.

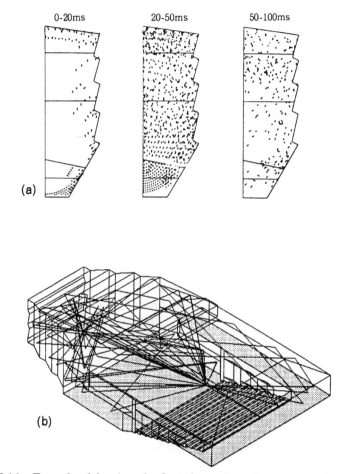

Fig. 8.16. Example of drawing of reflected sound rays by computer-simulation: (a) sound distribution over seating area for delay intervals by 'Ray tracing'; and (b) reflecting sound rays between source and receiver by 'Image method'.

In the 'Image method' as the order of reflections become higher the number of images becomes too large to deal with. Therefore, it is appropriate to investigate the configuration of lower order early reflections as shown in Fig. 8.16(b).

In both methods, the inner surface of the room is approximated by many flat planes. Although the approximation of the room shape improves with increasing number of planes, the errors increase because there are insufficient reflections from the planes whose dimensions are small compared with the wavelength. Moreover, the sound reflection coefficients must vary with incident angle but this variation is so difficult to define that the effect is neglected, hence the reflection coefficients are derived from the sound absorption coefficients obtained in the reverberation chamber. Consequently, it is rather difficult to give an indication of just how good the approximation of the sound field, obtained by the computer simulation, is for the room. It may, however, be an effective method of examining the room shape at an early stage in the architectural design. Recently an approximate method applying wave theory has been investigated (Sekiguchi et al. 1985).

b.   Sound Field Analysis Using Wave Theory
The analysis of room acoustics by wave theory is described in Chap. 3 but is limited to the simple case. However, due to the growth in computer technology and through the development of solutions to the wave equation based on integral equation analysis of large spaces, using the 'finite element method' or 'the boundary integral equation' (Sakurai 1987; Terai & Kawai 1990), we are now in a position to apply such mathematical techniques to the practical design of room acoustics.

B.   Acoustic Model Analysis
The changing of boundary conditions is so easy in computer simulation that it is a useful method of investigating room shapes at an early phase of design. At the detailed design stage however, acoustic measurements using a scale model are recommended to determine the shape and material for interior design. Historically many methods have been used in model studies which relate to the scale ratio.

a.   Ripple Tank Method (scale about 1 / 50)
In place of sound, ripples on a shallow water basin are used; the wavelength range to be handled is rather narrow to serve as an analogue of the sound wave and only the wave motion in two dimensions can be seen. Three-dimensional space can not be studied by this method; therefore, it is not used.

b.   Light Ray Method (scale 1 / 50–1 / 200)
Instead of sound, light rays are an effective means of reducing the problems encountered in the geometrical drawing of a complicated

shape. This method is often used to examine reflections in two dimensions and to investigate sound intensity distribution (using luminous intensity) in three-dimensional space (see Lit. A1). Although confined to geometrical acoustics new detailed investigations have been reported recently (Pinnington *et al.* 1993).

c. *Ultrasonic Wave Method*

Using a 1/30–1/8 scale model in which a spark pulse or a small speaker system generates a sound whose wavelength is of the same scale, impulse response, sound pressure distribution, echoes and reverberant-decay can be measured using small microphones. Applying this technique it is possible to investigate not only room shapes but materials for the room boundaries. To make a wavelength $1/n$ of the original means that the frequency must be n times larger than the original, i.e. in the supersonic range. Recently, measuring instruments in that frequency range have become sufficiently well developed.

The materials for the model are obtained by looking for other materials with an absorption coefficient appropriate to the scale frequency by measurements in a scale reverberation chamber, they are, of course, different from those building materials used in the actual room. Resonant absorbers may be designed in the normal way; porous absorbers tend to have a higher density and window panes can be simulated with thin panels made from aluminium and so on.

One major problem is that the attenuation coefficient m in eqn (3.31), due to air absorption, becomes very large in the ultrasonic range. Although the measurements are generally used for the investigation of room shape, even ignoring the above effect, the air absorption coefficient m must be n times larger in the $1/n$ scale model. Air absorption is due to both molecules of oxygen O_2 and moisture H_2O. However, since no absorption occurs in the absence of either oxygen or moisture, it seems reasonable to apply a method using either nitrogen or dry air. So far a method using dry air whose relative humidity is 2–3% has been used, although the effect on the model materials and instruments is still of concern (Spandök *et al.* 1967). But, by using nitrogen quite a good approximation to the air absorption is obtained in a 1/10 scale model though there is a possible risk of oxygen shortage for operators (Ishii & Tachibana 1974). Therefore, if these problems are solved, the sound field can be realised in a 1/10 model both in the frequency and time domain.

Fig. 8.17. Bunkamura Orchard Hall (2000 seats Tokyo, 1989): (a) 1/10 experimental scale model; and (b) finished hall.

Then, by using small microphones in both ears of a 1/10-scale dummy head, the impulse responses are measured in the model and multiplied by 10 in time scale in order to obtain the equivalent responses in the real room, so that more precise binaural auditory tests can be performed by convoluting dry music recorded in an anechoic chamber, with both impulse responses, using a computer (Els & Blauert 1986). Figure 8.17 shows an example of a real concert hall and the acoustic model on which it was based.

When the model scale is smaller than 1/20 useful information can still be obtained by objective testing such as observing the echo time pattern, for obtaining a uniform sound distribution and smooth decay curves at any position in the room (Barron & Chiney 1979). It may also be possible to theoretically correct the effect of air absorption using a computer.

8.5 PRACTICAL EXAMPLES OF ACOUSTIC DESIGN OF ROOMS

Some examples which present acoustically-interesting problems have been selected from the field of architecture and building.

A. School Classroom

When the number of students is less than 100, a rectangular room shape is acceptable, bearing in mind the three-dimensional proportions (see Section 8.2A,a). If the number is greater than 100 or 150 say, the room section in Fig. 8.18 is preferred. As this figure shows, if the first reflected sound is used properly, no sound-reinforcing system is necessary since the audience is provided with sufficient speech intelligibility so long as the background noise is low and there is a slightly longer reverberation time. However, when an audio-visual facility is required, or a sound reinforcement system is used with rather high background

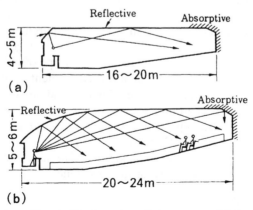

Fig. 8.18. Design of longitudinal section of class rooms: (a) for 150–300 seats; and (b) for 300–500 seats.

noise level, then it would be preferable to apply some absorptive treatment to the rear wall.

B. Gymnasium

Since a gymnasium has usually a large volume with relatively small seating area, the reverberation time tends to be very long and yet the space is frequently used as a multi-purpose hall, thus, it is usually difficult to provide satisfactory acoustics. Moreover, the use of an inappropriately designed electro-sound system adds to the problem as speech intelligibility may become considerably worsened due to the overlapping effect of delayed sound from distributed loudspeakers. Since the installation of a sound reinforcement system is indispensable in a room of large volume, the system design should be carried out according to the recommendation in Chap. 9. At the architectural design stage sufficient absorption should be provided to make the reverberation time as short as possible. For example, resonance absorption based on a slotted wainscotting and absorbent ceiling with glass fibre or rock wool are effective. Since the floor surface is always reflective, the ceiling and other surfaces can not have too much absorption. At the same time, the room plan and section should be closely examined to avoid any possible defects which could arise from parallel walls or domed ceiling and also from flutter echoes as shown in Fig. 8.3.

C. Theatre

There is a wide range of theatre design possible, depending not only on the type of play or drama it is intended to produce, but also on the style of production and direction. An overriding influence tends to be the priority given to visual rather than acoustic requirements. Therefore, the seating area is limited in distance from the stage and is often extended in a fan shape (Fig. 8.10), so that the shape of walls and ceiling must be treated as an essential acoustic component. Although actors require the natural voice to be intelligible and an electro-acoustic system is used for background sound, because these may be musical performances, it is also important that the reverberation time is chosen from the middle of C and D in Fig. 3.21 in Chap. 3. As regards the electro-acoustic system, the loudspeaker installation should be such that the audience is not made aware of their existence.

D. Concert Hall

This is a hall whose main objective is the performance of music. Some plans and sections of historically well-known halls are shown chronologically in Figs 8.19 and 8.20, respectively.

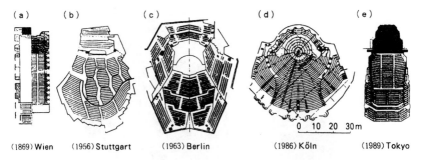

(a)	(b)	(c)	(d)	(e)
(1869) Wien	(1956) Stuttgart	(1963) Berlin	(1986) Kőln	(1989) Tokyo

0 10 20 30m

Fig. 8.19. Examples of concert-hall plans.

Part (a) in Figs 8.19, 8.20 and Fig. 8.21 shows a representative hall built in the 19th century which, because of its rectangular shape, is referred to as a 'shoebox', which has a rich sonority for many people. This basic design has been adopted all over the world; the one shown in Figs 8.17 and 8.19(e) is intended to be a descendant of it. In contrast to its 'end stage' an 'arena stage' is possible, as shown in Fig. 8.19(c). This is a descendant of the classic amphitheater in Greece; Fig. 8.19(d) shows a more faithful version of it. As for the directivity of musical instruments, the acoustic quality in the seating area must be changed according to its orientation with respect to the stage. Recently, halls of this type have been built throughout the world and may have been influenced by a desire for the performance to have visual as well as musical impact.

Note the longitudinal sections in Fig. 8.20. At the start of 'modern architectural acoustics' in 1900, a parabolic ceiling as in Fig. 8.20(c) was considered desirable as a means of effectively collecting sound from the

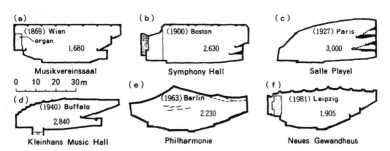

Fig. 8.20. History of longitudinal sections of concert halls, each number showing seating capacity.

Fig. 8.21. Grosser Musikvereinssaal Vienna.

stage and sending it to the audience but it creates problems by gathering the audience noise and concentrating it back on the stage.

In the next example (d) it was decided that acoustic quality could be improved by introducing many more reflections from surfaces divided into small diffusing elements rather than reflections from a larger continuous shallower concave surface to improve natural brilliance. The room shape of figure (e) was investigated by 1/8-scale acoustic model where reflecting panels, called 'clouds', were suspended above the stage where the ceiling became too high to reflect the stage sound with appropriate time delay. In the photograph (Fig. 8.22), we can see the ceiling reflectors and also the seating area which is divided into blocks like a terraced field. This is referred to as 'vineyard' seating intended to supply lateral reflections from the terrace walls which would otherwise be in short supply, caused by the rather wide plan as seen in Fig. 8.19(c) (Cremer, Lit. B27).

As regards Fig. 8.20(f), it would appear that the ceiling section is the successor to that in (d) and that the seating arrangement follows that in (e).

Now, as an important page of history, we must not forget the 'New York Philharmonic Hall' in the Lincoln Centre, shown in Fig. 8.23, which was completed in 1962, a year which also saw the publication of the well-known book by Beranek (Lit. A4). After several modifications, all of which did nothing to enhance its reputation, the Hall disappeared and was replaced by a new 'Avery Fisher Hall' of shoebox-type in 1976. During its short life, researchers were excited at discovering the reason

Fig. 8.22. Neue Philharmonie Berlin.

for the failure and, as a result of experiments, great strides were made in room acoustics (Lit. A11). Recently, computer simulation and acoustic model study have shown marked progress. However, exact prediction of room acoustics is still not easy and the designing of acoustic quality is a long way from becoming a scientific approach to the art of musical performance.

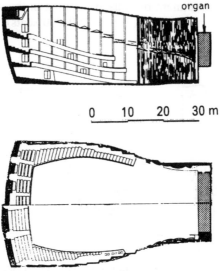

Fig. 8.23. New York Philharmonic Hall (1962–1975).

E. Multi-Purpose Hall

Public halls like civic centre auditoria and most commercial rental halls are for multi-purpose use so that the reverberation time has to be adequate for both music and speech, but priority must be given to the requirements of the most frequent performance, although, unfortunately, it is not easy to anticipate the true requirements. Once there was an inclination towards shorter reverberation times for the purpose of broadcasting, but nowadays almost all those in Japan aim at concert hall acoustics. This seems to be rather a quirk of fashion as concerts, especially in the provinces, are rare.

The style of auditorium should meet the requirements of the social activity in the locality in which it is situated. Although, in Japan, most multi-purpose halls have a stage for drama and fixed seats for the audience, and a concert stage with movable reflecting panel for an orchestra shell (Figs. 9.2, 9.3 in Chap. 9). In Europe there is usually a fixed concert stage, an organ and movable seats on a flat floor for the purpose of banquets and balls, etc. Figure 8.24 shows a European example which has 1400 seats for concerts.

As for variable reverberation time facilities, there are some problems as described in Section 8.3A, but, without any electronic hardware, the difference between stage with orchestra shell and drama stage having removed the reflecting panels gives about a 20–30% variation with highly absorptive treatment of walls and ceiling in the stage area. When the auditorium is not so large, (up to 500–600 seats), a curtain 2–3 m

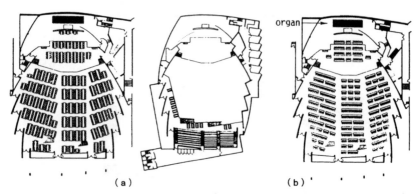

Fig. 8.24. Variable seating in Beethoven Halle in Bonn (seating capacity 1407): (a) banquette style for 960 seats; and (b) parliamentary style for 492 seats.

high above the floor improves speech intelligibility even if the variation in reverberation time is small.

Additionally, active control by electro-acoustic devices would be useful for changing the acoustic conditions of a hall to suit any performance.

PROBLEMS 8

1 When designing the shape of a room what is the fundamental strategy from the acoustical point of view?
2 Enumerate the important acoustical points starting from the basic design of a concert hall, giving the sequence.
3 When designing a multi-purpose hall, how do the acoustical requirements differ from a concert hall?
4 What acoustical problems should be given special consideration in the architectural design of the following rooms? (1) Conference room (about 40 persons); (2) small auditorium (approximately 500 seats); (3) Banqueting room (about 200 persons); (4) Gymnasium in a primary school; (5) Drawing office in a factory; (6) Large office (about 30 persons).

Chapter 9

ELECTRO-ACOUSTIC SYSTEM

Now we have reached the stage where there is no building type which does not possess an electro-acoustic system. Also, in the open air, the electro-acoustic system plays an important role as an information service in the outdoor environment. An architectural or environmental planner must, therefore, have a basic knowledge of that system sufficient to enable him to cooperate with an audio engineer. In this chapter we shall discuss several items which are closely related to the basic scheme for both the architecture and the environment, especially the sound reinforcement system which is the most important equipment as far as planning the electro-sound is concerned.

9.1   FUNCTIONS AND AIM OF ELECTRO-ACOUSTIC SYSTEMS

a.   Sound Reinforcement System

The system consists of a microphone, amplifier and a loudspeaker usually situated in the same acoustic environment. The microphone receives speech or music signals and the loudspeaker radiates the amplified sound. The system is useful for obtaining high articulation and intelligibility by raising the loudness when the sound pressure level of the original signal is insufficient or the SN ratio is too low due to background noise. The term SR (Sound Reinforcement) implies powerful radiation at high level, especially for modern music, and the term PA (Public Address) implies amplified speech, though there is no strict dividing line.

A major problem is that of 'howling'. This is an acoustic phenomenon which totally swamps the ability to hear due to an oscillatory sound caused by feedback which is linked with the radiated sound from the loudspeaker to the microphone. How to control it and still amplify without oscillation up to the required sound level is the most important problem, not only for the electro-acoustic but also the room acoustic design.

b. Sound Reproducing System

The system has additional means of reproducing recorded tape or discs, but the original sources are in a different space from the listeners as with radio, or cable transmission or sound effects in a drama theatre or cinema. There is no 'howling' so that it is much easier to obtain good quality with appropriate volume. In a public space, however, the sound system is seldom of high quality for the transmission of information and sometimes, regrettably, even gives rise to environmental pollution.

c. Sound Recording System

This system records the sound signals of not only musical performance but lectures and conference presentations. It is most important that the recording apparatus is carefully selected since there is a wide range of sophistication from a simple cassette recorder to a professional recorder for manufacturing commercial recordings.

d. Auxiliary Facility

There are several pieces of equipment attached to the sound reinforcement and reproducing systems with facilities for actively controlling the sound field. The time delay devices and reverberation equipment owe much to the rapid development of digital electronics. Table 9.1 shows the important electro-acoustic equipment categorised according to application, but it would be useful to look at it from the point of view of architectural design in the next section.

9.2 REINFORCEMENT SYSTEMS AND ARCHITECTURAL DESIGN

A. Layout of Loudspeakers

Generally the most important problem is planning the layout of the loudspeakers. The aims are as follows:

(1) uniform distribution of sufficient loudness for all listeners;
(2) natural directional perception of the original source, without giving the impression of sound coming from the existing loudspeakers.

Table 9.1
Principal Apparatuses for Electro-Acoustic System

Instruments	Purpose	Reinforcement system			Reproducing system		Recording system	
		Lecture	Conference	Music	Announcement	Effect Sound	Music	Speech
Input system	Microphones	○	○	○	○		○	○
	Wireless microphones	○	○	○				○
	Mic. hydraulic suspension for jack	○		○			○	
	3 point (hanger) of mic.			△				
	Record players	○	○	○	○	○	○	○
	Tape recorders	○	○	○	○	○	○	○
Control system	Mixing console	○	○	○	○	○	○	○
	Time-delay machines	○		○	△	○	△	
	Reverb. machines			○		○	○	
	Sound image control	△	△	△		○		
	Effects console					○		
	Tape recorders	○	○	○	○	○	○	○
Output system (loudspeakers & amplifiers)	Audience area Centralized system	○	△	○	△			
	Distribution system	△	○		○	○		
	On the stage for Music			○				
	Fold back	○		○				
	Lobby, Foyer	○	○	○	○	○		
	Monitor in control room	○	○	○	○	○	○	○
Simultaneous interpretation system		○	○					○

○ : necessary;   △ : need to consider.

In addition, it is important to control the accompanying echo and howling. Depending on the purpose and taking into account the shape, size and reverberation time of the room, two system layouts are used.

a. Centralised System

One or two loudspeaker systems having proper directivity are situated as close to the original source as possible. This arrangement is commonly used in auditoria, lecture halls and gymnasiums, etc. Its merits are as follows:

(1) good localisation of the source is easy to obtain for the listeners;
(2) prevention of echo is fairly simply achieved by controlling the directivity so that the direct sound is not too incident on ceiling or walls but only on the audience and by sound absorptive treatment on the rear wall;
(3) speech intelligibility can be raised by the amplified direct sound, making the virtual reverberation time short by means of the proper loudspeaker arrangement described above;
(4) the likelihood of howling can be more or less totally overcome by considering both the directivities of the microphone and loudspeakers, and selecting their position accordingly; in practice attention should be given to the microphone position.

b. Distribution System

When the same signal is fed to two loudspeakers some distance from each other, a listener sitting equidistant from the two loudspeakers will perceive a sound image which appears to be at the midpoint between them. But, if the distances are different, the sound image appears to be situated at the nearest loudspeaker, by the 'law of the first wave front' (see Chap. 1, Section 1.12), and the other loudspeaker seems to be silent. When the difference of arrival time is in the range of several to slightly more than 20 ms, colouration is caused by phase interference more than 30–50 ms and echos will occur (Chap. 3, Fig. 3.30). As shown in Fig. 9.1, when the same signal is fed to many distributed loudspeakers, the sound pressure distribution of continuous noise becomes uniform in the steady state. However, if the signal is meaningful sound such as speech or music, many different time delay of arriving signals will interfere with each other in a complicated way and reduce articulation. Sometimes listeners cannot understand anything at all. Therefore the indispensable fundamental design parameters in the distributed loudspeaker system are as follows:

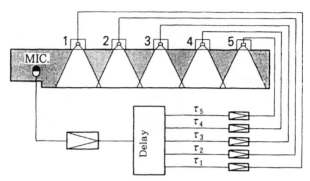

Fig. 9.1. Distributed loudspeakers with a time-delay system for controlling of the localisation of a sound source.

(1)   The service area of each loudspeaker must be limited in terms of its directivity, and the sound level should be controlled in order not to disturb adjacent areas. The articulation will be raised by this procedure.

(2)   The proper time delay should be given to each loudspeaker by using an electronic delay as shown in Fig. 9.1, so each listener receives sound from the nearest loudspeaker a few seconds after the arrival of the direct sound from the original source.

This localises the sound image in the original source direction by the 'law of the first wave front', and gives the listener good directional perception of high quality.

c.   Combination of Centralised and Distribution Systems

In practice the design layout of the loudspeaker system depends on the size and shape of the room as well as the specific purpose for which it is intended. Generally, a centralised system is recommended with the system as a basic principle and distributed loudspeakers added at spots where there is a poor supply of sound. In this case, also, deliberate consideration needs to be given to the control of the defects in the distribution system described above.

The example shown in Fig. 9.2 has a main loudspeaker 'Center Sp' at the centre of the proscenium intended to amplify the sound of the original sources on the stage for the benefit of the whole audience, and additional loudspeakers are distributed at dark spots, i.e. 'Front Sp' at the front of the stage for the front seats, and 'Foldback Sp' on the stage

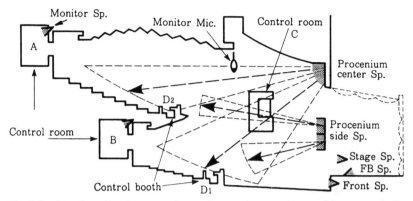

Fig. 9.2. Loudspeaker layout and sound control rooms in a multi-purpose hall.

for folding back to the performers. In Fig. 9.3, the proscenium side speakers, indicated by 'Side Sp' are used not only to reproduce stereo music, but also to control the sound image of 'Center Sp', to shift it down to a lower position with the cooperation of the 'Front Sp's'.

For sound effects in drama and cinema, many loudspeakers may be distributed in the walls and ceiling or floor. In this case, it is necessary to have a skilled operator to control the effects console. Therefore, deliberate planning is required, taking into account the purpose, frequency of usage and technical ability of the operator employed by the hall.

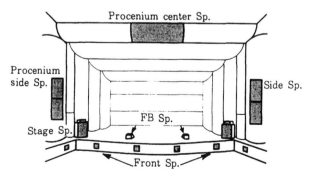

Fig. 9.3. Loudspeaker layout around the stage in an auditorium.

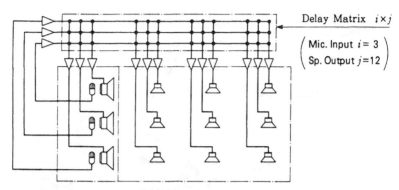

Fig. 9.4. Basic principle of 'delta stereophony' for good localisation of the distributed sound sources (G. Steinke 1983).

d. Distribution System for Sound Field Control

The sound field control includes localisation of the sound images and the adding of reflections and reverberation, etc.

(1) *Control of localisation of the sound images*: In order to localise the sound images at the positions of the original sound sources, the arrival time and sound level of each signal from many loudspeakers should be controlled at each listening point. The situation with a single original source on the stage has been covered in the above. If there are many original sources on a wide stage, a 'Delta sterephony system' is applicable, though it is complicated. The basic principle is shown in Fig. 9.4. The stage sound is received by i distributed microphones and fed to j distributed loudspeakers through an $(i \times j)$ matrix circuit consisting of delays and level controllers, with which the sound images are controlled, so that they are localised at the microphone positions. In order to amplify the direct sounds i of the j, loudspeakers are situated close to the microphones. Also in this case, it is important to realise the indispensable fundamentals, (1) of Section b, described above. When the ceiling is too high the loudspeakers may be better installed in chairs or on the floor.

(2) *Enhancement of sound reflection and reverberation*: In order to improve the sound field in a room, the early sound reflection is sometimes reinforced at the seats where there is a shortage of the latter by an electro-acoustic device, as shown in Fig. 9.5. This device is called an 'active reflector' since the sound pressure received by a microphone situated on the wall surface is amplified and emitted from a loudspeaker

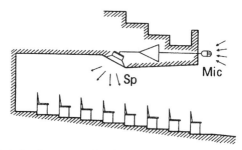

Fig. 9.5. Reinforcing a sound reflection by an electro-acoustic system.

on the wall. By combining many such devices, prolongation of the reverberation time has been attempted. The most difficult problem is to suppress the howling, and many systems for resolving it have been developed. The longest established successful system is in the Royal Festival Hall in London (1964), with more than 150 channels with microphones, each limited within a very narrow frequency band by a Helmholtz resonator. Normal modes of room vibration are enhanced, hence the system is called 'assisted resonance'. Later, systems which have wider frequency bands, and which combine the electronic reverb-machine or a signal-processing device for adding many sound reflec-tions, have appeared. All of them have many distributed loudspeakers and their layout plays a very important role (Berkhout 1988).

B. Planning of Sound Control Rooms
All electro-acoustic equipment except the loudspeakers is installed in a sound control room in which the whole system is operated in such a way as to give full play of its functions. The basic guidelines for planning this room are as follows:

(1)   an extensive view of the whole audience, including stage, and good contact with the stage;
(2)   the possibility of monitoring the sound in the audience area as realistically as possible.

a. *Layout and Design of Sound Control Room*
In Fig. 9.2, 4 positions of the sound control room are shown. Position A in the figure satisfies the condition (1) but the distance to the stage is too large. Position B is best though the balcony seats are out of view. Position C is prefered, especially in public halls, because it is easy to

manage the stage preparation with a small number of staff through close contact with the stage. 10–15 m² of floor area is needed for a mixing console and accompanying instruments and, additionally, 5–10 m² for an annex room.

The best position for the window is in front of the operator's seat and of sufficient size to give a good view of the stage floor and suspended microphones and should have an openable sash and curtain. The interior must be treated with absorbent, both for sound and light, in order to avoid leakage to the audience area, and the room should have an independent air-conditioning system. Positions D1 and D2 in Fig. 9.2 are ideal for satisfying condition (2), since these are representative of what the audience receives, though several of the best seats are missing.

According to the character and use of the hall and after studying the operation system, the position of control room should be selected at A, B, or C. Positions D1 or D2 are also possible for auxiliary use.

b. Monitoring System in the Control Room
All control work, generally, should have a perfect real-time monitoring system which gives an instant response to a control operation in order to feed back to the next operation. However, a monitoring system which is conscious of the feedback loop is rare. Apart from positions D1 or D2 inside the auditorium, a monitor system which gives virtual reality for the operator is the most important instrument, playing the role of nerve centre. Its indispensable functions are as follows:

(1)   the sound pressure level (dBA) value at the representative audience seat should be indicated on the main part of the mixing console;

(2)   the sound indicated above should be heard with a binaural or stereo system.

An indicator is required to cover a wide range from 50–100 dBA with no switching and a binaural listening system is desirable for virtual reality. The monitor microphone, also called an air-monitor, may be hung from the lighting bridge on the ceiling and close to the stage in the directional zone of the main loudspeaker system in the centre of the proscenium arch. The best position would be slightly off the centre line of the hall in order not to interfere with the spotlight on the stage or offend the eye of the audience.

Ideally, the system should be able to monitor all sound not only that from the loudspeakers, and indicate to the sound operator the sound pressure level in the audience area. For this purpose the directivity of the monitor microphone might be useful.

c. Annex Rooms

It is desirable that the electro-acoustic hardware such as amplifiers, etc., is installed in a separate room or enclosed by a glass screen for observation so as to isolate the cooling fan noise. It is also a good idea to enclose the control cubicle with a glass wall with a good view from the control console. The storeroom for microphones, cables, microphone stands, recording tapes, etc., depending on the scale of the equipment, should be located close to the control room. It is important that the room containing the microphones and recording tapes is air-conditioned as they can be damaged by dust and moisture.

C. Installation of Microphones and Loudspeakers

a. Wiring and Microphone Arrangement

The microphone elevator on the stage should be planned in cooperation with the architect so that the mechanism does not foul any structural component such as a beam and should have a clearance of $2 \cdot 6$ m below the stage floor to allow for a hydraulic jack. A three-point hanging microphone has three winches attached to the ceiling so that it can be easily moved to any position within a triangular area limited by the three locating points of the winches.

There should be many microphone sockets set not only in the stage but also in the floor, wainscot, in the ceiling and in the audience area for performances which require amplification of sounds which occur there. After collecting the microphone inputs on a socket panel at the side of the stage, they are fed to an input board in the control room. Their cables should be laid out so they do not run close to power lines and loudspeaker cables and are shielded from stray electromagnetic fields in order to avoid induced signals, particularly from the lighting controller.

b. Loudspeaker Arrangement

The loudspeaker system is generally installed in a large cabinet measuring between several tens of centimetres to more than one metre and weighing several tens of kilograms. When it is hung from the ceiling, proscenium, etc., it is important that the loudspeaker is separated from its surroundings and supported by means of a vibration isolating rubber suspension system (Fig. 9.6).

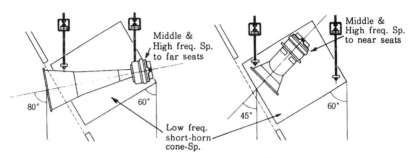

Fig. 9.6.   Suspending the proscenium loudspeakers.

The loudspeaker should be fully exposed to the auditorium so as not to impair the sound quality. If, for aesthetic reasons, it is necessary to hide it in the ceiling or walls, the front face should be as open as possible and covered with a sound transparent coarse cloth and should not be obstructed with either a perforated board or dense grill. Moreover, for ease of maintenance, the loudspeaker should be constructed so that it can be lowered to the floor or accessible from a catwalk, etc.

9.3   PREVENTION OF HOWLING

'Howling' should not occur under any conditions. In the feedback loop in Fig. 9.7 howling will occur when the loop gain exceeds 1, i.e. when the sound pressure received from the loudspeaker at the microphone becomes greater than the initial sound pressure received by the microphone. Therefore, the loop gain should be kept as low as possible in order to obtain stable operation.

a.   Reduction of Direct Sound
The direct sound level L_d from the loudspeaker (Sp) to the microphone (Mic), shown in Fig. 9.7, should be reduced. In order to satisfy this:

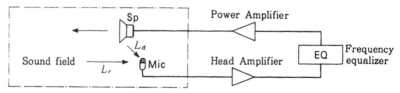

Fig. 9.7.   Feedback loop of a sound reinforcement system.

(1) Sp and Mic should be separated by a distance from each other, paying attention to the directional perception of the audience;
(2) a barrier such as a wing wall is useful;
(3) the microphone should be outside the area covered by the loudspeaker's directivity;
(4) a unidirectional microphone should be used.

b. Reduction of Reflected and Diffused Sound

The reflected and diffused sound level L_r to Mic, Fig. 9.7, should be reduced. For this purpose:

(1) the direct sound from the loudspeaker should be directed to the audience area or other absorptive surfaces, and not to the reflective walls or ceiling;
(2) the total absorption in the room should be increased, resulting in a shorter reverberation time;
(3) the surfaces surrounding the microphone, especially the surface covered by the microphone's directivity, should be absorptive, i.e. the stage wall should be treated with sound absorbent.

c. Flattening of Frequency Characteristics

The total frequency response of the feedback loop should be flat. If there is a peak, oscillations will occur at that frequency. Therefore, all instruments such as microphones and loudspeakers, etc., should be of high grade and with flat frequency responses. Standing waves in the room should be eliminated using sound absorptive treatment. Furthermore, a frequency equaliser (EQ), in Fig. 9.7, is useful for obtaining flat frequency characteristics in the loop gain.

d. Receiving of High Signal Level

The direct sound of the original source should be received at high sound pressure level. For this purpose the microphone should be as close as possible to the source. For instance, it is very useful to attach a small microphone to the speaker's lapel.

9.4 ELECTRO-ACOUSTIC EQUIPMENT

The instruments which are frequently used are listed in Table 9.1 according to their purpose. Basically, the received sound signals from microphones and recordings are fed into the input system, after mixing

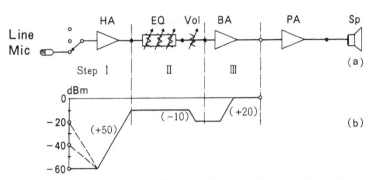

Fig. 9.8. (a) Basic circuit; and (b) level diagram of a sound reinforcement system.

and amplifying to the proper level, then sent to the output system which supplies enough power to the loudspeakers for sound radiation. An outline of the equipment is described below.

A. Basic Construction of Reinforcement Systems

A diagram of a simple reinforcement system is shown in Fig. 9.8: (a) is a block diagram of the circuit of the system; and (b) shows the level diagram of its performance. The reference value of 0 dB is the voltage of $0·775$ V which supplies an electric power of 1 $mW = 1/1000$ W to a circuit of 600 Ω impedance. Generally, since line input levels from records, etc, are higher than microphones, a step attenuator and phase selector is set up (Step I in Fig. 9.8) and Head Amplifier (HA) amplifies the signal. The EQ (Step II) controls sound quality of the signal and the attenuator or fader (Vol) controls the sound volume from it. The Boost amplifier or Buffer amplifier (BA) (Step III) amplifies the signal to the standard input level of the Power Amplifier (PA). The PA sends the signal to the loudspeaker (Sp) with sufficient electric power to drive it and radiate the sound, with impedance matching between the output of PA and the input of the loudspeaker. Actually, Steps I, II and III are constructed compactly into one 'input-module' (Fig. 9.9) with a number of microphone and record channels placed in a row for creating a mixing console with which the signals are selected, mixed and controlled by the operator.

Fig. 9.9. Example of an input module of a sound mixing console.

B. Sound Control Equipment

Through a matrix circuit shown in Fig. 9.10, which receives a number of input channels i and mixes into j group channels, the mixed signals are controlled for sound quality and volume purposes with 'group-modules' similar to Fig. 9.9. An output signal from the group-module is fed to a power amplifier which drives a loudspeaker system. Recently, since the number of channels both of input and output are increased, by using a $j \times k$ matrix circuit j output signals are often rearranged into k 'program-modules' for connecting the outputs to the power amplifiers.

The associated delay-system or reverb-machine, etc., called 'effector', generally receives the signal from a group-module and feeds back to the same group-module after processing it. The attenuator of the group-module is called a 'master-fader' and plays an essential role in sound control. Additionally, the mixing console has a 'talkback-module' for audience announcement, a 'phones-module' which, with headphones, enables an arbitrary channel to be selected and monitored, and also VU meters which indicate the working level of every channel.

Many mixing-consoles are manufactured not for the control of a sound system situated in a control room separated from the sound fields of the auditorium, but for field-mixing of popular music performances.

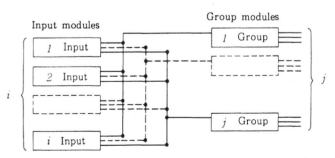

Fig. 9.10. Matrix circuit for grouping j channels from i input channels.

Therefore, if it is used in the control room, separated from the auditorium, then a monitor system, as described above, needs to be consciously designed.

The graphic equaliser (GEQ) is used to comprehensively control the transmission-frequency characteristics of each loudspeaker channel, including the sound field in the room, by changing the gain of each 1/3 octave band placed in close proximity to each other's channel.

As mentioned above, the number of operating switches and variety of control knobs becomes very large, since each one of more than 20–30 modules has several tens of them arranged in a line in an operating panel of the control console. The control console, therefore, should be designed for ease of operation and to simplify and automate it so that it is well within the capabilities of the operator. It is desirable that, for example, there is a semi-transparent cover for most of the control switches and knobs except those such as faders, which are frequently used. Moreover, there should be illuminated spots on the graphically-displayed circuit to prevent mistakes in operation and make the system user friendly. Fig. 9.11 is an example of a well-designed operating panel of a mixing console for a sound control room in a public auditorium designed to seat 1200. Recently, automatic control facilities, made possible by the development of digital technology, have become avail-

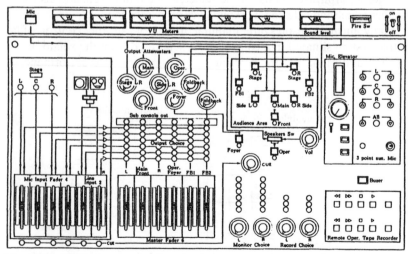

Fig. 9.11.   Example of a graphically-displayed control panel of a sound mixing console for a multipurpose hall.

able, complete with memory of the use pattern determined by the program.

C. Equipment for Input and Output Systems

a. Microphone

The construction of three of the most popular types of microphone are illustrated in Figs 9.12–9.14, and their features shown in Table 9.2. A single stereo condenser microphone is also available for music. Until now dynamic microphones and, more recently, electret condenser microphones, have been the most popular and are inexpensive. However,

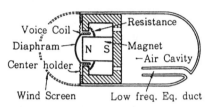

Fig. 9.12. Section of a dynamic-microphone.

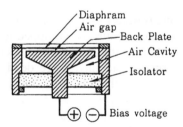

Fig. 9.13. Section of a condenser-microphone.

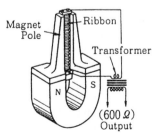

Fig. 9.14. Construction of a velocity-microphone.

Table 9.2

Microphones—their Types and Features

Types and directional characteristics	Features
Dynamic microphones (moving coil type) uni- and omni-directional	Strong construction easy operation with stable performance; various styles for many purposes; also varied ability of performance.
Condenser microphones uni- and omni-directional (also variable)	Flat frequency characteristics; needs of bias voltage and installation of a head amplifier; high output level; sensitive to moisture; simple usage for electret type with a dry cell; very popular because of small size and low pric
Velocity microphone (ribbon type) bidirectional (figure of eight)	Favourite sound quality for human voice and music; large in size and weight; low-output level; low-frequency enhancement as microphone approached. Easily affected by air flow, studio use only.

both their price and characteristics are wide-ranging so it is important to obtain expert opinion in order to make a sensible choice.

b.   Wireless Microphone

The wireless microphone is widely used as it is free to move without any restriction. The special receiver must be equipped for receiving VHF or UHF, which is transmitted by the microphone. General problems are tone quality and performance stability. Since dead spots occur due to standing waves in the room, the 'diversity receiving system', which automatically selects the stronger signal from double antennae, is recommended. Since again the quality and price vary widely, choice needs to be made with great care.

c.   Record Player

The 45–$33\frac{1}{3}$ rev./min disks which have been used until recently are being rapidly replaced by compact disk (CD). In the near future, reproduction of video-disks might be required.

d.   Tape Recorder

The compact-cassette recorder is commonly used; however, the open-reel tape recorder is also employed because of its convenience for editing and cueing. Nowadays, the digital audio tape (DAT) recorder developed from digital technology is much in favour because of its high

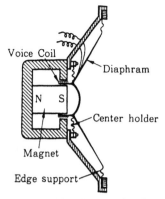

Fig. 9.15. Section of a cone loudspeaker.

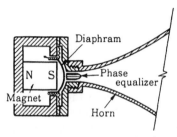

Fig. 9.16. Section of a horn loudspeaker.

quality. On the other hand, the recordable-erasable CD is expected to come into general use. The all electro-sound systems should always have the capability of accepting the latest equipment as part of the overall system.

e. Loudspeaker

Currently, cone- and horn-type loudspeakers, shown in Figs. 9.15 and 9.16, are widely used. The cone loudspeaker radiates directly from a diaphragm made of paper or plastic. The efficiency is so low, however, that the acoustic power output is about 1% of the electrical input power. The horn loudspeaker consists of a diaphragm made from plastic or light metal and a horn in front of the diaphragm. The efficiency is significantly increased by more than a factor of 10 by the horn as an acoustic transformer. The electrical impedance of both types is as low as a few to tens of ohms.

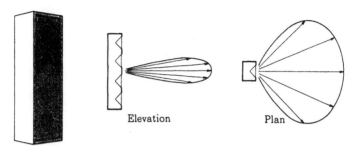

Fig. 9.17. Line (column) speaker and its directivity.

The smaller loudspeakers of a distributed system usually comprise a single- or double-cone of 10–30 cm diameter driven by a high-impedance constant voltage line through transformers and cover the full-frequency range 100–10 000 Hz with electrical power of 3–50 W. The larger loudspeakers of a centralised system usually consist of a multi-way arrangement, i.e. a cone loudspeaker, of 30–45 cm diameter in a cabinet with a short horn for low frequencies up to 200–1000 Hz and one or more horn loudspeakers for higher frequency ranges. They are directly driven by low-impedance lines from the power amplifier output which has a nominal power of more than several hundred watts.

The control of its directivity is achieved by means of the shape of the throat and horn. There are various kinds of loudspeaker systems on the market and choice is possible on the basis of appropriate design data. Where speech is the main requirement, a line-array (column) loud-speaker of several cone loudspeakers, as shown in Fig. 9.17, is frequently used. The directivity does not spread vertically and has the same pattern as a single loudspeaker in the horizontal plane. Therefore, effective radiation to the audience area is obtained without harmful sound radiation to the ceiling which would increase the reverberant sound. Consequently, high intelligibility may be obtained.

For the purpose of PA in the open field, a folded-horn loudspeaker called a 'trumpet-speaker', which has a frequency range of about 200–5000 Hz, is frequently used because it is weatherproof, but there are often problems due to sound quality.

The tone quality of the cone loudspeaker is subjectively pleasing, with a natural soft sound, especially for the human voice. However, greater power is needed in a large space for the reinforcement of modern music, hence the horn loudspeaker has become indispensable because of its high efficiency.

f. Power Amplifier

A power amplifier should have an output with sufficient electrical power and appropriate impedance in the audio-frequency range to match the input of the loudspeaker system. The maximum power output should have sufficient margin so as not to distort peak signals and have a protection circuit to deal with extravagant inputs. Furthermore, the SN ratio, dynamic range, percentage distortion and damping factor (load impedance/internal impedance), etc., are all part of the technical specification. The distortion should be small but the larger the other parameters the better.

The power output has grown over the years and now several hundred watts are available. But, it is desirable to drive a complex system of many loudspeaker units with a multi-amplifier system so that each speaker unit is directly driven by an independent power amplifier with a low impedance line in order to obtain high-quality sound. Since the total power consumption becomes considerable, a cooling fan is indispensable. Do not forget to control the fan noise and to deal with the heat load on the air conditioning system.

9.5   PERFORMANCE TEST OF ELECTRO-ACOUSTIC SYSTEMS

The performance of a first class electro-acoustic system should satisfy the following requirements: (a) high intelligibility of speech; (2) rich and high quality music sound; and (3) safe handling without howling. After the hearing test, including various kinds of short samples of music and speech, several physical measurements are carried out as follows.

A.   Measurement of Maximum Sound Pressure Level

'Pink noise' in the frequency range 63–8000 Hz is played in place of music, or 125–4000 Hz in place of speech from the main loudspeaker system. The long-term stability of the maximum sound pressure level (10–30 min) at the centre of audience area should be measured and should satisfy the recommended values in Table 9.3.

Table 9.3
Recommended Maximum Sound Pressure Levels with
Electro-acoustic Systems dB*

Lecture room	75–80
Conference room or banquet room	80–85
Sports facilities in open field	85–90
Multi-purpose auditorium (popular music)	90–95
Disco (Rock music)	105–110

*Average values: equipment must not distort at a peak of more
than 10 dB higher.

B. Transmission Frequency Characteristics

The measurement described in Chap. 3, Section 3.6.5B is carried out at
the centre of the audience area.

The measured values should be compared with the recommended
ranges in Fig. 9.18. For a monitor loudspeaker system in a small studio
or listening room, flat characteristics are desirable. In a large auditorium, however, it would sound so unnatural that the frequency characteristics would be better controlled to produce natural sounding
music and speech and improved intelligibility obtained by using a
graphic equaliser.

In order to check intelligibility, as an alternative to direct measurement of the 'percentage-articulation' described in Chap. 1, Section
1.14A, measurements of 'STI' or 'RASTI' (see Section 3.6.5C) have
become more common.

C. Sound Pressure Distribution in Steady State

The measurement described in Section 3.6.7A is carried out in the
room. The uniform distribution in the whole audience area might be
ideal, but it is acceptable that measured values fall in the range of 6 dB

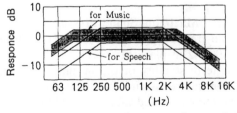

Fig. 9.18. Recommended transmission frequency characteristics in auditoria.

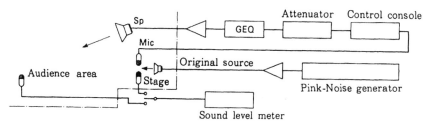

Fig. 9.19. Block diagram for measuring the 'safe amplifying gain' of a sound reinforcement system.

or so. Irregularities of the distribution are liable to be caused by standing waves at low frequencies and by the directivities of loudspeakers at high frequencies. Therefore, it makes sense to control the directivity of loudspeakers at high frequencies.

D.   Safe Amplifying Gain for Reinforcement
In the circuit shown in Fig. 9.7, when the loop gain is set at -6 dB from the howling point (called 'howling margin' $= -6$ dB), the sound pressure level at a representative seat of audience area, referred to the sound pressure level at the microphone, is called the 'safe amplifying gain'. The higher this value the better, but should generally equal -10 dB at least. Though it varies with the directivity of the microphone, etc., the sound level of -10 dB is equivalent to an attenuation with distance of a factor of 3. Therefore, when a man speaks at 30 cm from the microphone, the listener in the seat can hear at a sound level equivalent to the distance of 90 cm from the speaker. This measurement is undertaken after the completion of all other measurements and controls mentioned above. As shown in Fig. 9.19, in place of the original speaker a small loudspeaker radiates pink noise at a distance of 30–50 cm from the stage microphone, at two different sound pressure levels at the stage microphone position and at the audience seat shall be measured.

E.   Remaining Noises
Noises can occur associated with power supply, i.e. hum at low frequencies and random noise from circuit elements at high frequencies. The noise level caused by the loudspeaker system should be lower than the threshold of hearing (Chap. 2, Fig. 2.7) whilst the system is in operation. The highest noise level must be 10 dB lower than the recommended values shown in Table 2.6.

PROBLEMS 9

1 When planning the equipment of an electro-acoustic system in an auditorium, list those items which the architect needs to consider.

2 In planning a public address system for a room, compare the merits and demerits of the centralised system and the distribution system of loudspeakers and describe how to organise both systems.

3 Enumerate all procedures necessary to control 'howling' of a sound reinforcement system.

4 'Difficult to make it howl' is an important ability of a reinforcement system. What should be measured in order to evaluate this?

5 When a mixing console is installed in a control room, separated from an auditorium, what consideration needs to be given to the monitoring system?

Chapter 10

ADDENDA

10.1 WAVE EQUATIONS (Lit. B7, B13, B20, B32, etc.)

A. Bulk Modulus

The changes in pressure when a sound wave travels through the air are, in general, so rapid that heat cannot be exchanged between different volume elements. Consequently, the changes are adiabatic. When air, whose initial pressure and volume are P_0 and V_0 are changed to $(P_0 + p)$ and $(V_0 + \Delta V)$, respectively, due to sound pressure p, the following relationship is obtained:

$$P_0 V_0^\gamma = (P_0 + p)(V_0 + \Delta V)^\gamma$$

$$\therefore \quad 1 + \frac{p}{P_0} = \left(1 + \frac{\Delta V}{V_0}\right)^{-\gamma}$$

where γ is the ratio of specific heats at constant pressure and constant volume. If $V_0/\Delta V$ is very small, then expanding the right-hand side of the above equation and approximating, it follows that:

$$\frac{p}{P_0} = -\gamma \frac{\Delta V}{V_0}$$

$$\therefore \quad p = -\gamma P_0 \frac{\Delta V}{V_0}$$

Putting

$$\kappa = \gamma P_0 \tag{10.1}$$

$$p = -\kappa \frac{\Delta V}{V_0} \tag{10.2}$$

Therefore, sound pressure is proportional to volume change. κ is called the 'bulk modulus of elasticity' or 'volume elasticity'.

B. Plane Wave Equation

Consider a tube of unit cross-sectional area with its axis parallel to the direction of propagation of a plane wave, as shown in Fig. 10.1, where the plane at x is displaced by ξ and the plane at $(x + \delta x)$ is displaced by

$$\xi + \delta \xi = \left(\xi + \left(\frac{\partial \xi}{\partial x} \right) \delta x \right)$$

This means that the original volume $V = \delta x$ contained between the two planes has been increased by

$$\Delta V = \left(\frac{\partial \xi}{\partial x} \right) \delta x$$

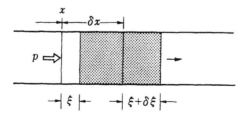

Fig. 10.1. Plane wave propagation.

due to the passage of the sound wave. Thus, the fractional increase in volume becomes

$$\frac{\Delta V}{V} = \frac{\partial \xi}{\partial x}$$

which is the so-called equation of continuity. Substituting this into eqn (10.2) gives

$$p = -\kappa \frac{\partial \xi}{\partial x} \tag{10.3}$$

When the sound pressure p acts on the plane at x, then

$$\left(p + \left(\frac{\partial p}{\partial x} \right) \delta x \right)$$

acts on the plane at $(x + \delta x)$. The differential pressure

$$\left(\frac{\partial p}{\partial x} \right) \delta x$$

sets in motion the mass of air between the two planes. If ρ is the average density of the air, then the mass between the two planes is $(\rho \, \delta x)$. Hence, using Newton's second law, which states force equals mass $\times$ acceleration, we have

$$\rho \, \delta x \frac{\partial^2 \xi}{\partial t^2} = -\frac{\partial p}{\partial x} \cdot \delta x$$

$$\therefore \quad \rho \frac{\partial^2 \xi}{\partial t^2} = -\frac{\partial p}{\partial x} \tag{10.4}$$

This is the equation of motion.

Differentiating both sides of eqn (10.3) with respect to t and eqn (10.4) with respect to x and eliminating ξ,

$$\frac{\partial^2 p}{\partial t^2} = \frac{\kappa}{\rho} \frac{\partial^2 p}{\partial x^2} \tag{10.5a}$$

or

$$\frac{\partial^2 p}{\partial t^2} = c^2 \frac{\partial^2 p}{\partial x^2} \tag{10.5b}$$

where

$$c = \sqrt{\frac{\kappa}{\rho}}$$

This is the wave equation in terms of sound pressure. Similarly, eliminating p, the wave equation, in terms of the displacement ξ, is obtained in the same form. Then, introducing a new function, the velocity potential φ which is defined by eqn (3.2) in Chap. 3,

$$\left.\begin{aligned} \frac{\partial \xi}{\partial t} &= -\frac{\partial \varphi}{\partial x} \\ p &= \rho \frac{\partial \varphi}{\partial t} \end{aligned}\right\} \tag{10.6}$$

and using the fundamental equation eqn (10.3), the following is obtained

$$\frac{\partial^2 \varphi}{\partial t^2} = c^2 \frac{\partial^2 \varphi}{\partial x^2} \tag{10.7}$$

This has exactly the same form as eqn (10.5) for sound pressure.

If the sound wave behaves as a simple harmonic vibration, then the function may be written as $\varphi e^{j\omega t}$ where ω is the angular frequency, then eqn (10.7) may be written

$$\left(\frac{d^2}{dx^2} + k^2\right)\varphi = 0 \tag{10.8}$$

where

$$k = \frac{\omega}{c}$$

k is called the 'wavelength constant' or 'wave number'.

C. Characteristic Impedance of Media

The solution of eqn (10.8) can be expressed in the form

$$\varphi = C_1 e^{j(\omega t - kr)} + C_2 e^{j(\omega t + kr)}$$

where C_1 and C_2 are constants. The first term describes a wave propagating in the positive x direction, while the second term describes a wave propagating in the negative x direction.

When there is only one wave propagating in one direction, i.e. a progressive plane wave, $C_2 = 0$; therefore

$$\varphi = C_1 e^{j(\omega t - kx)} \tag{10.9}$$

So from eqn (10.6)

$$v = \frac{\partial \xi}{\partial t} = jkC_1 e^{j(\omega t - kx)}$$

$$p = \rho j\omega C_1 e^{j(\omega t - kx)}$$

Thus, the impedance is a real number only,

$$Z = \frac{p}{v} = \rho c \qquad (10.10)$$

This is called the 'characteristic impedance' of a medium, but it must be noted that this is for a plane wave in a homogeneous medium of infinite extent.

D.   Wave Equation in 3-Dimensional Space
In order to derive the wave equation for the propagation of a plane wave in three-dimensional space, we use the same principles as for the one-dimensional case applying the equations of continuity and motion of the medium. Then it follows

$$\frac{\partial^2 \varphi}{\partial t^2} = c^2 \left(\frac{\partial^2 \varphi}{\partial x^2} + \frac{\partial^2 \varphi}{\partial y^2} + \frac{\partial^2 \varphi}{\partial z^2} \right) \qquad (10.11)$$

Using the Laplace Differential Operator

$$\nabla^2 \equiv \frac{\partial^2}{\partial x^2} + \frac{\partial^2}{\partial y^2} + \frac{\partial^2}{\partial z^2}$$

Eq (10.11) becomes

$$\frac{\partial^2 \varphi}{\partial t^2} = c^2 \nabla^2 \varphi \qquad (10.12)$$

When the sound wave is a simple harmonic motion, since φ can be replaced by $\varphi e^{j\omega t}$ the above equation may be written

$$(\nabla^2 + k^2) \varphi = 0 \qquad (10.13)$$

where $k = \omega/c$.

E.   Spherical Wave Equation and Acoustic Impedance
In order to derive a wave equation we transform to a spherical coordinate system with polar coordinates (r, θ, ψ) in which the wave function does not depend on θ or ψ but on r and t. Hence the wave equation may be written

$$\frac{\partial^2(\varphi r)}{\partial t^2} = c^2 \frac{\partial^2(\varphi r)}{\partial r^2} \qquad (10.14)$$

A general solution of this equation, which is finite everywhere except at $r = 0$, is

$$\varphi = \frac{1}{r} F(ct - r) + \frac{1}{r} G(ct + r)$$

In free space, since the sound wave is radiated outward from the sound source, the first term alone exists, and, in the case of simple harmonic motion, the above expression reduces to

$$\varphi = \frac{A}{r} e^{j(\omega t - kr)}$$

From eqn (10.6) the following are obtained

$$v = -\frac{\partial \varphi}{\partial r} = \left(\frac{1 + jkr}{r}\right) \frac{A}{r} e^{j(\omega t - kr)} \tag{10.15a}$$

$$p = \rho \frac{\partial \varphi}{\partial t} = j\omega\rho \frac{A}{r} e^{j(\omega t - kr)} \tag{10.15b}$$

Therefore, the acoustic impedance density becomes

$$Z = \frac{p}{v} = \frac{j\omega\rho r}{1 + jkr} = \rho c \frac{jkr}{1 + jkr} \tag{10.16}$$

When the distance r is very large ($kr \gg 1$), the impedance density approaches ρc, which is equivalent to the case of a plane wave, although it must be noted that, in the near field of the sound source, this situation does not hold true. Also, the sound pressure, i.e. eqn (10.15b), is inversely proportional to r, while the particle velocity given by eqn (10.15a) is inversely proportional to r^2 in the near field with $kr \ll 1$. This is the reason why low-frequency sounds are unnaturally emphasized when a velocity microphone is brought too close to any sound source, e.g. the mouth, often a problem in practice.

10.2 ANALOGY BETWEEN ELECTRICAL, MECHANICAL AND ACOUSTIC SYSTEMS AND TIME CONSTANT (Lit. B13, B40, etc.)

A. Correspondence between Electrical and Mechanical Systems

When an electromotive force $E(t)$ is applied to an inductance, as shown in Fig. 10.2, an electric current i is generated according to Faraday's Law as follows:

$$L\frac{di}{dt} = E(t) \tag{10.17}$$

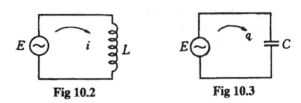

Fig 10.2   **Fig 10.3**

The electric charge q in this circuit is related to the current by

$$i = \frac{dq}{dt} \tag{10.18}$$

therefore

$$L\frac{d^2q}{dt^2} = E(t) \tag{10.19}$$

Also, when $E(t)$ is applied to a capacitor C as shown in Fig. 10.3, the generated electric charge q will be given by

$$\frac{q}{C} = E(t) \tag{10.20}$$

and the relation with the electric current i is

$$\frac{1}{C}\int i\,dt = E(t) \tag{10.21}$$

On the other hand, when an external force $F(t)$ acts on a mass m, a velocity v results (see Fig. 10.4). According to Newton's Second Law, mass velocity and force are related by

$$m\frac{dv}{dt} = F(t) \tag{10.22}$$

Expressing this in terms of displacement ξ,

$$m\frac{d^2\xi}{dt^2} = F(t) \tag{10.23}$$

Fig. 10.4   Fig. 10.5

Also, when $F(t)$ acts on a spring whose elastic modulus is k, producing a displacement ξ at the end, as shown in Fig. 10.5

$$k\xi = F(t) \tag{10.24}$$

If v is the velocity at the tip then

$$k\int v\,dt = F(t) \tag{10.25}$$

Now comparing eqns (10.17)–(10.19) and (10.20)–(10.21) with eqns (10.22)–(10.23) and (10.24)–(10.25), respectively, and the corresponding terms shown in Table 10.1, it can be seen that the equations for both electrical and mechanical systems have exactly the same form. Therefore, if the solutions of eqns (10.17)–(10.19) and (10.20)–(10.21) are found, those of eqns (10.22)–(10.23) and (10.24)–(10.25) are also known. In this case, these two systems are said to be equivalent and, furthermore, a problem in one system can be solved by analogy with the other. Thus, mechanical or acoustical vibrating systems can often be solved easily using alternating current theory if they are replaced by an equivalent electrical circuit, since circuit theory has been extremely well developed.

Table 10.1
Analogy between Electrical and Mechanical Systems

Electrical system	*Mechanical system*
Inductance, L	Mass, m
Current, i	Velocity, v
Charge, q	Displacement, ξ
Electromotive force, $E(t)$	External force, $F(t)$
Reciprocal of electrostatic capacitance, $1/C$	Elastic modulus, k

B. Simple Resonant System

The equation of motion of a single resonance system with a mass on a spring, as discussed in Chap. 6, Section 6.4, is

$$m\frac{d^2\xi}{dt^2} + r\frac{d\xi}{dt} + k\xi = F(t) \tag{10.26}$$

Re-writing the above in terms of velocity v,

$$m\frac{dv}{dt} + rv + k\int v\,dt = F(t) \tag{10.27}$$

The system is illustrated in Fig. 10.6(a).

It can be seen by comparing eqns (10.17) and (10.22) that, in the first term of the above equation, the mass m is equivalent to induction and, by comparing eqns (10.21) and (10.25), the modulus of elasticity k in the third term is equivalent to the reciprocal of capacitance, that velocity v corresponds to the current i and, hence, frictional resistance in a mechanical system corresponds to electrical resistance in an electrical system. Therefore the following equation corresponding to eqn (10.27) is obtained

$$L\frac{di}{dt} + Ri + \frac{1}{C}\int i\,dt = E(t) \tag{10.28}$$

So the equivalent circuit is a well-known L–R–C circuit as shown in Fig. 10.6(b). If the electromotive force E is a simple harmonic alternation

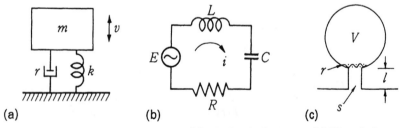

(a)   (b)   (c)

Fig. 10.6. Single resonance system: (a) Mechanical system; (b) Electrical system; and (c) Acoustical system.

then $E(t) = Ee^{j\omega t}$ where $\omega = 2\pi f$. Remembering $d/dt = j\omega$ eqn (10.28) becomes

$$i\left(j\omega L + R + \frac{1}{j\omega C} \right) = Ee^{j\omega t} \qquad (10.29)$$

Hence, the solution is

$$i = \frac{Ee^{j\omega t}}{R + j(\omega L - (1/\omega C))} \qquad (10.30)$$

where

$$Z_e = R + j\left(\omega L - \frac{1}{\omega C} \right) \qquad (10.31)$$

is the electrical impedance of this circuit, and, at the frequency at which the imaginary part $(\omega L - 1/\omega C)$ becomes zero, resonance occurs. Namely, when

$$\omega L = \frac{1}{\omega C} \qquad \therefore \quad \omega^2 = \frac{1}{LC}$$

The resonance frequency is therefore

$$f_r = \frac{1}{2\pi} \sqrt{\frac{1}{LC}} \qquad (10.32)$$

The mechanical impedance of the mechanical system of eqn (10.27) is by analogy

$$Z_m = r + j\left(\omega m - \frac{k}{\omega} \right) \qquad (10.33)$$

And, similarly, setting the imaginary part equal to zero, the resonance frequency is

$$f_r = \frac{1}{2\pi} \sqrt{\frac{k}{m}} \qquad (10.34)$$

The vibration velocity is

$$v = \frac{1}{Z_m} \cdot Fe^{j\omega t} \qquad (10.35)$$

The displacement is

$$\xi = \frac{v}{j\omega} = \frac{1}{j\omega Z_m} \cdot Fe^{j\omega t} \qquad (10.36)$$

and the acceleration is obtained as follows:

$$\frac{dv}{dt} = j\omega v = \frac{j\omega}{Z_m} \cdot Fe^{j\omega t} \tag{10.37}$$

C. Frequency Characteristics (See Fig. 5.29)

We now consider how the characteristics of the mechanical impedance $Z_m = j\omega m + r + k/_{j\omega}$ may change when subject to a wide range of frequency variation.

(i) When the frequency is lower than the resonance frequency

$$f = \frac{1}{2\pi}\sqrt{\frac{k}{m}}$$

the first term is much smaller than the third term so that over a certain range of frequencies

$$Z_m \simeq \frac{k}{j\omega} \tag{10.38}$$

In this range, since the vibration is determined by the elastic modulus k, the vibration is referred to as 'stiffness controlled' under which condition the displacement is constant eqn (10.36).

(ii) Near the resonance frequency, the imaginary part, i.e. the sum of the first and third terms, approaches zero; hence

$$Z_m \simeq r \tag{10.39}$$

which is independent of frequency. In this frequency range, since displacement, velocity and acceleration amplitude are determined by resistance, the vibration is said to be 'resistance controlled' and, as can be seen in eqn (10.35), velocity is constant.

(iii) In the range where the frequency is much higher than the resonance frequency, the first term becomes quite large, then the impedance may be approximated as follows:

$$Z_m \simeq j\omega m \tag{10.40}$$

This condition is then referred to as 'inertia controlled' or 'mass controlled' and from eqn (10.37) the acceleration dv/dt is constant.

D. Acoustic Vibration System

As discussed in Chap. 4, Section 4.5, the Helmholtz resonator, as shown in Figs. 10.6(c), corresponds to the mechanical and electrical systems illustrated in Figs 10.6(a) and 10.6(b).

Consider a single degree of freedom resonance system in which the mass m of air in the neck vibrates on the air cushion in the cavity which acts like a spring, where the entrapped air has a bulk modulus κ. Equations (10.26) and (10.27) apply to this system. In the resonator the mass m of the air in the neck is given by

$$m = sl\rho \qquad (10.41)$$

when s is the cross-sectional area of the neck, l the effective length and ρ the density of the air.

In order to determine the elastic modulus of the volume V of air in the cavity we first assume a piston whose area is s and which is subjected to an inward displacement x. So the trapped air is compressed due to a pressure increase

$$p = \kappa \frac{sx}{V}$$

Then, from eqn (10.2), the force F applied to the piston is given by

$$F = sp = \kappa \frac{s^2 x}{V}$$

but the elastic modulus

$$k = \frac{F}{x}$$

$$\therefore \quad k = \frac{\kappa s^2}{V} \qquad (10.42)$$

Furthermore, due to the resistance r per unit area of the neck, the viscous loss is srv. On the other hand, since the external force acting on the resonator is due to an alternating sound pressure $pe^{j\omega t}$ per unit area, the following equation is obtained

$$sl\rho \frac{dv}{dt} + srv + \frac{s^2\kappa}{V} \int v \, dt = spe^{j\omega t} \qquad (10.43)$$

From this, comparing with eqn (10.33), the following expression

$$Z_m = \frac{sp}{v} = sr + j\left(\omega sl\rho - \frac{s^2\kappa}{\omega V}\right) \qquad (10.44)$$

is the mechanical impedance of the resonator.

Since the acoustic impedance Z_a is defined as the ratio of sound pressure to volume velocity

$$Z_a = \frac{p}{sv} = \frac{Z_m}{s^2} \qquad (10.45)$$

It follows therefore that the specific acoustic impedance Z_{sp} is

$$Z_{sp} = \frac{p}{v} = sZ_a = \frac{Z_m}{s} \qquad (10.46)$$

The resonant frequency of this resonator is thus

$$\omega^2 = \frac{s\kappa}{l\rho V}$$

Since the imaginary part of any impedance is zero at resonance.
From eqn (10.5)

$$\kappa = \rho c^2 \qquad \therefore \quad \omega^2 = \frac{sc^2}{lV}$$

$$\therefore \quad f_r = \frac{c}{2\pi}\sqrt{\frac{s}{lV}} \qquad (10.47)$$

When handling further more complicated acoustic vibration systems than this example, one can appreciate that such an analogous solution based on corresponding mechanical or electrical system analogy becomes much more effective.

E. Time Constant of an Integrating Circuit

(a) Let us consider the transient phenomenon when a direct current voltage E is applied to the input of a series RC circuit as shown in Fig 10.7. From Fig. 10.3 and eqns (10.2), (10.4)

$$R\frac{dq}{dt} + \frac{1}{C}q = E \qquad (10.48)$$

The solution of this equation is

$$q = CE + Ke^{-t/RC} \qquad (10.49)$$

This is called a 'delay system of the 1st order', which means the exponential term is of the 1st order. Since the integration constant K is determined by the initial condition, putting $q = 0$ at $t = 0$, it follows that $K = -CE$

$$\therefore \quad q = CE(1 - e^{-t/RC}) \qquad (10.50)$$

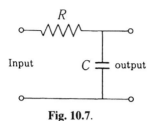

Fig. 10.7.

The output voltage is

$$e_0 = \frac{q}{C} = E(1 - e^{-t/RC}) \tag{10.51}$$

where

$$RC = T \tag{10.52}$$

the so-called 'time constant'.

The output voltage varies as shown in Fig. 10.8, $e_0 \to E$ at $t \to \infty$. If a line tangent to the curve at $t = 0$ is drawn it intercepts $e_0 = E$ at angle θ. The point of interception is A of which the corresponding point on the abscissa is B as shown in the figure. Differentiating eqn (10.51)

$$\tan \theta = \frac{de_0}{dt} = \frac{E}{RC} = \frac{AB}{OB} \qquad \therefore \quad OB = RC = T$$

and when $t = T$, the output voltage becomes

$$e_0 = E(1 - e^{-1}) = 0 \cdot 632E \tag{10.53}$$

i.e. $63 \cdot 2\%$ of the steady state value.

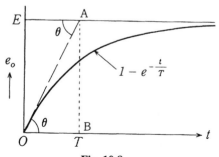

Fig. 10.8.

(b) When a fluctuating voltage $E(t)$ is applied to the circuit shown in Fig. 10.7, from eqn (10.48)

$$\frac{dq}{dt} + \frac{q}{T} = \frac{1}{R}E(t) \qquad (10.54)$$

When T is sufficiently large the second term on the left-hand side of the equation can be neglected; hence

$$q \simeq \frac{1}{R}\int E(t)\,dt$$

$$\therefore \quad e_0 = \frac{q}{C} \simeq \frac{1}{T}\int E(t)\,dt \qquad (10.55)$$

The output voltage is proportional to the integral of the input voltage, therefore the RC circuit shown in Fig. 10.7 is called an 'integrating circuit'.

(c) The indicator of a sound-level meter or a vibration-level meter consists of a squaring circuit and RC-integrating circuit in order to give the root mean square value of the signal, and time-weighting characteristics, as defined by the time constant of the integrating circuit. Therefore, the peak value of the input of the tone burst signal is shown in Fig. 10.9, which is a transformed presentation in dB of the curve in Fig.10.8. When the duration of the tone burst signal is the same as the time constant of the circuit the peak value is 2 dB below the steady state value according to eqn (10.53)

(d) In the frequency domain, since the impedance of this circuit is $Z = R + 1/j\omega C$, at the frequency where $R = 1/\omega C$

$$\omega = 1/RC = 1/T$$

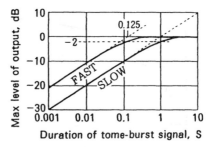

Fig. 10.9.

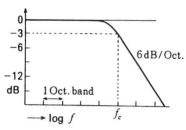

Fig. 10.10.

and the output power is $1/2$ the input power and the circuit functions as a 'low pass filter' with a cut off frequency

$$f_c = \frac{1}{2\pi . T} \qquad (10.56)$$

as shown in Fig. 10.10.

10.3 FOURIER TRANSFORMATION AND CORRELATION
FUNCTION (Lit. B39, B40, etc.)

The basic components of signal processing which are frequently applied in acoustic measurements are formulated here but with the omission of mathematical proof.

A. Fourier Transform

Generally, a time function $f(t)$ can be expressed using the Fourier Integral as follows,

$$f(t) = \frac{1}{2\pi} \int_{-\infty}^{\infty} F(\omega) e^{j\omega t} \, d\omega \qquad (10.57)$$

and the function $F(\omega)$ is given by

$$F(\omega) = \int_{-\infty}^{\infty} f(t) e^{-j\omega t} \, dt \qquad (10.58)$$

This is called the 'Fourier transform' of $f(t)$, and $f(t)$ is called the 'Inverse Fourier transform' of $F(\omega)$. Both are complex functions of amplitude and phase, and have perfectly reciprocal relations.

The coefficient $1/2\pi$ in eqn (10.57) can be removed and shifted to eqn (10.58), or $1/\sqrt{2\pi}$ can be used as a coefficient for both eqns (10.57) and (10.58), in other words, the product of the two coefficients should be $1/2\pi$.

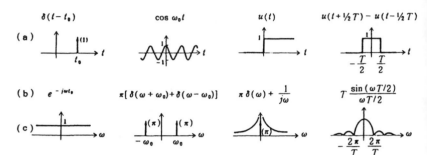

Fig. 10.11. Examples of wave forms and spectrums: (a) Wave form $f(t)$; (b) Fourier transform $F(\omega)$; and (c) Amplitude spectrum.

In physical terms, the Fourier transform $F(\omega)$ of a waveform $f(t)$ in the time domain becomes a frequency spectrum. Fig. 10.11 shows representative wave forms and their frequency spectra. The absolute value of $F(\omega)$ is called the 'amplitude spectrum' and its square the 'power spectrum'.

B.   Unit Impulse Function and Convolution Integral

A unit impulse function is called a delta (δ) function and is defined mathematically as

$$\delta(t - t_0) = 0 \qquad t \neq t_0 \tag{10.59a}$$

also

$$\int_{-\infty}^{\infty} \delta(t - t_0)\, dt = 1 \tag{10.59b}$$

δ is a time function, having the integral value of unit area, but an amplitude which is zero everywhere except at $t = t_0$ where the amplitude is infinite.

When unit impulse $\delta(t)$ is fed to a linear transmission system S, the output signal is called the 'impulse response' of the system. Then, if a signal $x(t)$ is fed to this system the output is expressed by

$$y(t) = \int_{-\infty}^{\infty} x(\tau)h(t - \tau)\, d\tau = \int_{-\infty}^{\infty} x(t - \tau)h(\tau)\, d\tau = x(t) * h(t) \tag{10.60}$$

This is called a 'convolution integral' and is often expressed by $*$. Fig. 10.12 gives a visual explanation of this, applied to the principle of superposition in a linear system. This relation plays a very important and widely-applicable role in various linear systems.

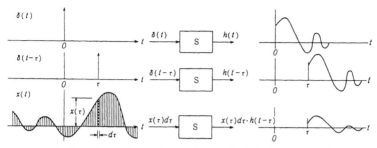

Fig. 10.12. Explanation of 'convolution integral' with the superposition theorem.

When the impulse response is expressed in the form of a Fourier integral, a pair of Fourier transforms is obtained as follows:

$$h(t) = \frac{1}{2\pi} \int_{-\infty}^{\infty} H(\omega) e^{j\omega t} \, d\omega \tag{10.61}$$

$$H(\omega) = \int_{-\infty}^{\infty} h(t) e^{-j\omega t} \, dt \tag{10.62}$$

where $H(\omega)$ is called a 'system function' or 'transfer function'.

If the Fourier transform $X(\omega)$ of the input signal $x(t)$ is known, then the Fourier transform $Y(\omega)$ of the output $y(t)$ becomes

$$Y(\omega) = X(\omega) \cdot H(\omega) \tag{10.63}$$

This means that the output in the frequency domain is obtained simply by multiplying the Fourier transform of the input signal by the transfer function.

C. Autocorrelation Function

In order to express the properties of a time-variant waveform, the 'autocorrelation function' as defined by eqn (10.64) is used:

$$\varphi_{11}(\tau) = \int_{-\infty}^{\infty} f_1(t) f_1(t + \tau) \, dt, \tag{10.64}$$

especially for an irregular function,

$$\varphi_{11}(\tau) = \lim_{T \to \infty} \frac{1}{2T} \int_{-T}^{T} f_1(t) f_1(t + \tau) \, dt \tag{10.65}$$

It may be sufficient to integrate over one period if the function is periodic, and over a finite time function, e.g. several or several tens of

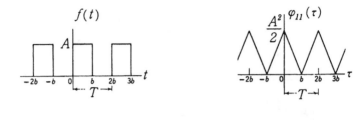

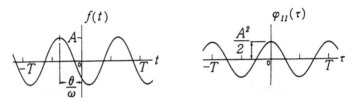

Fig. 10.13. Example of autocorrelation function of periodic waves.

milliseconds for the aperiodic function, music or speech. Fig. 10.13 shows examples of the autocorrelation functions of simple periodic functions.

Since the value of $\varphi_{11}(\tau)$ is a maximum at $\tau = 0$, the normalised form with maximum value

$$\phi_{11}(\tau) = \frac{\varphi_{11}(\tau)}{\varphi_{11}(0)} \quad (10.66)$$

is often used. Fig. 10.14 shows examples of the autocorrelation function of noise, music and speech displayed by eqn (10.66).

The autocorrelation function $\varphi_{11}(\tau)$ and the power spectrum $\Phi_{11}(\omega)$ make a pair of Fourier transforms as follows:

$$\varphi_{11}(\tau) = \int_{-\infty}^{\infty} \Phi_{11}(\omega) e^{j\omega t} \, d\omega \quad (10.67)$$

$$\Phi_{11}(\omega) = \frac{1}{2\pi} \int_{-\infty}^{\infty} \varphi_{11}(\tau) e^{-j\omega t} \, d\tau \quad (10.68)$$

When $\tau = 0$ the autocorrelation function becomes an integral of the square of $f_1(t)$

$$\varphi_{11}(0) = \int_{-\infty}^{\infty} f_1^2(t) \, dt \quad (10.69)$$

This gives the total energy of $f_1(t)$.

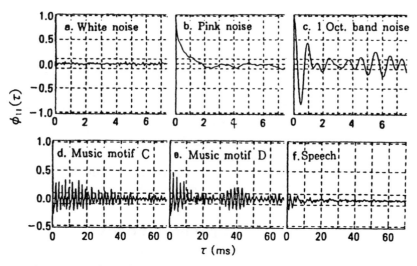

Fig. 10.14. Examples of autocorrelation function of aperiodic signals.

D. Crosscorrelation Function

In order to express the similarity of two time functions $f_1(t)$ and $f_2(t)$, the 'cross-correlation function' $\varphi_{12}(\tau)$, generally defined by eqn (10.70), is frequently used.

$$\varphi_{12}(\tau) = \lim_{T \to \infty} \frac{1}{2T} \int_{-T}^{T} f_1(t) f_2(t + \tau) \, dt \qquad (10.70)$$

In practice the normalised form of the above, i.e. eqn (10.71) is often used

$$\phi_{12}(\tau) = \frac{\varphi_{12}(\tau)}{\sqrt{\varphi_{11}(0)\,\varphi_{22}(0)}} \qquad (10.71)$$

The results of psychoacoustic research on room acoustic assessment show that the less the degree of similarly between signals $f_l(t)$, and $f_r(t)$, which are received by the left and right ears, respectively, i.e. the lower the value of $\phi_{12}(\tau)$ the larger the spatial impression. Ando (see Lit. B33) defined the IACC (Inter-Aural Cross-Correlation) as follows,

$$\text{IACC} = |\varphi_{lr}(\tau)|_{\max}, \qquad |\tau| \le 1 \text{ ms} \qquad (10.72)$$

This is used as a parameter for the evaluation of sound fields (see Section 3.6.8). Fig. 10.15 shows an example of this.

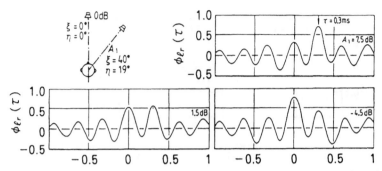

Fig. 10.15. Example of calculated results of IACC when the intensity of a single reflection is changed (Y Ando).

10.4   OUTLINE OF AUDITORY ORGAN

(Chap. 4, etc., Lit. B5, B28, B34)

The structure of the human ear is shown in Fig. 10.16. The sound collected by the 'pinna' (ear lobe) passes through the outer ear canal and oscillates the eardrum which is at the entrance to the middle ear. The oscillation of the eardrum is transferred by three bones called ossicles in the middle ear to the 'oval window' which closes the entrance

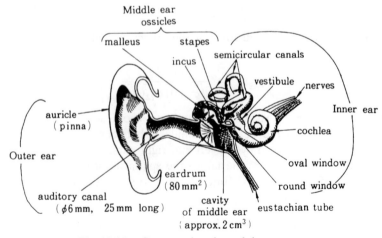

Fig. 10.16. Cross section through human ear.

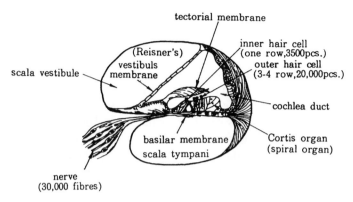

Fig. 10.17. Cross section through the cochlea.

to the inner ear. Three ossicles, 'malleus' (hammer), 'incus' (anvil), and 'stapes' (stirrup), which are of different lengths, create a lever ratio (impedance transformer) which provides impedance matching between the air oscillation on a large area and the motion on a small area of 'lymph' (fluid) in the 'cochlea' which comprises the inner ear.

The cochlea is coiled like a snail shell whose cross section consists of three 'scalae (canals)' as shown in Fig. 10.17. The extended length of it is about 35 mm while the 'scala vestibuli' and the 'scala tympani' are connected with the 'helicotrema', a small window at the apex of the cochlea as shown in Fig. 10.18. Another 'scala media' is separated from the other two scalae by the 'Reissner's membrane and the 'basilar membrane' and is filled with lymph as shown in Fig 10.17. The basilar membrane is loaded with the 'organ of Corti' which has sensory 'hair

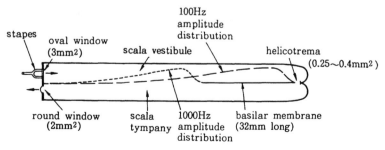

Fig. 10.18. Schematic representation of unrolled cochlea.

cells' embedded at both sides of the 'trigonal pillar'. The hairs of both inner and outer hair cells are in touch with the 'tectorial membrane'.

When the oval window receives an oscillation, transferred from the middle ear, the travelling wave produces a vertical displacement, which occurs in the basilar membrane with the lymph in the scala media; then the hairs are bent by the relative displacement of hair cells and tectorial membrane. Then, 'spikes' (electric pulses) are 'fired' electro-physiologi- cally in the auditory nerves which transmit the spikes to the brain.

The amplitude of displacement of the basilar membrane is small near the oval window, but the position of maximum displacement depends on the frequency, as shown in Fig. 10.18, where the higher the frequency the closer to the oval window is the maximum displacement. It is considered that, to some extent, a frequency analysis is performed. Although the variation of electric potential produced by the hair cells is related to the sound wave as if the cochlea plays a similar role to that of a microphone, the electric pulses transmitted to the brain are quite a different style. Therefore, the generation mechanism, transmission sys- tem in the auditory nerves and the faculty of auditory sensation in the cerebral cortex are being researched under the umbrella of electro- physiology.

10.5 CALCULATION OF LOUDNESS LEVEL (PHON)

Though human sensory perception cannot be directly measured, several methods have been proposed in order to measure the physical magni- tude of stimulus. From 1940 onwards S.S. Stevens continued his re- search on the subject and published a series of reports from Mark I (1956) to Mark VII (1972). The procedure is pursued as follows: first, find the Loudness Index S_i (sone) from measured values, in either 1, 1/2 or 1/3 octave bands of the objective noise, using Fig. 10.19, and obtain the maximum value of S_m. Then the total loudness S_t for the entire frequency range is given by

$$S_t = S_m + F(\Sigma S_i - S_m) \text{ sone} \qquad (10.73)$$

where

$$\begin{cases} F = 0\cdot 3 & (1 \text{ Oct. band}) \\ F = 0\cdot 2 & (1/2 \text{ Oct. band}) \\ F = 0\cdot 15 & (1\cdot 3 \text{ Oct. band}) \end{cases}$$

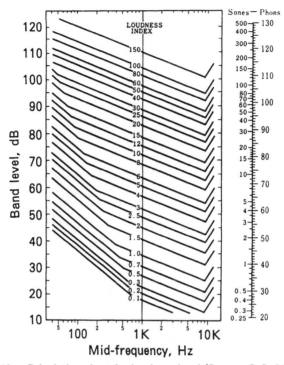

Fig. 10.19. Calculation chart for loudness level (Stevens S. S., Mark VI).

From the above, the Loudness Level, LL (phon) can be calculated by

$$LL = 40 + 10 \log_2 S_t = 40 + \frac{10}{0 \cdot 3} \log_{10} S_t \qquad (10.74)$$

Also the scale provided at the right-hand side of Fig. 10.19 may be used conveniently for conversion between sones and phons. Equation (10.73) is a simplified version, taking into account the masking effect due only to the frequency band which has the maximum stimulus. In addition to this method, ISO standard 532 (1966) has also adopted another method developed by E. Zwicker (1960) to calculate masking more accurately. Stevens (1972) also published Mark VII as a synthesized evaluation scale combining not only Loudness but also Noisiness and Annoyance, which is called 'Perceived Level' represented by a chart similar to Fig.

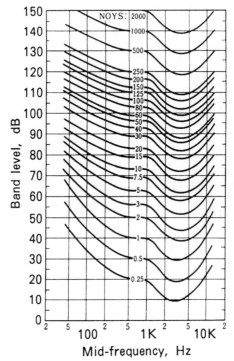

Fig. 10.20. Calculation chart for perceived noise level (Kryter K. D.).

10.20 with folded lines and not curves, though its applicability requires further investigation (See Lit. B24).

10.6 CALCULATION OF NOISINESS (PNdB)

K.D. Kryter (1960–64) realised by experiments on auditory perception that actual noisiness is different from loudness level (phon) and established a calculation method for PNL (Perceived Noise Level) by constructing equal noisiness curves following the S.S. Stevens' method.

The procedures are exactly the same as in Stevens' method, using eqns (10.73) and (10.74), except employing Fig. 10.20 in place of Fig. 10.19 and also instead of Loudness Index S using the values N called Noy, hence PNL (PNdB) is obtained. The values for the range from 500 to 1000 Hz in Fig 10.20 correspond to eqn (10.74) (see Lit. B21, B24).

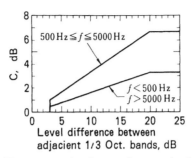

Fig. 10.21. Tone correction factors for perceived noise level.

10.7 WECPNL AND L_{eq} (16 h) FOR AIRCRAFT NOISE ASSESSMENT (Lit. B24)

A. EPNL (Effective PNL)

This scale was recommended as ISO-R507 1970 and ICAO Annex 16, 1971, for assessment of aircraft noise following the American method and practice, which is based on the total noise power for a fixed-time duration, modified to take into account human sensation and psychology.

Assuming access to computer processing, first a 1/3 octave-band analysis of the fluctuating noise is carried out at 0·5-s intervals, then, after applying pure tone correction due to adjoining band level differences using Fig. 10.21, PNdB is obtained from Fig. 10.20. The resultant value is called PNLT (Tone corrected PNL) and the peak value when the total energy approximated in practice by the integrated value in the duration D in eqn (10.75) is transformed into an equivalent rectangular shape within the prescribed duration time T_0 (here 10 s) is referred to as EPNL (Effective PNL). The main purpose of this method is to certify the noise generated by newly manufactured civil aircraft. The following eqn (10.75) seems, however, appropriate as an approximation for general noise monitoring and land-use planning

$$\text{EPNL} = \text{PNL} + C + 10\log_{10}\frac{D}{20} \qquad (10.75)$$

where PNL = PN dB, obtained from the peak value of 1 oct band analysis; C = pure tone correction, $+2$ dB, only for landing of turbofan aircraft; and D = duration in seconds when the level is 10 dB lower than the peak value. The third term, i.e. duration correction, is based on the assumption of a triangular shape for level change.

As a further simplification instead of analysis, if the peak level dBD or dBA is measured using a sound level meter, then PNL may be obtained with the use of eqns (2.3) or (2.4).

B. ECPNL (Equivalent Continuous PNL) and WECPNL (Weighted ECPNL)

For the purpose of assessment of environmental noise, ECPNL is defined as the energetic average of EPNL for a certain time period T.

$$\text{ECPNL} = 10 \log_{10} \sum_i 10^{\text{EPNL}_i/10} + 10 \log_{10} \frac{T_0}{T} \qquad (10.76)$$

T is usually considered for a full day (seconds). However, WECPNL is a weighted ECPNL which takes into account the life-cycle variation depending on the time of day such as daytime (0700–1900 h), evening (1900–2200 h) and night (2200–0700 h), thus the weighting is $+5$ dB for evening and $+10$ dB for night referred to daytime, and they are identified by subscripts d, e and n, respectively,

$$\text{WECPNL} = 10 \log_{10} \left[\frac{4}{8} \cdot 10^{\text{ECPNL}_d/10} + \frac{1}{8} \cdot 10^{(\text{ECPNL}_e + 5)/10} \right.$$
$$\left. + \frac{3}{8} \cdot 10^{(\text{ECPNL}_n + 10)/10} \right] \qquad (10.77)$$

Since the generated engine noise depends on the air temperature, further correction is sometimes required as shown in Table 10.2.

For simplification, using the energetic average value EPNL obtained from the observed EPNLi for the total number of aircraft N in a full day (86 400 s).

$$\text{ECPNL} = \text{EPNL} + 10 \log_{10} N - 39 \cdot 4 \qquad (10.78)$$

Table 10.2
Seasonal Adjustment for Aircraft Noise

	(dB)
For months having less than 100 h at or above 20°C	−5
For months having more than 100 h at or above 20°C and less than 100 h at or above 25.6°C	0
For months having more than 100 h at or above 25.6°C	+5

Hence using eqn (2.4) and weighting with the number of events N eqn (2.12) is derived.

The above evaluation method is based on computer calculation which facilitates the estimation; however, the relationship to social response is not yet clear, thus further study is necessary.

C. L_{eq} (16 h)

In 1984 the U.K. Aircraft Noise Index Study was carried out by the Civil Aviation Authority and came to the conclusion that a good fit to aircraft noise annoyance response was given by L_{eq} (24 h). The daytime L_{eq} (16 h) does correlate about as well with aircraft noise disturbance as the L_{eq} (24 h) (daytime is from 0700 to 2300 local time).

L_{eq} (16 h) was officially introduced as the UK index of aircraft noise exposure in 1990.

Aircraft noise contours are determined by calculating values of $L_{eq}(T)$ at a large number of grid points on the map based on the approximation

$$L_{eq}(T) = \overline{L_{AE}} + 10\log N - 10\log(T \times 3600)$$

where N is the number of aircraft events, T is the time period in hours and $\overline{L_{AE}}$ is the logarithmic average sound exposure level of the N events (Cadoux 1992).

10.8   REVERBERATION IN A COUPLED ROOM

Generally a theatre has two major spaces, stage and seating area, linked via a proscenium opening. Therefore, when calculating reverberation time of the seating area, the proscenium opening is considered as an absorptive surface, the absorption coefficient of which is assumed. Sometimes, for instance, when the reverberation time is measured at some stage during construction, the calculated values never agree with those measured due to the fact that the absorption in the stage space is much lower compared with that in the seating area, as described in Chap. 3, Section 3.3D. Therefore, we must examine the situation where two spaces exchange acoustic energy mutually through the opening between them. Such a combined space is called a 'coupled room' for which Eyring (1931) developed a solution. The basic principle of dealing with this problem is simply explained as follows:

As shown in Fig. 10.22, a room R_1 is coupled with another R_2 through the opening F. We then assume that (1) both rooms have completely diffuse sound fields and (2) the acoustic energy density changes abruptly at the opening between both rooms.

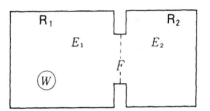

Fig. 10.22. Coupled room.

When the source located in room R_1 generates acoustic power W, the energy density becomes E_1 and E_2 in both rooms whose surface areas, except for area of the opening, are S_1 and S_2 with average absorption coefficients α_1 and α_2, respectively. Hence the energy absorbed in the room R_1 is $cE_1(S_1\alpha_1 + F)/4$, whereas the energy returned from room R_2 is $cE_2F/4$ (see Section 3.3B). Therefore the total energy in room R_1 changes according to the following equation:

$$V_1\frac{\mathrm{d}E_1}{\mathrm{d}t} = W - \frac{cE_1(S_1\alpha_1 + F)}{4} + \frac{cE_2F}{4} \tag{10.79}$$

Similarly, in room R_2

$$V_2\frac{\mathrm{d}E_2}{\mathrm{d}t} = -\frac{cE_2(S_2\alpha_2 + F)}{4} + \frac{cE_1F}{4} \tag{10.80}$$

These two equations should be solved simultaneously.

In the steady state

$$\frac{\mathrm{d}E_1}{\mathrm{d}t} = \frac{\mathrm{d}E_2}{\mathrm{d}t} = 0$$

While, during decay, $W = 0$. Hence the form of solution is

$$\begin{cases} E_1 = Ae^{-\beta_1 t} + Be^{-\beta_2 t} & (10.81) \\ E_2 = Ce^{-\beta_1 t} + De^{-\beta_2 t} & (10.82) \end{cases}$$

Thus, the problem is reduced to finding values of A, B, C, D, β_1 and β_2 which satisfy eqns (10.79) and (10.80).

Equations (10.81) and (10.82) show that the situation in both rooms can be expressed by the summation of two exponential terms; consequently, the decay curve should be bent unless β_1 and β_2 are equal and, furthermore, the profile of the bent curve is changed according to the magnitudes of A and B or C and D.

10.9   NEW METHOD OF MEASURING REVERBERATION TIME

Schroeder (1965) presented a new method of measuring reverberation time on the basis that a simple integration taken over the squared impulse response in a single measurement yields the ensemble average of the decay curves, which, in themselves, are unstable, and where measurements using the conventional method require the taking of the average of a number of measurements.

Assume $n(t)$ to be a 'stationary white noise'. It's 'autocovariance' function $\langle n(t_1) \cdot n(t_2) \rangle$ depends only on the time difference $(t_2 - t_1)$ since it is 'stationary', and is zero everywhere except for $t_1 = t_2$ since it is 'white'. Thus, we can write

$$\langle n(t_1) \cdot (t_2) \rangle = N \cdot \delta(t_2 - t_1) \qquad (10.83)$$

where the brackets $\langle \ \rangle$ denote 'ensemble average', $N =$ noise power/1 Hz, $\delta(t_2 - t_1) =$ delta function as defined in Section 10.3B.

When the band noise is switched off at $\tau = 0$ after the 'steady state' is reached, the signal received at a point is expressed by a convolution integral,

$$S(t) = \int_{(-\infty)}^{0} n(\tau) \cdot h(t - \tau) \, d\tau \qquad (10.84)$$

where $h(t)$ is the impulse response from the source to the receiving point including all related factors. The lower limit $(-\infty)$ in the integral means that sufficient time is needed to build up to the 'steady state'. The decay of sound energy represented by the square of the received signal is written as a double integral as follows:

$$S^2(t) = \int_{(-\infty)}^{0} d\tau \int_{(-\infty)}^{0} d\theta n(\tau) \cdot n(\theta) \cdot h(t - \tau) \cdot h(t - \theta) \quad (10.85)$$

Applying eqn (10.83) to the ensemble average of eqn (10.85)

$$\langle S^2(t) \rangle = \int_{(-\infty)}^{0} d\tau \int_{(-\infty)}^{0} d\theta N \cdot \delta(\theta - \tau) \cdot h(t - \tau) \cdot h(t - \theta) \quad (10.86)$$

Since $\delta(\theta - \tau)$ vanishes except when $\theta = \tau$, and since the integral becomes unity, integration over θ yields

$$\langle S^2(t) \rangle = N \int_{(-\infty)}^{0} h^2(t - \tau) \, d\tau \qquad (10.87)$$

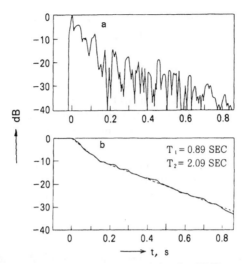

Fig. 10.23. Reverberation curves measured in the Philharmonic Hall, New York (Schroeder M. R.). (a) Tone-burst response curve showing sound pressure decay; (b) Squared tone-burst response integrated from time t to 1 s. T_1 and T_2 show reverberation times obtained by straight-line fits to first 10 dB and remainder of the decay respectively.

or, using the new integration variable $x = t - \tau$

$$\langle S^2(t) \rangle = N \int_t^{(\infty)} h^2(x)\, \mathrm{d}x \qquad (10.88)$$

This equation shows that the ensemble average of the squared noise decay, which would require a large number of measurements, may be obtained by only a single measurement of the impulse response. Figure 10.23 shows an example of measurement by this method.

10.10   SOUND ABSORPTION CHARACTERISTICS OF MULTI-LAYERED ABSORBENTS

A.   Characteristics of Sound Absorbing Material   (Lit. B8, B22)
Since a sound wave is attenuated during transmission through an absorptive material, the sound pressure p of a plane wave propagating

in the x-direction is expressed as a function of distance x follows:

$$\left.\begin{array}{l} p = p_0 e^{-\gamma x} \\ \gamma = \alpha + j\beta \end{array}\right\} \tag{10.89}$$

where p_0 = sound pressure at $x = 0$, γ = propagation constant, α = attenuation constant, $\beta = \omega/c$ = phase constant and c = sound speed in the material. When $\alpha = 0$, i.e. with no attenuation, β is synonymous with the wavelength constant k.

As regards particle velocity, if the medium is homogeneous and of density ρ, from eqn (10.4) in Section 10.1, $\partial v/\partial t = -1/\rho \cdot \partial p/\partial x$ and in the case of a sinusoidal wave $\partial/\partial t = j\omega$, then

$$v = -\frac{1}{j\omega\rho}\frac{\partial p}{\partial x} \tag{10.90}$$

Assuming the same relationship in an absorptive material, from eqn (10.89) and (10.90)

$$v = \frac{\gamma}{j\omega\rho}p,$$

Hence the characteristic impedance of the medium is

$$Z = \frac{p}{v} = \frac{j\omega\rho}{\gamma} \tag{10.91}$$

Thus, any spatial and time conditions of a sound wave in an infinitely continuous medium can be determined completely by two quantities, i.e. the propagation constant γ and the characteristic impedance Z of the medium.

B. Single-layer Absorbent
When a single layer of homogeneous material which has thickness l, propagation constant γ and characteristic impedance Z exists with $x = 0 \sim l$, as shown in Fig. 10.24, and is faced with a surface whose impedance is Z_2 at $x = l$, then what will be the impedance Z_1 at $x = 0$?

If the sound wave propagation in the positive x direction has sound pressure p_i at $x = l$ and the reflected wave returning in the reverse

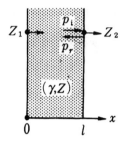

Fig. 10.24. Single layer absorbent.

direction has pressure p_r at the same point, the sound wave through the material may be expressed as follows:

$$\begin{cases} p(x) = p_i e^{\gamma(l-x)} + p_r e^{-\gamma(l-x)} & (10.92) \\ v(x) = \dfrac{P_i}{Z} e^{\gamma(l-x)} - \dfrac{P_r}{Z} e^{-\gamma(l-x)} & (10.93) \end{cases}$$

From the boundary condition $p(l)/v(l) = Z_2$, the relation

$$p_r/p_i = (Z_2 - Z)/(Z_2 + Z)$$

is obtained. Substituting this into eqns (10.92) and (10.93), the impedance at $x = 0$ is

$$Z_1 = \frac{p(0)}{v(0)} = Z \cdot \frac{Z_2 \cosh \gamma l + Z \sinh \gamma l}{Z_2 \sinh \gamma l + Z \cosh \gamma l} \qquad (10.94)$$

The particular conditions which apply to the above equation are as follows:

(1) when the material thickness is infinitely large, $Z_2 = Z$, $\therefore Z_1 = Z$;
(2) if the material is fastened to a rigid wall:

$$Z_2 = \infty \quad \therefore \quad Z_1 = Z \coth \gamma l \qquad (10.95)$$

(3) when an air space, whose thickness is $\lambda/4$, is provided between the material and the rigid wall, using $\gamma = jk$ and eqn (10.95) and the assumption that there is no attenuation in the air,

$$Z_2 = Z \coth j \frac{\pi}{2} = 0 \quad \therefore \quad Z_1 = Z \tanh \gamma l \quad (10.96)$$

From these relationships the propagation constant γ and characteristic impedance Z of the material can be obtained by measurements which satisfy the requirements of eqns (10.95) and (10.96).

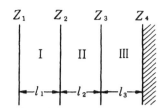

Fig. 10.25.   Multi-layered absorbent.

After the acoustic impedance Z_1 of the material surface has been determined from eqn (10.94) the absorption coefficient can be obtained from eqn (1.34).

C.   Multi-layered Absorbents

In the case of a multi-layered construction, for example, where a composite panel consisting of three kinds of material is directly mounted on a rigid wall, as shown in Fig. 10.25 and where each material's propagation constant and characteristic impedance is known, then applying the method described above, firstly the impedance Z_3 can be determined from eqn (10.95) with $Z_4 = \infty$, then substituting Z_3 in eqn (10.94) Z_2 is obtained, and finally Z_1 can be obtained in the same way from eqn (10.94) by substituting Z_2. As a basic principle for any number of layers, the impedance at the surface of the composite wall can be calculated by repeating the above process using eqn (10.94) for the layer which lies at the back. Then the absorption coefficient of the composite wall can be determined from eqn (1.34), although a new calculation method has been published (Mechel 1988).

10.11   SMITH CHART AND STANDING WAVE METHOD

A.   Configuration of Smith Chart

Expressing the sound pressure reflection complex coefficient as

$$|r_p|e^{j\Delta} = p + jq \tag{10.97}$$

and from eqns (4.5) and (4.6) the acoustic impedance ratio may be written

$$r + jx = \frac{1 + (p + jq)}{1 - (p + jq)}$$

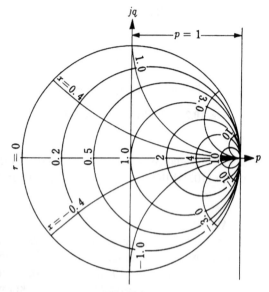

Fig. 10.26.

Therefore, equating real and imaginary parts of both sides, the following relationships are obtained:

$$\left(p - \frac{r}{r+1}\right)^2 + q^2 = \frac{1}{(r+1)^2} \tag{10.98}$$

$$(p-1)^2 + \left(q - \frac{1}{x}\right)^2 = \frac{1}{x^2} \tag{10.99}$$

As shown in Fig. 10.26, eqn (10.98) is the locus of $r =$ constant with a circle of radius $1/(r+1)$ whose centre has coordinates $p = r/(r+1)$, $q = 0$, while eqn (10.99) is the locus of $x =$ constant with a circle of radius $1/x$ whose centre has coordinates $p = 1$, $q = 1/x$.

Since eqn (10.97) yields $|r_p| = \sqrt{p^2 + q^2}$, the locus of $|r_p| =$ constant is a circle whose centre is at the origin of the coordinates and where all the values should be within the circle whose radius is 1 because $|r_p| < 1$. The phase angles are shown in Fig. 10.27 where $q/p = \tan \Delta$. Figure 10.28 is a Smith Chart which combines Figs 10.26 and 10.27 although concentric circles are omitted and, instead of an angle scale, there is a wave number scale (d/λ) where d is the distance to the first minimum

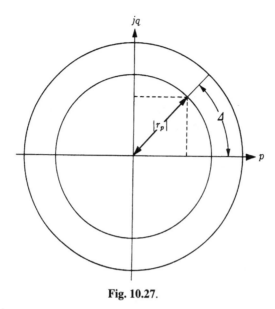

Fig. 10.27.

of a standing wave from the specimen surface, shown in Fig. 4.5, and λ is the wavelength.

B. Using a Smith Chart

The chart was intended to be used for calculations on communication transmission lines, providing double scales for wave number towards the load and in the opposite direction towards the generator, although in determinations of acoustic impedance derived from standing waves generated in the tube method, only the outer scale (towards the load) is used.

Wave numbers are graduated from 0 to $0 \cdot 5$ for one rotation starting at the negative end of the real axis in Fig. 10.26; then, in the case of a perfect reflection, the first standing wave minimum is at $d/\lambda = 0 \cdot 25$, which coincides with the positive end of the real axis, thus $\Delta = 0$ in Fig 10.27. In general, d/λ for a material is obtained from the measured value d and then by connecting the relevant point on the circumference of the circle to the centre Δ is obtained. Therefore, depending on $d/\lambda \lessgtr 0 \cdot 25$ the phase angle of the reflected wave $\Delta \gtrless 0$ and the imaginary part of the impedance is given by $x \gtrless 0$.

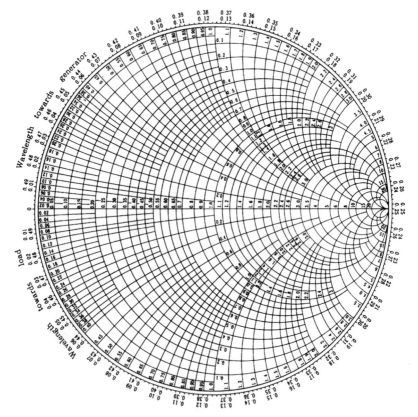

Fig. 10.28. Smith chart.

Next, plotting the measured value of the standing wave ratio n on the real axis, we allow the concentric circle through n to intersect the radius at angle Δ obtained above. The point of intersection gives the acoustic impedance ratio. When the standing wave ratio is measured on the dB scale, the value of n or the radius $|r_p|$ of the concentric circle can be found from Table A.1 in the Appendices. The absorption coefficient can immediately be obtained from the same table.

[Ex. 10.1] The measurement of the acoustic impedance of a material is to be carried out using a standing wave tube. Let us suppose that the room temperature is 15°C and a standing wave is produced in the tube

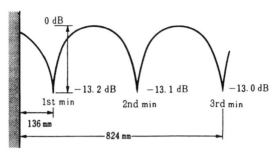

Fig. 10.29. Example of the standing wave.

at a frequency of 500 Hz by a tone generator. The results obtained are shown in Fig. 10.29 and from Table A.1 it can be seen that:

(1) With a standing wave ratio -13.2 dB (with the minimum which is closest to the sample) $n = 4 \cdot 57$.

(2) The normal incidence absorption coefficient $\alpha_0 = 58 \cdot 9\%$.

(3) The absolute value of the sound pressure reflection coefficient is

$$|r_p| = 0 \cdot 64$$

(4) The phase angle from eqn (4.4) is given by

$$\Delta = 4\pi\delta/\lambda$$

where λ is the distance from the first to the third minimum, i.e. $824 - 136 = 688$ mm. Therefore $\lambda/4 = 172$ mm and so subtracting $d = 136$ mm from this

$$\delta = -36 \text{ mm} \quad \text{(see Fig. 4.5)}$$

and hence $\Delta = -360° \times 2 \times 36 \div 688 = -37 \cdot 5°$. Using the Smith Chart $d/\lambda = 136/688 = 0 \cdot 198$ is plotted on the wave number scale towards load and joined to the centre; $\Delta = -37 \cdot 5°$ is obtained with a protractor. The minus sign indicates a delay of the reflected sound wave at the sample surface.

(5) To obtain acoustic impedance from the Smith Chart, we draw a concentric circle through $n = 4 \cdot 57$ on the real axis to intersect a radius at angle Δ, namely the point corresponding to $0 \cdot 64$ of the radius from the centre. For this point $r = 1 \cdot 5$ and $x = -2 \cdot 0$ which gives the acoustic impedance ratio at the specimen surface.

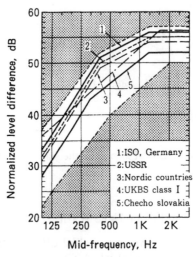

Fig. 10.30. Criteria for airborne sound insulation of walls in several countries.

10.12   SOUND INSULATION CRITERIA FOR BUILDING IN DIFFERENT COUNTRIES

A.   Airborne Sound Insulation Criteria for Walls

The field measuring method of airborne sound insulation is described in Chap. 5 (see Section 5.2C) and the evaluation of the sound insulation of a wall is given by eqns (5.30) or (5.31), i.e. normalised sound level difference. Following on from this, the ISO single number rating method is described in Section 5.2D. Here the representative curves of the criteria for the evaluation of sound insulation of walls in many countries are shown in Fig. 10.30.

B.   Impact Sound Insulation Criteria for Floors

The field measurement of the impact sound insulation of floors is presented as a 'normalised impact sound level', as described in Chap. 6 (see Section 6.3B), and the ISO single number rating is derived as described in Section 6.3C.

Here the representative curves of the criteria for evaluation of impact sound insulation of floors in many countries are shown in Fig. 10.31 in 1 octave band levels; the values are, therefore, 5 dB higher than those in Fig. 6.11.

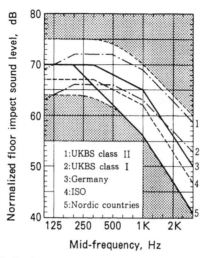

Fig. 10.31. Criteria for impact sound insulation of floors in several countries.

C. STC (Sound Transmission Class) and IIC (Impact Insulation Class) Used in the U.S.A.

STC and IIC are different from the preceding European standards. The single number rating called STC is recommended in the U.S. for rating the airborne sound insulation of walls and is described in ASTM E90-66T. The process of obtaining an STC number is almost the same as ISO 717 described in Section 5.2D except that, when the reference curve (called the sound transmission class contour which is the same as

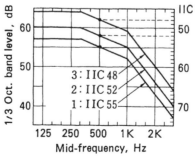

Fig. 10.32. IIC contours for classification of impact sound insulation of floors recommended in U.S.A.

Table 10.3

Recommendation for STC and IIC Class in Various Environments by F.H.A. in U.S.A.

Class	STC & IIC	Environmental condition	Outdoor noise level in night (dBA)
1	55	Rural or high class residential	< 40
2	52	Suburban common residential	40–45
3	48	Urban general area	> 45

Fig. 5.20 but with the frequency range changed to 125 Hz–4 kHz) is shifted towards the measured curve, the maximum unfavourable deviation does not exceed 8 dB at any single frequency.

In order to obtain the rating of the impact sound insulation of a floor, the reference curve is the same as Fig. 6.11. However, another scale IIC is added as seen at the right-hand side of Fig. 10.32. The reference curve is shifted towards the measured curve of normalised impact sound levels using the same procedure as for STC described above. Figure 10.32 shows 3 reference curves which are recommended by the Federal Housing Administration (FHA) for use in different environments as shown in Table 10.3. This classification is also applied with the same number to STC for airborne sound insulation. The measured STC and IIC numbers for many building materials and constructions have been quoted and illustrated in a convenient way for use in noise control (see Lit. A6).

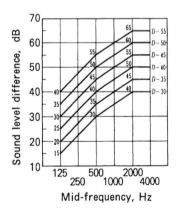

Fig. 10.33. Classification of airborne sound insulation with level difference between rooms in Japan.

Table 10.4
Recommendation for Average Sound Level Difference between Rooms
by A.I.J. (Architectural Institute of Japan) in Japan (1979)

Buildings	Rooms	Parts	S better	1 normal	2 acceptable	3 minimum
Apartment houses	Living	Party wall and floor between dwellings	D-55	D-50	D-45	D-40
Hotel	Bedroom	Party wall and floor	D-50	D-45	D-40	D-35
Office	Office meeting room	Party wall	—	D-40	D-35	D-30
	Needed more privacy	Party Wall	D-50	D-45	D-40	—
School	Classroom		D-45	D-40	D-35	D-30
		Party wall				
	Lecture room		D-50	D-45	D-40	D-35

D. Sound Insulation Criteria in Japan

a. Criteria for Airborne Sound Insulation

In order to evaluate the airborne sound insulation between rooms, the sound level difference, eqn (5.29), is used and the insulation criteria determined, as shown in Fig. 10.33 in JIS (Japanese Industrial Standard) 1419, and the appropriate classification is recommended by the Architectural Institute of Japan as shown in Table 10.4. Building law ensures that the partition wall between dwellings in flats matches the values equivalent to curve D-40.

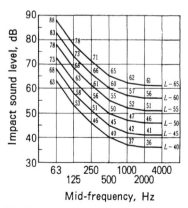

Fig. 10.34. Classification of impact sound insulation of floors in Japan.

Table 10.5
Recommendation for Impact Sound Insulation of Floors
by A.I.J. in Japan (1979)

Buildings	Rooms	Building component	Class			
			S	1	2	3
Apartments	Living	Party floor	L-40	L-45	L-50, 55	L-60
Hotel	Bedroom	Party floor	L-40	L-45	L-50	L-55
School	Classroom	Party floor	L-50	L-55	L-60	L-65

b.   Criteria for Impact Sound Insulation
In Japan, not only the tapping machine but also a heavy-weight impact source is standardised (JIS 1418) as a simulation of a child jumping. The standard is based on the principle that the jump is equivalent to the impact of an automobile tyre, having a weight $7 \cdot 3 \pm 0 \cdot 4$ kg at a pressure of $(1 \cdot 5 \pm 0 \cdot 1) \times 10^5$ Pa, falling from a height of $0 \cdot 9 \pm 0 \cdot 1$ m on the floor but bouncing once only.

A sound level meter and 1 octave band analyser are used as sound receiver and for measuring the peak values of each single impact with a time weighting of 'F'. The measured curve is then evaluated with the aid of reference curves in Fig. 10.34, which are an upside-down version of 'A' weighted curves which simulate human hearing. Shown in Table 10.5 is the appropriate classification based on the use of buildings and their locations which is recommended by the Architectural Institute.

10.13   MEASUREMENT OF POWER LEVEL AND DIRECTIVITY OF SOUND SOURCE

As discussed in Chap. 5 (see Section 5.1), it is convenient to express the sound source output in terms of power level in order to calculate the sound level at a receiving point. Now, let us consider how to obtain the sound power level in principle. For further detail the reader should refer to ISO 3740.

A.   Sound Pressure Measurement in Free Field
Using eqns (5.2), (5.6) and (5.11) the power level L_w can be calculated on the assumption that the sound source is omni-directional and the reflected sound has no effect on the field, as would be the case in an anechoic chamber.

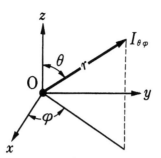

Fig. 10.35. Coordinates showing directivity of a sound source.

When the sound source is directional and the intensity at the point of distance r in the direction θ, φ is $I_{\theta\varphi}$, as shown in Fig 10.35, the total energy radiated for the whole solid angle is given by the following integral

$$W = \int I_{\theta\varphi} r^2 \, d\omega \qquad (10.100)$$

where $d\omega$ is an infinitesimal unit angle. In practice this may be approximated by the following expression where the solid angle is divided into small portions $\Delta\omega$

$$W = \Sigma I_{\theta\varphi} \, \Delta\omega \qquad (10.101)$$

If the measured sound pressure level at a distance r is $L_{\theta\varphi}$ the intensity $I_{\theta\varphi}$ is obtained from eqn (1.18).

$$I_{\theta\varphi} = \log_{10}^{-1} \frac{L_{\theta\varphi}}{10} \times 10^{-12} \qquad (10.102)$$

Substituting this into eqn (10.101),

$$L_\omega = 10 \log_{10} \left(\Sigma \log_{10}^{-1} \frac{L_{\theta\varphi}}{10} \Delta\omega \right) + 20 \log_{10} r \text{ dB} \qquad (10.103)$$

[Ex. 10.2] When the sound source has an axi-symmetrical directivity, locating the measured point in the plane including the axis of symmetry (e.g. z-axis), the individually-assigned solid angle $\Delta\omega$ may be obtained from

$$\Delta\omega = \int_{\theta_1}^{\theta_2} 2\pi \sin\theta \, d\theta$$

Table 10.6
Axi-symmetrical Case

Measuring point θ	$\Delta\omega$
0°	0·214
30°	1·63
60°	2·82
90°	3·25
120°	2·82
150°	1·63
180°	0·214

For example, if every measuring point is taken at 30° spacing, $\pm 15°$ is to be assigned at the boundaries for each division; thus $\Delta\omega$ for each measuring point will be given by Table 10.6

[Ex. 10.3] If a point source is located on the ground it is possible to make n equal divisions of hemi-spherical surface 2π; then eqn (10.100) becomes

$$W = \sum^{n} I_{\theta\varphi} r^2 \frac{2\pi}{n} \qquad \therefore \quad \frac{W}{2\pi r^2} = \frac{\sum^{n} I_{\theta\varphi}}{n}$$

Table 10.7
Coordinates of Measuring Points Dividing Hemisphere
of Unit Radius into Equal Surface Area

Division numbers	No.	x	y	z
	1	0	0.82	
	2	0.82	0	
4	3	0	−0.82	0.58
	4	−0.82	0	
	1	0	0.89	
	2	0.85	0.28	
6	3	0.53	−0.72	0.45
	4	−0.53	−0.72	
	5	−0.85	0.28	
	6	0	0	1

Thus, W is simply obtained from the average value of n intensities provided the measuring points follow the specified coordinates indicated in Table 10.7

B. Sound Power Measurement in a Reverberation Room

When a sound source of sound power W is situated in a room with a high degree of diffusion, the average energy density E in the steady state in the room is expressed by eqn (3.20); therefore

$$W = \frac{EcA}{4} \tag{10.104}$$

where Ec is the sound intensity from eqn (1.16). Then, by measuring the average sound pressure level $\overline{L}_p$ in the room, the power level is obtained from eqns (1.14) and (1.18) as follows,

$$L_\omega = 10\log_{10}\frac{W}{10^{-12}} = \overline{L}_p - 6 + 10\log_{10} A \tag{10.105}$$

where A can be determined from eqn (3.23) by measuring the reverberation time T.

This method is easily employed since it does not depend on the directivity. However, it is essential to be sure that the sound field is, in fact, diffuse.

C. Method of Intensity Measurement

The indirect methods are described above where the sound power is calculated from measured sound pressure. When the sound power is measured directly by a sound-intensity measuring system, many benefits accrue as follows: the effect of ambient noise can be cancelled in the steady state. In addition to measurements at fixed points, such as those shown in Tables 10.6 and 10.7, by sweeping the intensity probe over the surface enclosing the sound source, the single-value spatial average intensity is easily obtained. Therefore, it has become possible to measure the sound power emitted by a sound source in a noisy environment. Standardisation of this method will appear in due course.

D. Determination of Directivity Factor

When an omni-directional point-sound source is located in free space, the directivity factor $Q = 1$. The ratio of the sound intensity in a particular direction to that of an omni-directional source of the same total power is defined as the directivity factor $Q_{\theta\varphi}$ in that direction. The measurement of directivity should be performed in an anechoic room or the open air with no reflected sound.

[Ex. 3]   The sound pressure level is measured as 94 dB at 2 m from a sound source whose sound power level is known and is 105 dB. Let us find the directivity factor in that direction.

If the sound source is omni-directional, from eqn (5.2)

$$L = 105 - 11 - 20 \log_{10} 2 = 88 \text{ dB}$$

The required directivity factor Q is obtained from eqn (5.3) as follows:

$$10 \log_{10} Q = 94 - 88 = 6 \text{ dB}$$

The value expressed in dB is called the 'directivity gain'. Thus, the directivity factor $Q = 4$.

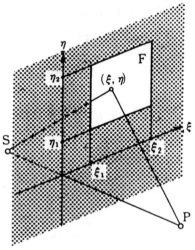

Fig. 10.36.

10.14   SOUND DIFFRACTION AROUND A SCREEN AND OTHER BARRIERS

A.   General Approximation for Sound Diffraction

Consider the application of the Fresnel-Kirchhoff approximate theory of diffraction in optics, to an infinite screen, which exists between sound source S and receiving point P and which has an open area F as shown in Fig. 10.36 The sound pressure $U(p)$ at the receiving point may be expressed as follows with the condition that the dimensions of the open area are sufficiently small compared to the distances to S and P.

$$U(p) = B \int \int_F e^{jkf(\xi,\eta)} \, d\xi \, d\eta \qquad (10.106)$$

where B is regarded as a constant though it depends on the source power, wavelength, distances between source, receiving point and the screen, and other geometrical relations. $k = 2\pi/\lambda$, ξ, η are the coordinates in the plane of the screen, and $f(\xi,\eta)$ is a contribution function to the point P. Integration is over the open area F.

When the open area is defined by ξ_1, ξ_2, η_1 and η_2, as shown in Fig. 10.36,

$$U(p) = B \int_{\xi_1}^{\xi_2} d\xi \int_{\eta_1}^{\eta_2} d\eta \cdot e^{jkf(\xi,\eta)} \qquad (10.107)$$

Transforming the variables from $\xi \to u$ and $\eta \to v$, and using an appropriate form of the function $f(\xi,\eta)$ following Kirchhoff's diffraction theory,

$$U(p) = jA \int_{u_1}^{u_2} e^{j(\pi/2)u^2} \, du \int_{v_1}^{v_2} e^{j(\pi/2)v^2} \, dv \qquad (10.108)$$

where A is a similar constant to B and the two integrals have the same form. The integrals are closely related to Fresnel's integral defined as the following:

$$\int_0^{u_1} e^{j(\pi/2)u^2} \, du = C(u_1) + jS(u_1) \qquad (10.109)$$

$$\left.\begin{aligned} C(u_1) &= \int_0^{u_1} \cos\left(\frac{\pi}{2}u^2\right) du \\ S(u_1) &= \int_0^{u_1} \sin\left(\frac{\pi}{2}u^2\right) du \end{aligned}\right\} \qquad (10.110)$$

These quantities are illustrated in the curve of Fig. 10.37 which is known as 'Cornu's Spiral' where u is the arc length from the origin.

When $u_1 \to \pm\infty$,

$$\left.\begin{aligned} C(\pm\infty) &= \pm\tfrac{1}{2} \\ S(\pm\infty) &= \pm\tfrac{1}{2} \end{aligned}\right\} \qquad (10.111)$$

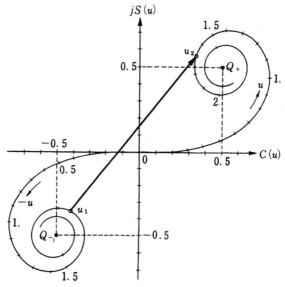

Fig. 10.37. Cornu's spiral.

Thus the values converge to the points of $Q\pm$.
    Further

$$\int_{u_1}^{u_2} e^{j(\pi/2)u^2}\, du$$

expresses a vector connecting two points u_1 and u_2 on the curve. This means that amplitude and phase are indicated simultaneously.

Then, assuming that S and P are situated in free space without any barrier, $u_1 = -\infty$, $v_1 = -\infty$, $u_2 = +\infty$, $v_2 = +\infty$, eqn (10.108) becomes

$$U_0 = -jA\{2C(\infty) + 2jS(\infty)\}^2 = -jA(1+j)^2 = 2A$$

Therefore, the diffraction factor [DF], which is the ratio of sound pressure when a screen exists to sound pressure in free space, may be expressed as follows:

$$[\text{DF}] = \frac{U(p)}{U_0} = \frac{-j}{2}\int_{u_1}^{u_2} e^{j(\pi/2)u^2}\, du \int_{u_1}^{u_2} e^{j(\pi/2)v^2}\, dv$$

$$= \frac{-j}{2}\big[\{C(u_2) - C(u_1) + j(S(u_2) - S(u_1))\}$$

$$\times \{C(v_2) - C(v_1) + j(S(v_2) - S(v_1))\}\big] \quad (10.112)$$

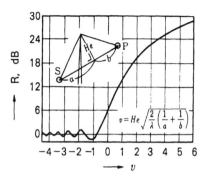

Fig. 10.38. Kirchoff's approximate theory of diffraction.

B. Semi-Infinite Thin Screen

When a semi-infinite thin screen exists between S and P, the integration of eqn (10.108) is carried out over the remaining semi-infinite open surface. In this case, in Fig. 10.36, $\xi_1 \to -\infty$, $\xi_2 \to +\infty$, and $\eta_2 \to +\infty$, so that, in eqn (10.112) $u_1 = -\infty$, $u_2 = +\infty$, and $v_2 = +\infty$ and hence

$$[DF] = \frac{-j}{2}\{1+j\}\{(\tfrac{1}{2} - C(v_1)) + j(\tfrac{1}{2} - S(v_1))\} \quad (10.113)$$

The attenuation caused by the screen in this condition in decibel form $[\text{Att}]_{1/2}$ is thus

$$[\text{Att}]_{1/2} = -10\log_{10}|[DF]|^2$$
$$= -10\log_{10}\tfrac{1}{2}\left\{(\tfrac{1}{2} - C(v_1))^2 + (\tfrac{1}{2} - S(v_1))^2\right\} \text{ dB} \quad (10.114)$$

where the bracketed terms correspond to the square of the absolute value of the vector from v_1 to Q_+ on the Cornu's Spiral shown in Fig. 10.37. The graph of $[\text{Att}]_{1/2}$ vs v in eqn (10.114) is shown in Fig 10.38.

C. Interpretation of Fresnel's Integral

It is necessary to understand the geometrical meaning of the integral variable v. For this purpose, use of the concept of Fresnel zones is appropriate.

Consider a spherical surface whose centre is at a sound source S with radius r_0 as shown in Fig. 10.39. According to Huygens' principle, the sound wave reaching the point P must be a synthesis of secondary wavelets emitted from the spherical surface. Taking the reference point as M_0 on the line SP, the wavelets emitted from other points are

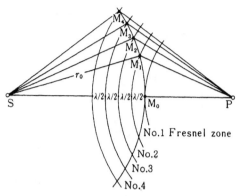

Fig. 10.39.

reduced in amplitude due to path difference δ, and their phases delayed by $k\delta$ ($k = 2\pi/\lambda$). When the secondary wavelets are expressed in the form of vectors, addition of these vectors leads to Cornu's Spiral.

When a tangent is drawn at a point v on the spiral, making an angle ψ with the $C(v)$ axis, from eqn (10.110),

$$\tan\psi = \frac{dS(v)}{dC(v)} = \frac{dS(v)/dv}{dC(v)/dv} = \frac{\sin((\pi/2)v^2)}{\cos((\pi/2)v^2)} = \tan\left(\frac{\pi}{2}v^2\right)$$

$$\therefore \quad \psi = \frac{\pi}{2}v^2 \tag{10.115}$$

Taking the secondary wave vector from M_0 as the origin, put $\psi_{M_0} = 0$. Then the phase lag ψ due to the path difference δ becomes

$$\psi = \frac{\pi}{2}v^2 = \frac{2\pi}{\lambda}\delta \quad \therefore \quad v = 2\sqrt{\frac{\delta}{\lambda}} \tag{10.116}$$

Hence it is found that v is related to path difference δ and wavelength λ.

In Fig 10.39 by plotting $M_1, M_2, \ldots, M_n$ on the spherical wave surface with the path differences $\delta_n = n \cdot \lambda/2$, $n = 1, 2, 3, \ldots$, divided annular regions $M_0 - M_1$, $M_1 - M_2, \ldots$ are created called Fresnel's zones. So, in

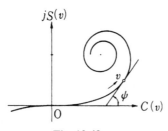

Fig. 10.40.

order to express the relationship between δ and λ the following general parameter is introduced,

$$N = \delta \cdot \frac{2}{\lambda} \tag{10.117}$$

called a Fresnel's zone number (or Fresnel Number). From eqns (10.116) and (10.117) we obtain $N = v^2/2$, and, changing the variable with the aid of this relation, Fig 10.38 can be rearranged to provide the dotted line values in Fig. 5.38 with parameter N in a form which is convenient for practical calculations. In practice, in place of eqn (10.114), it is more convenient and reliable to use the values from the solid line in Fig. 5.38 since it has been corrected by experiment.

D. Screen of Finite Length

As shown in Fig. 10.41, dividing the surface not obstructed by the screen into region $[A]$ as semi-infinite and regions $[B]$ and $[C]$ as quarter-infinite and integrating eqn (10.112) for each region, the results can be combined. In the case of noise, their energies are summed, neglecting their phases, since they are incoherent. While, in region $[A]$, eqn

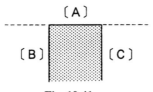

Fig. 10.41.

(10.114) is used, for a quarter-infinite zone, substituting $u_2 = +\infty$, $v_2 + \infty$ into eqn (10.112) the attenuation denoted by $[\text{Att}]_{1/4}$ is obtained

$$[\text{Att}]_{1/4} = -10 \log_{10} \tfrac{1}{2} \left\{ \left(\tfrac{1}{2} - C(u_1)\right)^2 + \left(\tfrac{1}{2} - S(u_1)\right)^2 \right\}$$
$$- 10 \log_{10} \tfrac{1}{2} \left\{ \left(\tfrac{1}{2} - C(v_1)\right)^2 + \left(\tfrac{1}{2} - S(v_1)\right)^2 \right\} \quad (10.118)$$

Thus, the procedure involved the summation of two terms of the same form as eqn (10.114). Fig. 5.38 is applicable in either case. Therefore, an approximate calculation for diffraction due to a finite screen is possible by simply taking the values from the solid line in Fig. 5.38 several times and summing them up.

E. Thickness and Edge Section of Barriers
So far the thickness of the screen has been neglected. However, in practice it will have a finite thickness and the section of the edge which

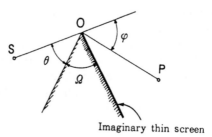

Fig. 10.42. Diffraction by a wedge.

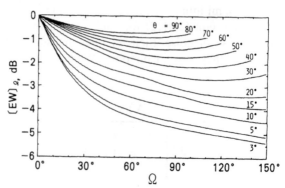

Fig. 10.43. Effect of wedge angle Ω on attenuation by diffraction with source angle θ as parameter.

produces diffraction may be simply described as a wedge of a certain apex angle. The effects of these characteristics on sound attenuation by diffraction can be expressed as correction terms which should be added to the approximate calculation described above. They are derived by taking the difference between the approximate approach and a rigorous solution of the wave theory.

a. Effect of Wedge Angle

On the surface on the receiver side of a wedge an imaginary thin screen is assumed as shown in Fig. 10.42. Sound attenuation by diffraction of the wedge $[\text{Att}]_\Omega$ can be expressed as

$$[\text{Att}]_\Omega = [\text{Att}]_0 + [\text{EW}]_\Omega \qquad (10.119)$$

where $[\text{EW}]_\Omega$ is the effect of wedge angle Ω. The first term is obtained from Fig. 5.38, while the second term can be obtained from Fig. 10.43 (Maekawa *et al.* 1985).

b. Effect of Thickness of Screen

In the same way as in the foregoing section, an imaginary thin screen is assumed on the surface on the receiver side of a thick barrier as shown in Fig. 10.44. The effect of thickness b on noise attenuation $_n[\text{ET}]_b$ is obtained as a correction term, so that the noise attenuation by the thick barrier is

$$_n[\text{Att}]_b = [\text{Att}]_0 + {}_n[\text{ET}]_b \qquad (10.120)$$

where

$$_n[\text{ET}]_b = K \log_{10}(kb) \qquad (10.121)$$

K is obtained from Fig. 10.45 (Fujiwara *et al.* 1977a).

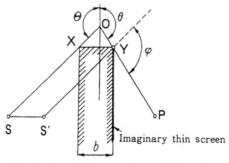

Fig. 10.44.   Diffraction by a thick barrier.

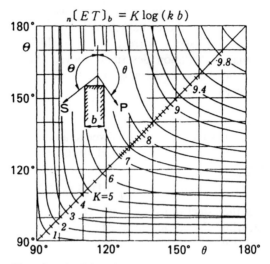

Fig. 10.45. Chart for obtaining the effect of thickness b of a noise barrier.

F. Effect of Surface Absorption

All screens or barriers discussed above are assumed to have a rigid surface. But, barriers which have sound absorbent treatment are widely

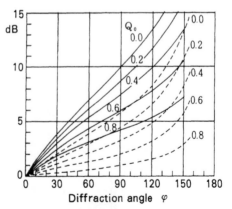

Fig. 10.46. Effect of surface absorption on barrier attenuation calculated for a thin half plane diffraction. Solid curves apply to a line source, dotted curves apply to a point source, Q_0 is the sound pressure reflection coefficient.

used. The effect of this is obtained from Fig. 10.46 which is derived from exact theory with some approximation for simple conditions. The correction term is usually not so large. This fact suggests that absorptive treatment is to be used, not for reducing the diffracted sound, but for suppressing the reflected sound (Fujiwara *et al.* 1977b).

G. Treatment of Large Noise Source

It has been assumed that the sound is propagated from a point source. If a large extended noise source is assumed to be an ensemble of many incoherent point sources, the sound energy received is obtained by summing the sound energies at the receiver from each point source as follows,

$$[\text{Att}] = 10 \log_{10} \left\{ \frac{\sum\limits_{i=1}^{n} \dfrac{K_i}{d_i^2}}{\sum\limits_{i=1}^{n} \dfrac{K_i}{d_i^2} \log_{10}^{-1} \dfrac{-[\text{Att}]_i}{10}} \right\} \text{dB} \qquad (10.122)$$

where K_i is the power factor, d_i the distance to the receiver and $[\text{Att}]_i$ the value of attenuation due to the barrier for each point source (Maekawa *et al.* 1971).

For the special case of a street or a highway, the source can be treated as many point sources in a line parallel to the edge of the barrier. The result is shown by a dashed curve in Fig. 5.38.

H. Effect of Ground Absorption

The calculation of sound attenuation by diffraction with a screen on the ground is performed in Fig. 5.39 under conditions of perfect reflection at the ground surface. The ground, however, generally has a finite acoustic impedance so that sound attenuates as it propagates over the ground without any barrier as shown in Fig. 5.14 in Chap. 5. If there is a barrier on the ground, the insertion loss of the barrier is obtained by subtraction of the ground attenuation from the barrier attenuation. The value of insertion loss may then possibly be negative. Figure 10.47 shows an example of the calculation of insertion loss by a barrier. We have to pay attention to the fact that the performance of a barrier on absorptive ground may be worse than expected (Isei *et al.* 1980).

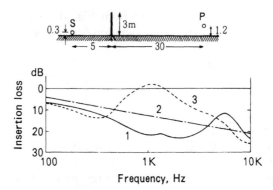

Fig. 10.47. Calculated insertion loss of a barrier on the ground. The line source is above a hard surface, and the ground on the receiver side of the barrier is hard in Curve 1 and 2 but soft, grass-covered, in Curve 3. Curves 1 and 3 show exact results from wave theory, while Curve 2 is an approximate value estimated using the dashed curve in Fig. 5.38 [Ex. 5.5].

10.15   PRINCIPLE OF SEA (STATISTICAL ENERGY ANALYSIS)

Transmission of structure-borne sound in buildings is very difficult to solve analytically since most practical structures have complicated systems, each of which have resonant modes of vibration. So a statistical approximate calculation of energy flow has been developed called SEA (Statistical Energy Analysis).

Considering two systems I and II, coupled as shown in Fig. 10.48 where P_{1in}, P_{2in} are input powers, P_{1d}, P_{2d} are dissipating powers and the power flow between two systems is P_{12}: from system I to system II, and P_{21} is the power flow from system II to system I, respectively. Then

$$P_{1in} = P_{1d} - P_{12} + P_{21} \qquad (10.123)$$

$$P_{2in} = P_{2d} - P_{21} + P_{12} \qquad (10.124)$$

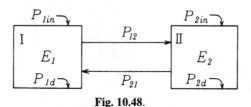

Fig. 10.48.

where the energy dissipated in each system P_{id} at angular frequency ω is

$$P_{id} = E_i \omega \eta_i \qquad (10.125)$$

where E_i is the energy stored in one cycle of vibration, η is the dissipation loss factor in each system respectively.

Assuming further that the waves transmitting and exchanging energy through each system are uncorrelated with each other, we can separate the power flow as

$$P_{12} = E_1 \omega \eta_{12} \qquad (10.126)$$

$$P_{21} = E_2 \omega \eta_{21} \qquad (10.127)$$

where η_{12} is the coupling loss factor from system I to system II and η_{21} is the coupling loss factor from system II to system I.

Then the net power flow between the two systems is

$$\bar{P}_{12} = P_{12} - P_{21} = \omega(E_1 \eta_{12} - E_2 \eta_{21}) \qquad (10.128)$$

Here we have assumed that each resonant mode within a narrow frequency band $\Delta \omega$ has the same energy, and also that the coupling of the individual resonant modes of both systems is approximately the same.

Now, defining the modal energy as

$$E_m = \frac{E(\Delta \omega)}{n(\omega) \Delta \omega} \quad (\text{W s/Hz}) \qquad (10.129)$$

where $E(\Delta \omega)$ is the total energy in angular frequency band $\Delta \omega$ and $n(\omega)$ is the modal density, i.e. the number of modes in unit band width ($\Delta \omega = 1$) centred on ω.

From this definition, assuming equal distribution of energy in the modes and the same coupling-loss factor,

$$\eta_{12} \cdot n_1(\omega) = \eta_{21} \cdot n_2(\omega) \qquad (10.130)$$

therefore, combining eqns (10.128) and (10.130) gives

$$\bar{P}_{12} = \omega \eta_{12} n_1(\omega)[E_{1m} - E_{2m}] \Delta \omega \ (\text{W}) \qquad (10.131)$$

where E_{1m}, E_{2m} are modal energies for systems 1 and 2 respectively (W s/Hz). This is the fundamental equation of the SEA method. It shows that the power flow is from the system with higher modal energy to that with lower modal energy. It does not depend on any dynamic variables, but is similar to the equation for heat flow due to temperature difference. Though it is a very simple equation, there are many problems to be investigated such as the validity of simplifying assumptions, determination of loss factors, modal densities and modal energies and so on. (See Lit. B19, B22).

APPENDICES

Table A.1
Standing Wave Ratio and Related Coefficients

$20\log n$ (dB)	n	α_0 (%)	$\lvert r_p \rvert$ (%)	$20\log n$ (dB)	n	α_0 (%)	$\lvert r_p \rvert$ (%)
0·0	1·000	100·0	0·0	7·0	2·239	85·4	38·3
0·2	1·023	100·0	1·1	7·2	2·291	84·6	39·2
0·4	1·047	99·9	2·3	7·4	2·344	83·8	40·2
0·6	1·072	99·9	3·5	7·6	2·399	83·1	41·2
0·8	1·096	99·8	4·6	7·8	2·455	82·3	42·1
1·0	1·122	99·7	5·8	8·0	2·512	81·5	43·1
1·2	1·148	99·5	6·9	8·2	2·570	80·7	44·0
1·4	1·175	99·4	8·1	8·4	2·630	79·8	44·9
1·6	1·202	99·2	9·2	8·6	2·692	79·0	45·8
1·8	1·230	98·9	10·3	8·8	2·754	78·2	46·7
2·0	1·259	98·7	11·5	9·0	2·818	77·3	47·6
2·2	1·288	98·4	12·6	9·2	2·884	76·5	48·5
2·4	1·318	98·1	13·7	9·4	2·951	75·6	49·4
2·6	1·349	97·8	14·9	9·6	3·020	74·7	50·3
2·8	1·380	97·5	16·0	9·8	3·090	73·9	51·1
3·0	1·413	97·1	17·1	10·0	3·162	73·0	52·0
3·2	1·445	96·7	18·2	10·2	3·236	72·1	52·8
3·4	1·479	96·3	19·3	10·4	3·311	71·3	53·6
3·6	1·514	95·8	20·5	10·6	3·388	70·4	54·4
3·8	1·549	95·3	21·5	10·8	3·467	69·5	55·2
4·0	1·589	94·8	22·8	11·0	3·548	68·6	56·0
4·2	1·622	94·4	23·7	11·2	3·631	67·7	56·8
4·4	1·660	93·8	24·8	11·4	3·715	66·8	57·6
4·6	1·698	93·3	25·9	11·6	3·802	65·9	58·4
4·8	1·738	92·8	27·0	11·8	3·890	65·1	59·1
5·0	1·778	92·2	28·0	12·0	3·981	64·2	59·9
5·2	1·820	91·5	29·1	12·2	4·074	63·3	60·6
5·4	1·862	90·9	30·1	12·4	4·169	62·4	61·3
5·6	1·905	90·3	31·2	12·6	4·266	61·5	62·0
5·8	1·950	89·6	32·2	12·8	4·365	60·7	62·7
6·0	1·995	89·0	33·2	13·0	4·467	59·8	63·4
6·2	2·042	88·3	34·3	13·2	4·571	58·9	64·1
6·4	2·089	87·6	35·3	13·4	4·677	58·0	64·8
6·6	2·138	86·9	36·3	13·6	4·786	57·2	65·4
6·8	2·188	86·1	37·3	13·8	4·898	56·3	66·1

Table A.1—*contd.*

$20\log n$ (dB)	n	α_0 (%)	$\lvert r_p \rvert$ (%)	$20\log n$ (dB)	n	α_0 (%)	$\lvert r_p \rvert$ (%)
14·0	5·012	55·5	66·7	22·0	12·59	27·3	85·3
14·2	5·129	54·6	67·4	22·5	13·34	25·9	86·1
14·4	5·248	53·8	68·0	23·0	14·13	24·7	86·8
14·6	5·370	52·9	68·6	23·5	14·96	23·5	87·5
14·8	5·495	52·1	69·2	24·0	15·85	22·3	88·1
15·0	5·623	51·3	69·8	24·5	16·79	21·2	88·8
15·2	5·754	50·5	70·4	25·0	17·78	20·2	89·4
15·4	5·888	49·7	71·0	25·5	18·84	19·2	89·9
15·6	6·026	48·8	71·5	26·0	19·95	18·2	90·5
15·8	6·166	48·0	72·1	26·5	21·13	17·3	91·0
16·0	6·310	47·2	72·6	27·0	22·39	16·4	91·5
16·2	6·457	46·5	73·2	27·5	23·71	15·5	91·9
16·4	6·607	45·7	73·7	28·0	25·12	14·7	92·3
16·6	6·761	44·9	74·2	28·5	26·61	14·0	92·8
16·8	6·918	44·1	74·7	29·0	28·18	13·2	93·2
17·0	7·079	43·4	75·2	29·5	29·85	12·5	93·5
17·2	7·244	42·6	75·7	30·0	31·62	11·9	93·9
17·4	7·413	41·9	76·2	31·0	35·48	10·7	94·5
17·6	7·586	41·2	76·7	32·0	39·81	9·6	95·1
17·8	7·762	40·4	77·2	33·0	44·67	8·6	95·6
18·0	7·943	39·7	77·6	34·0	50·12	7·7	96·1
18·2	8·128	39·0	78·1	35·0	56·23	6·9	96·5
18·4	8·318	38·3	78·5	36·0	63·10	6·2	96·9
18·6	8·511	37·6	79·0	37·0	70·79	5·5	97·2
18·8	8·710	37·0	79·4	38·0	79·43	4·9	97·5
19·0	8·913	36·3	79·8	39·0	89·13	4·4	97·8
19·2	9·120	35·6	80·2	40·0	100·0	3·9	98·0
19·4	9·333	35·0	80·6	42·0	125·9	3·1	98·4
19·6	9·550	34·3	81·0	44·0	158·5	2·5	98·8
19·8	9·772	33·7	81·4	46·0	199·5	1·9	99·0
20·0	10·000	33·1	81·8	48·0	251·2	1·6	99·2
20·5	10·59	31·5	82·7	50·0	316·2	1·3	99·4
21·0	11·22	30·0	83·6	55·0	562·3	0·7	99·6
21·5	11·89	28·6	84·5	60·0	1000·0	0·4	99·8

Table A.2
Sound Absorption Coefficients
2.A   Common Building Materials

No.	Materials	Frequency (Hz)					
		125	250	500	1 k	2 k	4 k
1	Brick, bare concrete surface	0·01	0·02	0·02	0·02	0·03	0·04
2	Mortal smooth finishing, Plaster, Marble, Ceramic-tile finishing	0·01	0·01	0·02	0·02	0·02	0·03
3	Cloth-finishing on concrete wall	0·03	0·03	0·03	0·04	0·06	0·08
4	Plastic-tile on concrete floor	0·01	0·02	0·02	0·02	0·03	0·04
5	Wood-floor (parquet, or flooring on stud)	0·16	0·14	0·11	0·08	0·08	0·07
6	Needle-punch carpet	0·03	0·04	0·06	0·10	0·20	0·35
7	Pile carpet 10 mm thick	0·09	0·10	0·20	0·25	0·30	0·40
8	Glass-wall 10 mm thick	0·15	0·06	0·04	0·03	0·02	0·02
9	Window-glass (in wooden-frame)	0·35	0·25	0·18	0·12	0·07	0·04
10	Plexiglass for illuminating (910 × 910 × 2 mm)	0·40	0·25	0·20	0·20	0·22	0·25
11	Velvet-curtain (with no drape)	0·05	0·07	0·13	0·22	0·32	0·35
12	Velvet-curtain draped to half its area (100 mm air space)	0·10	0·25	0·55	0·65	0·70	0·70
13	(500 mm air space)	0·15	0·25	0·50	0·75	0·80	0·85
14	Gravel 150 mm thick	0·15	0·30	0·80	0·42	0·61	0·72
15	Sand (dried) 125 mm thick	0·24	0·34	0·45	0·62	0·76	0·95
16	Water surface	0·01	0·01	0·01	0·02	0·02	0·03
17	Reflecting panels (of plywood with dumping sheet) on stage	0·20	0·13	0·10	0·07	0·06	0·06
18	Equivalent absorption coefficient of virtual surface without the reflecting panels on stage	0·40	0·50	0·60	0·60	0·60	0·60
19	Proscenium opening	0·30	0·35	0·40	0·45	0·50	0·55
20	Lighting opening (of non absorptive treated booth)	0·10	0·15	0·20	0·22	0·25	0·30
21	Opening for ventilation ducts, etc.	0·75	0·80	0·80	0·80	0·85	0·85
		Absorption Area (m^2/p)					
22	Plywood-chair	0·02	0·02	0·02	0·04	0·04	0·03
23	Theatre chair covered with vinyl leather	0·04	0·13	0·22	0·17	0·16	0·11
24	Theatre chair upholstered with moquette	0·14	0·25	0·30	0·30	0·30	0·30
25	Person sitting on the upholstered chair	0·25	0·35	0·40	0·40	0·40	0·40

Table A.2—*contd.*

2.B   Sound Absorption Coefficients of Porous Materials

No.	Materials	Thick (mm)	Air layer (mm)	125	250	500	1 k	2 k	4 k
				Frequency (Hz)					
1	Glasswool 16–24 (kg/m³)	25	0	0·10	0·30	0·60	0·70	0·80	0·85
2		50	0	0·20	0·65	0·90	0·85	0·80	0·85
3		100	0	0·60	0·95	0·95	0·85	0·80	0·90
4		25	40	0·15	0·40	0·70	0·85	0·90	0·95
5		50	40	0·25	0·80	0·95	0·90	0·85	0·90
6		25	100	0·22	0·57	0·83	0·82	0·90	0·90
7		50	100	0·45	0·97	0·99	0·85	0·80	0·92
8		25	300	0·65	0·70	0·75	0·80	0·75	0·85
9		50	300	0·75	0·85	0·85	0·80	0·80	0·85
10	Glasswool 32–48 (kg/m³)	25	0	0·12	0·30	0·65	0·80	0·85	0·85
11		50	0	0·20	0·65	0·95	0·90	0·80	0·85
12		25	40	0·12	0·45	0·85	0·90	0·85	0·90
13		50	40	0·28	0·90	0·95	0·87	0·85	0·94
14		25	100	0·25	0·70	0·90	0·85	0·85	0·90
15	Glasswool 32–40 (kg/m³)	100	0	0·70	1·00	0·98	0·85	0·70	0·80
16		100	40	0·78	1·00	0·99	0·94	0·90	0·90
17	(with glass-cloth cover)	100	100	0·80	1·00	0·99	0·93	0·84	0·84
18	Rockwool 40–140 (kg/m³)	25	0	0·10	0·30	0·70	0·80	0·80	0·85
19		50	0	0·20	0·65	0·95	0·90	0·85	0·90
20		25	40	0·20	0·65	0·90	0·85	0·80	0·80
21		50	40	0·35	0·85	0·95	0·90	0·85	0·85
22		25	100	0·35	0·65	0·90	0·85	0·85	0·80
23		50	100	0·55	0·90	0·95	0·90	0·85	0·85
24		25	300	0·65	0·85	0·85	0·80	0·80	0·85
25		50	300	0·75	0·95	0·95	0·85	0·85	0·90
26	Soft Urethane foam	20	0	0·07	0·20	0·40	0·55	0·70	0·70
27		20	40	0·10	0·25	0·60	0·90	0·80	0·85
28	Polystyrene foam	25	0	0·04	0·05	0·06	0·14	0·30	0·25
29	Sprayed rockwool	12	0	0·05	0·12	0·40	0·55	0·70	0·75
30		25	0	0·12	0·35	0·80	0·88	0·85	0·90
31	Sprayed Pearlite plaster	5	0	0·04	0·10	0·17	0·17	0·19	0·20
32	Cemented fine-excelsior board	25	0	0·03	0·14	0·30	0·55	0·65	0·60
33	Cemented chipped-wood board	50	0	0·15	0·20	0·70	0·80	0·70	0·85
34	Rockwool board	12	300	0·35	0·30	0·40	0·55	0·65	0·70
35	(over gypsum board)	12	300	0·20	0·20	0·40	0·60	0·70	0·75
36	Ceramic board 1·36 (g/cm³)	20	0	0·05	0·10	0·20	0·40	0·80	0·60
37	(with air space behind)	20	200	0·40	0·90	0·80	0·55	0·55	0·70

Table A.2—*contd.*

2.C Sound Absorption Coefficients of Board Form Materials

No.	Materials	Thick (mm)	Air layer (mm)	125	250	500	1 k	2 k	4 k
1	Gypsum board	9 ~ 12 ⎱	⎧ 45	0·26	0·13	0·09	0·05	0·05	0·05
2	Flexible cement board	3 ~ 5 ⎰	⎨ 90	0·23	0·12	0·08	0·06	0·05	0·05
3	Calcium Silicate board	6 ~ 8 ⎰	⎩ 180	0·18	0·10	0·08	0·06	0·06	0·05
4	Lauan plywood	3	45	0·45	0·16	0·10	0·08	0·07	0·08
5		6 ~ 9	45	0·15	0·28	0·12	0·07	0·07	0·08
6		6 ~ 9	90	0·25	0·17	0·09	0·07	0·07	0·08
7		12	45	0·25	0·14	0·07	0·04	0·07	0·08
8	Particle-wood board	20	45	0·27	0·08	0·08	0·06	0·08	0·07
9	Corrugated Polyester board		90	0·26	0·41	0·22	0·12	0·10	0·15

Table A.2—*contd.*

2.D Slit-Resonator Type Sound Absorbing Structures

No.		Slit Width (mm)	Air Space (mm)	125	250	500	1 k	2 k	4 k
1		4·5	80	0·08	0·35	0·22	0·15	0·15	0·15
2		4·5	180	0·22	0·33	0·17	0·24	0·14	0·12
3		20·0	80	0·07	0·15	0·33	0·20	0·18	0·17
4		20·0	180	0·12	0·37	0·28	0·25	0·17	0·15
5		4·5	80	0·18	0·77	0·40	0·24	0·20	0·26
6		20·0	80	0·12	0·50	0·68	0·40	0·26	0·22
7		4·5	50	0·15	0·37	0·40	0·27	0·15	0·12
8		20·0	50	0·10	0·25	0·44	0·42	0·35	0·30
9		20·0	300	0·45	0·50	0·37	0·40	0·40	0·37
10		10·0	50	0·08	0·20	0·30	0·24	0·35	0·38
11		10·0	300	0·37	0·40	0·32	0·40	0·40	0·44

Table A.2—*contd.*

No.		Slit Width (mm)	Air Space (mm)	Frequency (Hz)					
				125	250	500	1 k	2 k	4 k
12		10·0	50	0·25	0·87	0·55	0·40	0·50	0·44
13		10·0	300	0·68	0·70	0·67	0·64	0·52	0·50
14		4·5	50	0·65	0·65	0·50	0·40	0·40	0·40
15		30·0	50	0·20	0·60	0·75	0·65	0·70	0·60

Table A.2—*contd.*

2.E   Sound Absorption Coefficient of Perforated Structures

No.	Diameter-pitch (perforation rate)	Thick. of board (mm)	Materials under the board (thickness; mm)	Air layer (mm)	Frequency (Hz)					
					125	250	500	1 k	2 k	4 k
1	4∅-15 (6%)	5	non	45	0·02	0·09	0·25	0·31	0·15	0·10
2			Glasswool (25)	45	0·15	0·35	0·82	0·52	0·23	0·22
3			non	180	0·12	0·45	0·30	0·25	0·23	0·16
4			non	500	0·45	0·31	0·31	0·30	0·30	0·28
5			Glasswool (25)	500	0·87	0·61	0·70	0·65	0·46	0·33
6	6∅-22 (6%)	9	non	45	0·03	0·09	0·46	0·31	0·15	0·15
7			Rockwool (25)	45	0·09	0·50	0·94	0·44	0·22	0·21
8			non	300	0·35	0·37	0·25	0·22	0·23	0·22
9			Rockwool (25)	300	0·68	0·82	0·58	0·53	0·33	0·23
10	6∅-15 (13%)	5	non	45	0·02	0·08	0·16	0·31	0·20	0·18
11			Glasswool (50)	45	0·13	0·32	0·78	0·69	0·40	0·31
12			non	500	0·35	0·29	0·30	0·35	0·36	0·39
13			Glasswool (25)	500	0·87	0·68	0·76	0·82	0·71	0·50
14	8∅-16 (20%)	4	non	300	0·22	0·30	0·29	0·23	0·19	0·28
15			Glasswool (25)	300	0·61	0·73	0·64	0·61	0·62	0·58
16			Rockwool (25)	300	0·85	0·94	0·83	0·75	0·66	0·60
17	9∅-15 (28%)	5	non	45	0·01	0·05	0·11	0·21	0·16	0·13
18			Glasswool (50)	45	0·15	0·30	0·68	0·78	0·59	0·58
19		6	Rockwool (25)	45	0·08	0·25	0·71	0·91	0·78	0·72
20		5	non	500	0·30	0·25	0·27	0·36	0·39	0·42
21			Glasswool (25)	500	0·83	0·72	0·80	0·90	0·87	0·70

Table A.3
Average Transmission Loss of Various Constructions

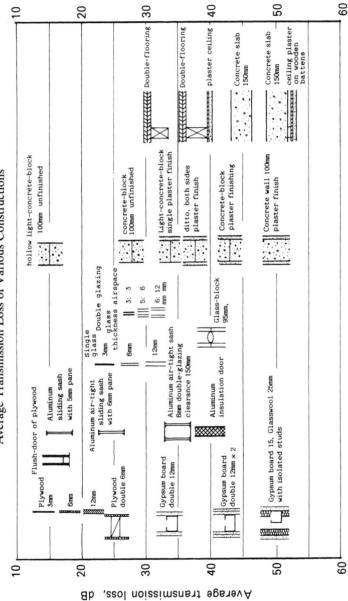

Average transmission loss, dB

Table A.3—*contd.*

3.A   Transmission Loss of Single Boards (dB)

No.	Materials	Thick. (mm)	Surface density (kg/m²)	Frequency (Hz) 125	250	500	1 k	2 k	4 k	Average 125 ~ 4 k
1	Lauan Plywood	6	3·0	11	13	16	21	25	23	17
2		12	8·0	18	20	24	24	25	30	22
3		40	24	24	25	27	30	38	43	29
4	Particle-wood board (Homogen)	20	13	24	27	26	27	24	33	26
5	(Novopan)	35	17	21	23	27	28	24	29	25
6	Parlite board	12		17	18	24	30	33	30	24
7	Flexible cement board	4	7·1	18	22	23	28	33	36	25
8		6	11	19	25	25	31	34	28	27
9	Gypsum board	9	8·7	15	20	25	28	34	25	25
10	Sheet metals: Aluminium	1·2		8	11	14	21	27	30	18
11	Steel	0·7	5·6	9	14	20	26	30	37	20
12	Lead	1·0	11·3	25	25	29	33	38	43	32
13	Glass pane	3	7·5	15	18	22	28	32	24	23
14		6	15	17	23	28	29	25	36	26
15		10	25	21	27	31	29	33	42	31
16	Double glazing: 6–18 mm airspace between double panes of 5 mm	16 ~ 28		16 ~ 18	17 ~ 21	27 ~ 31	32 ~ 34	28 ~ 30	30 ~ 32	26
17	Glass block 145 × 145	95	97	30	32	38	46	53	39	40
18	Ordinary concrete surface unfinished	120		32	40	46	53	59	64	49
19		150		35	40	49	55	60	65	51
20	Foamed concrete (ALC)	150		33	33	30	42	50	55	41
21	ditto resin-plaster 3 mm both sides	150		31	33	40	46	52	56	43
22	Concrete-block bare surface	100	160	19	24	28	32	36	40	28
23	ditto oil-paint both sides	100	160	32	36	40	48	54	51	41
24	ditto plaster 15 mm both sides	100	160	33	37	42	49	56	57	43
25	ditto mortal-finish both sides	150	180	31	35	45	52	56	56	44

Table A.3—*contd.*

3.B   Transmission Loss of Double Leaf Walls (dB)

No.	Materials and Structures	Surface density (kg/m²)	125	250	500	1 k	2 k	4 k	Averages 125–4 k
	Surface material (thickness-airlayer-thickness) + absorbing materials inside (mm)								
1	Plywood 5-75-5		13	17	25	31	40	40	28
2	ditto + Glasswool 25		20	17	31	36	46	47	33
3	Novopan 8-45-8		5	11	22	31	37	33	20
4	8-100-8		14	21	31	40	50	36	31
5	Gypsum board 9-42-9		15	22	27	33	30	32	28
6	ditto + Glasswool 25		16	28	32	37	33	34	32
7	Gypsum board 12-65-12	18·6	15	21	30	40	40	42	33
8	ditto + Rockwool 50	20·6	15	32	48	54	50	45	43
9	Gypsum board 12×2-65-12×2	39·2	20	33	40	50	50	50	43
10	Heavy gypsum board + GW50	49·0	30	40	50	57	55	52	50
11	Gypsum board 15×2-65-15×2	43·6	25	35	43	53	50	55	45
12	GW-Gyp. board 15×3-65-15×3	75·0	28	40	49	57	57	56	50
13	Silicate Calcium board $6 + 8 - 75 - 8 + 6$	42·6	27	35	43	48	53	59	45
14	ditto $8 \times 3 - 65 - 8 \times 3$	43·0	29	41	47	51	54	54	47

Table A.3—*contd.*

3.C   Transmission Loss of Sandwich Panels (dB)

No.	Materials and Constructions	125	250	500	1 k	2 k	4 k	Averages 125–4 k
	Surface material (thickness—that of core—that of surface) Core Material							
1	Plywood (6-50-6) Polyurethane foam	14	18	20	16	32	32	22
2	Plywood (3-60-3) Polystyrene foam	19	21	24	22	30	38	24
3	Gypsum board (7-50-7) Polyurethane foam	16	20	21	22	40	45	27
4	Fiber cement slate (6-50-6) Polyurethane foam	20	21	19	30	37	44	28
5	Flexible cement board (3-20-3) Polystyrene foam	21	18	23	24	22	45	25
6	ditto (3-25-3) Cemented excelsior board	26	25	27	30	35	40	30
7	ditto (3-30-3) Foamed concrete board	30	32	33	35	43	47	36
8	ditto (3-40-3) Pearlite grain	26	27	29	31	36	38	31
9	ditto (5-40-5) Glasswool	21	26	35	38	45	37	33
10	Plywood (4-25-4) Paper honeycomb	11	13	16	18	22	30	18
11	Gypsum board (9-20-9) ditto	15	22	27	30	32	31	26
12	Aluminium plate (1-25-1) ditto	16	15	17	17	21	23	18

Table A.3—*contd.*
3.D Transmission Loss of Window and Openings (dB)

No.	Materials and Constructions	*Frequency (Hz)* 125	250	500	1 k	2 k	4 k	*Averages* 125–4 k
1	Popular sliding aluminium sash (glass 5 mm)	18	20	23	21	22	25	22
2	Airtight aluminium sash (glass 5 mm)	20	23	27	29	29	30	26
3	Sliding aluminium sash double (air layer 100)	18	22	26	25	21	32	24
4	ditto (air layer 200 mm)	25	27	32	26	24	32	27
5	Airtight aluminium sash double (air layer 100)	27	31	31	34	34	36	32
6	ditto (air layer 200 mm)	27	34	40	45	50	50	41
7	2 mm steel flash door with air layer 45 mm	25	30	34	37	36	35	32
8	Aluminium insulation door for studio use	30	42	45	47	57	55	45

Table A.4
Physical Dimensions and Units

	MKS → cgs	*cgs → MKS*	*Dimension*
Density	$1\ kg/m^3 = 10^{-3}\ g/cm^3$	$1\ g/cm^3 = 10^3\ kg/m^3$	ML^{-3}
Surface density	$1\ kg/m^2 = 10^{-1}\ g/cm^2$	$1\ g/cm^2 = 10\ kg/m^2$	ML^{-2}
Speed	$1\ m/s = 10^2\ cm/s$	$1\ cm/s = 10^{-2}\ m/s$	LT^{-1}
Acceleration	$1\ m/s^2 = 10^2\ cm/s^2$	$1\ cm/s^2 = 10^{-2}\ m/s^2$	LT^{-2}
Force	$1\ N = 10^5$ dyne ($\equiv 1\ kg.m/s^2$)	1 dyne $= 10^{-5}\ N$ ($\equiv 1\ g.cm/s^2$)	MLT^{-2}
Pressure (sound pressure)	$1\ N/m^2 = 10\ dyne/cm^2$ ($\equiv 10\ \mu bar$) $\equiv 1$ Pa	$1\ dyne/cm^2 = 10^{-1}\ N/m^2$ ($\equiv 1\ \mu bar$)	$ML^{-1}T^{-2}$
Work load (sound energy)	$1\ J = 10^7$ erg ($\equiv 1\ N.m$)	1 erg $= 10^{-7}\ J$ ($\equiv 1$ dyne.cm)	ML^2T^{-2}
Power (acoustic power)	$1\ W = 10^7\ erg/s$ ($\equiv 1\ J/s$)	$1\ erg/s = 10^{-7}\ W$	ML^2T^{-3}
Acoustic impedance-density or Specific-acoustic impedance (flow resistance)	1 MKS rayl $= 10^{-1}$ rayl ($\equiv 1\ N.s/m^3 \equiv 1\ kg/m^2\ s$)	1 rayl $= 10$ MKS rayl ($\equiv 1\ dynes/cm^3 \equiv 1\ g/cm^2\ s$)	$ML^{-2}T^{-1}$
Acoustic resistance (ac.ohm)	1 MKS ac.Ω $= 10^3$ cgs ac.Ω ($\equiv 1$ MKS rayl.$m^2 \equiv kg/s$)	1 cgs ac.Ω $= 10^{-3}$ MKS ac.Ω ($\equiv 1$ rayl.$cm^2 \equiv 1\ g/s$)	MT^{-1}

REFERENCE PAPERS

Ando Y. (1968) *IEEE: Electro. & Comm. Jpn.* 51A-8: 303–310.
Ando Y. & Hattori H. (1970) *J. Acous. Soc. Am.* 47(4): 1128–1130.
Ando Y. & Hattori H. (1977) *Bri. J. Obstetrics Gynae.* 84(2): 115–118.
Barron M. (1971) *J. Sound Vib.* 15: 475–494.
Barron M. & Chiney C. B. (1979) *Appl. Acous.* 12(5): 361–375.
Barron M. & Marshall A. H. (1981) *J. Sound Vib.* 77: 211–232.
Beranek L. L. *et al.* (1946) *J. Acous. Soc. Am.* 18(1): 140–150.
Beranek L. L. (1947) *J. Acous. Soc. Am.* 19: 556–568.
Beranek L. L. (1957) *Noise Control* 3: 19–27.
Berkhout A. J. (1988) *J. Aud. Eng. Soc.* 36(12): 977–995.
Breeuwer R. & Tuckker J. C. (1976) *Appl. Acous.* 9(2):77–101.
Cadoux R. E. (1992) *euro. noise '92, Proc. I.O.A.* Vol. 14 pt. 4: 41–47.
Cook R. K. *et al.* (1955) *J. Acous. Soc. Am.* 27: 1072.
Els H. & Blauert J. (1986) *Proc. Symp. Vancouver 12th ICA* 65–70.
Eyring C. F. (1931) *J. Acous. Soc. Am.* 3: 181.
Fujiwara K. *et al.* (1977a) *Appl. Acous.* 10(2): 147–159.
Fujiwara K. *et al.* (1977b) *Appl. Acous.* 10(3): 167–179.
Fujiwara K. *et al.* (1992) *Appl. Acous.* 35(2): 149–152.
Furukawa H. & Fujiwara K. *et al.* (1990) *Appl. Acous.* 29(4): 255–271.
Gomperts M. C. (1964) *ACUSTICA* 14: 1.
Gomperts M. C. & Kihlman (1967) *ACUSTICA* 18: 144.
Houtgast T. & Steeneken H. (1973) *ACUSTICA* 28: 66–73.
Hunt F. V. (1939) *J. Acous. Soc. Am.* 10: 216–227.
Ingard U. & Bolt R. H. (1951) *J. Acous. Soc. Am.* 23: 533–540.
Isei T. *et al.* (1980) *J. Acous. Soc. Am.* 67(1): 46–58.
Ishii K. & Tachibana H. (1974) *Proc. 8th ICA (London)* 2: 610.
Kosten C. W. (1960) *ACUSTICA* 10: 400.
Krokstad A. *et al.* (1983) *Appl. Acous.* 16(4): 291–312.
Larrson C. *et al.* (1988) *Appl. Acous.* 25(1): 17–31.
Leventhall H. G. (1987) *Proc. 4th Int. Meeting Low Freq. Noise Vib.* 2–5–1.
London A. (1950) *J. Acous. Soc. Am.* 22: 263.
Maekawa Z. (1968) *Appl. Acous.* 1(3): 157–173.
Maekawa Z. and Sakurai Y. (1968) *Proc. 6th ICA (Tokyo)* E–1–8.
Maekawa Z. *et al.* (1971) *Symp. Noise Prevention 7th ICA. (Miskolc)* 4·8: 1–7.
Maekawa Z. & Osaki S. (1983) *Proc. 11th ICA (Paris)* 72: 1–4.
Maekawa Z. & Osaki S. (1985) *Appl. Acous.* 18(5): 355–368.
Mechel F. P. (1988) *J. Acous. Soc. Am.* 83(3): 1002–1013.
Miwa T. & Yonekawa Y. (1974) *Appl. Acous.* 7(2): 83–101.
Pinnington R. J. & Nathanail C. B. (1993) *Appl. Acous.* 40(1): 21–46.
Rindel J. H. (1991) *Appl. Acous.* 34(1): 7–17.
Robinson D. W. (1971) *J. Sound Vib.* 14: 279–298.
Sakurai Y. (1987) *J. Acous. Soc. Jpn. (E)* 8(4): 127–138.

Schroeder M. R. (1965) *J. Acous. Soc. Am.* 38: 409–412.
Schroeder M. R. (1979) *J. Acous. Soc. Am.* 65(4): 958–963.
Sekiguchi K. Kimura S. *et al.* (1985) *J. Acous. Soc. Jpn. (E)* 6(2): 103–115.
Shioda M. (1986) *J. Low Freq. Noise Vib.* 5(2): 51–59.
Spandoek F. *et al.* (1967) *ACUSTICA* 18: 213–226.
Steinke G. (1983) *J. Audio Eng. Soc.* 31(7–8): 500–511.
Stevens S. S. (1972) *J. Acous. Soc. Am.* 51(2): 575–593.
Strube H. W. (1981) *J. Acous. Soc. Am.* 70(2): 633–635.
Tachibana H. Yamasaki Y. *et al.* (1989) *J. Acous. Soc. Jpn. (E)* 10(2): 73–85.
Terai T. & Kawai Y. (1990) *J. Acous. Soc. Jpn. (E)* 11(1): 1–10.
Watters B. G. (1959) *J. Acous. Soc. Am.* 31(7): 898–911.
West M. *et al.* (1991) *Appl. Acous.* 33(3): 199–228.
Wilson G. P. & Soroka W. (1965) *J. Acous. Soc. Am.* 37: 286.
Yamasaki Y. & Itow T. (1989) *J. Acous. Soc. Jpn. (E)* 10(2): 101–110.
Zwicker E. (1960) *ACUSTICA* 10: 304–308.

BIBLIOGRAPHY

Literature A: for Acoustic Design

1. V. O. Knudsen & C. M. Harris, *Acoustical Designing in Architecture* (1950, John Wiley; 1978, Acous. Soc. Am.).
2. F. Ingerslev, *Acoustics in Modern Building Practice* (1952, Architectural press).
3. P. H. Parkin & H. R. Humphreys, *Acoustics Noise and Architecture* (1958, Faber & Faber).
4. L. L. Beranek *Music Acoustics and Architecture* (1962, John Wiley).
5. A. Lawrence, *Architectural Acoustics* (1970, Elsevier).
6. L. L. Doelle, *Environmental Acoustics* (1972, McGraw-Hill).
7. ASHRAE Hand Book, *Systems Volume 1980*, The American Society of Heating, Refrigerating and Airconditioning Engineers Inc.).
8. D. Collison: Stage Sound (1982, Cassell pub.).
9. Acous. Soc. Am., ed., *Halls for Music Performance Two Decades of Experience 1962-1982* (1982, American Inst. Physics).
10. D. Lubman & E. A. Wetherill, ed., *Acoustics of Worship Spaces* (1985, Acous. Soc. Am.).
11. M. Forsyth: *Buildings for Music.* (1985, MIT Press).
12. R. H. Talaske & R. E. Boner, ed., *Theatres for Drama Performance* (1986, *Acous. Soc. Am.*).
13. P. Lord & D. Templeton, *The Architecture of Sound, Designing Places of Assembly* (1986, Architectural Press).
14. A. Lawrence, *Acoustics and the Built Environment* (1989, Elsevier Science Pub.).
15. J. Eargle, *Handbook of Sound System Design.* (1989, ELAR Pub.).
16. M. Barron, *Auditorium Acoustics and Architectural Design.* (1993, E & FN Spon).

Literature B: for Acoustic Research

1. Lord Rayleigh, *Theory of Sound I, II, 1877* (1945, Dover).
2. W. C. Sabine, *Collected Papers on Acoustics, 1923* (1964, Dover).
3. H. Lamb, *The Dynamical Theory of Sound, 1925* (1960, Dover).
4. V. O. Knudsen, *Architectural Acoustics* (1932, John Wiley & Son).
5. S. S. Stevens & H. Davis, *Hearing its Psychology and Physiology 1938* (1983, Acous. Soc. Am.).
6. P. M. Morse & R. H. Bolt, *Sound Waves in Rooms* (Review of Modern Physics Vol. 16, No. 2, April, 1944).
7. P. M. Morse: *Vibration and Sound, 2nd ed.*(1948 McGraw-Hill).
8. C. Zwikker & C. W. Kosten, *Sound Absorbing Materials* (1949, Elsevier).
9a. L. L. Beranek, *Acoustic Measurements*, (1949, John Wiley).
9b. Revised: *Acoustical Measurements* (1988, Am. Inst. Physics).
10. P. V. Brüel, *Sound Insulation and Room Acoustics* (1951, Chapman Hall).
11. H. Fletcher, *Speech and Hearing in Communication* (1953, Van Nostrand).
12. E. G. Richardson ed., *Technical Aspect of Sound, Vol. I* (1953, Elsevier).
13a. L. L. Beranek, *Acoustics* (1954, McGraw-Hill).
13b. L. L. Beranek, *Acoustics* (1987, Acous. Soc. Am.).
14a. C. M. Harris ed., *Handbook of Noise Control* (1957, McGraw-Hill).
14b. 2nd ed. (1979, McGraw-Hill).
15. H. F. Olson, *Acoustical Engineering* (1957, Van Nostrand).
16a. L. L. Beranek ed., *Noise Reduction* (1960, McGraw-Hill)
16b. L. L. Beranek ed., *Noise Reduction* Reprint (1991, Peninsula Pub.).
17. E. G. Richardson & E. Meyer ed., *Technical Aspect of Sound, Vol. III* (1962 Elsevier).
18. G. Kurtze, *Physik und Technik der Lärmbekämpfung 1964*, G. Braun).
19a. L. Cremer & M. Heckl, *Körpershall* (1967, Springer-Verlag).
19b. E. E. Ungar tr., *Structure-Borne Sound* (1973, Springer-Verlag).
20. M. Morse & U. Ingard: *Theoretical Acoustics* (1968, McGraw-Hill).
21. K. D. Kryter: *The Effects of Noise on Man* (1970, 2nd ed. 1985, Academic Press).
22a. L. L. Beranek ed., *Noise and Vibration Control* (1971, McGraw-Hill).
22b. Revised (1988, Inst. Noise Con. Eng.).
23. Eugen Skudrzyk, *The Foundations of Acoustics* (1971, Springer-Verlag).
24. T. J. Schultz: *Community Noise Rating* (1972, 2nd ed. 1982, Applied Science Pub.)
25a. J. Blauert, *Räumlichen Hören* (1974, Hirzel Verlag).
25b. J. Blauert, *Spatial Hearing* (1983, MIT Press).
26. R. W. B. Stephens ed., *Acoustics 1974* (1975, Chapman and Hall).
27. R. Mackenzie ed., *Auditorium Acoustics* (1975, Applied Science Pub.).
28. L. H. Schaudinischky, *Sound Man and Building* (1976, Applied Science Pub.).

29a. L. Cremer & H. A. Muller, *Die Wissenschaftlichen Grundlagen Der Raumakustik Vol. 1, Vol. 2* (1978, S. Hirzel Verlag).
29b. T. J. Schultz tr., *Principles and Applications of Room Acoustics Vol. 1, Vol. 2* (1982, Applied Science Pub.).
30a. H. Kuttruff, *Room Acoustics* 2nd ed. (1979, Applied Science Pub.).
30b. H. Kuttruff, *Room Acoustics* 3rd ed. (1991, Applied Science Pub.).
31. V. L. Jordan, *Acoustical Design of Concert Halls and Theatres* (1980, Applied Science Pub.).
32a. A. D. Pierce, *Acoustics, an Introduction to its Physical Principles and Applications* (1981, McGraw-Hill).
32b. Revised (1989, Am. Inst. Physics).
33. Yoichi Ando, *Concert Hall Acoustics* (1985, Springer Verlag).
34. A. Lara Saenz & R. W. B. Stephens ed., *Noise Pollution* [SCOPE 24] (1986, John Wiley).
35. D. Davis & C. Davis, *Sound System Engineering*, 2nd ed. (1987, Haward W. Sams, Macmillan).
36. P. M. Nelson, *Transportation Noise Reference Book* (1987, Butterworths).
37. K. U. Ingard, *Fundamentals of Wave and Oscillation* (1988, Cambridge University Press).
38. F. J. Fahy, *Sound Intensity* (1989, Elsevier Science Pub.).
39. Y. W. Lee, *Statistical Theory of Communication* (1960, John Wiley).
40. W. H. Hayt, Jr. & J. E. Kemmerly, *Engineering Circuit Analysis* (1978, McGraw-Hill).
41. F. J. Fahy, *Sound and Structural Vibration* (1985, Academic Press).
42. J. O. Pickles, *An Introduction to the Physiology of Hearing*, 2nd ed. (1988, Academic Press).
43. B. C. J. Moore, *An Introduction to the Psychology of Hearing*, 3rd ed. (1989, Academic Press).

Index